"... And Then I Became Gay"

Books by Ritch C. Savin-Williams

The Lives of Lesbians, Gays, and Bisexuals: Children to Adults
(with K. M. Cohen) (1996)

Beyond Pink and Blue: Exploring Our Stereotypes of
Sexuality and Gender
A Program for Ages 13 to 15
(with T. Robinson-Harris) (1994)

Gay and Lesbian Youth: Expressions of Identity
(1990)

Adolescence: An Ethological Perspective
(1987)

". . . And Then I Became Gay"

Young Men's Stories

Ritch C. Savin-Williams

ROUTLEDGE
New York and London

Published in 1998 by
Routledge
29 West 35th Street
New York, New York 10001

Published in Great Britain in 1998 by
Routledge
11 New Fetter Lane
London EC4P 4EE

Printed in the United States of America on acid-free paper
Design: Jack Donner

Library of Congress Cataloging-in-Publication Data

Savin-Williams, Ritch C.
    "...And then I became gay": young men's stories / Ritch C. Savin-Williams
        p.   cm.
    Includes bibliographical references and index.
    ISBN 0–415–91676–3 — ISBN 0–415–91677–1
    1. Gay youth—United States.   2. Bisexual youth—United States.   3. Coming out
(Sexual orientation)—United States.   I. Title.
HQ76.2.U5S37   1997
305.235'08664—DC21   97–17062
                                                                              CIP

For Ken, For The Rest Of Our Lives

Contents

Suicide Risks
Reflections on a Positive Identity

Preface

Many gay and bisexual youths struggle for years to understand why they, of all boys their age, do not seem to fit in. During childhood and adolescence they may have felt and perhaps behaved differently, had persistent same-sex attractions that would not disappear despite vigorous efforts, and weathered the snide remarks of peers who seemed to know better than they did what they were. Then, the deniable became undeniable and suddenly all made sense. This was the experience of one particular youth who provided the title for this book. During his interview he spoke of battling to comprehend and defy his self-professed demons—his sexual fantasies of men. He finally stopped fighting and concluded, "and then I became gay." Never again would he pretend to himself that he was anything but gay. For him, "becoming" gay meant adopting a sexual identity or label that was consistent with and reflected his sexual orientation.

At the time of his revelation this youth was relatively unsophisticated about how he got to be gay or why he had to be the one who turned out gay. Like so many other youths, his sexuality simply felt natural, as much a part of him as his "love of beauty and my music playing." Being gay was not something that he had planned or would have selected for himself if given a choice, and he made repeated attempts during his childhood and early adolescence to convince himself that this could not possibly be the definitive outcome of his sexuality. He wanted "better" for himself. He wanted an easier life. But he also knew that he had no choice in the matter. Once he gave himself up to this genuine gay self he increasingly experienced happiness and self-acceptance. He ultimately came to celebrate his sexuality because of the uniqueness it bestowed on his life.

This youth's preadult years may have been common, but they certainly were not universal. Other youths knew "from birth" that their attractions were solely directed to other males; once they had the cognitive capacity to understand that this meant "gay," they were gay. The decisions to disclose this to others and to sexually act on their attractions were often independent of self-recognition and self-acceptance as gay. As adolescents, some gay/bisexual youths engaged girls in sex and romance—at varying ages, for singular or multiple occasions, and for an assortment of reasons. The same variability could also be noted in their child and adolescent sex with other boys and men.

This multiplicity or heterogeneity in the developmental trajectories of gay and bisexual youths is the most explicit theme of this book. During childhood, adolescence, and young adulthood the youths I interviewed lived both ordinary and intricate lives; as similar and dissimilar as their heterosexual peers; and, ultimately, as diverse as we would expect them to be. We would recognize many of them as our sons, brothers, grandsons, nephews, cousins, friends, and boys next door; others would be strangers to us.

The perspective that I propose in this book to account for this richness of diversity in the lives of gay and bisexual youths is *differential developmental trajectories.* The continuity and discontinuity in individual lives and the turning points that redirect or rechannel the meanings of experiences and feelings are the infrastructure for this conceptualization. In some respects, gay and bisexual youths are similar to all other contemporary adolescents, as well as like no other one who has ever lived. Gay/bisexual youths share commonalities that separate them from their heterosexual peers; they also diverge among themselves in their pathways to a sexual identity.

A second major objective of this book, perhaps more implied than explicitly argued, is to challenge the ways in which our culture thinks about sexual minority youths. We have imaginations of what it means to grow up gay during this historic time, and this is conveyed in no uncertain terms through religion, educational institutions, and the media. Sexual-minority youths are portrayed as victimized, suicidal individuals with low self-esteem who struggle to cope with an unwieldy modern universe that despises them and gives little hope that a good life can come to them. These beliefs in turn can affect the self-perception of gay youths and their expectations about the life they will have to lead. Despite the dearth of supporting *scientific* literature, educators, mental health care providers, parents, and sexual-minority youths often erroneously assume that gay/bisexual youths are inherently psychologically vulnerable. Researchers have been of little help in redressing this stereotype.

Too often ignored are the strengths and accomplishments of sexual-minority youths. In closing my previous book on gay youths, *Gay and Lesbian Youth: Expressions of Identity* (1990), I made this point in a section titled "The Promise of Lesbian and Gay Youth." I wish to reiterate the main points here because of their pertinence to the lives recounted in this book.

[Many] accept their homosexual feelings and attractions and lead successful, productive, nonneurotic lives as self-acknowledged gay men and lesbians. But social scientists, including lesbian and gay researchers, have focused almost exclusively on the "problems" at the expense of the "promises" of lesbian and gay youths. It is perhaps surprising that the results of the current study presented lesbian and gay adolescents as essentially psychologically and socially healthy individuals . . . [The research] does present another side of being young and gay—a positive and promising period of the life course. I believe that we need to say this loudly and clearly and to support it in the pages of our professional journals and in the media, such that we and our youth can hear it and believe it. (pp. 182, 185)

While interviewing gay/bisexual youths for this book, I have been impressed that the vast majority, similar to those in the earlier anonymous survey of sexual-minority youths, survived their adolescence with a healthy sense of self and of being gay. Indeed, their lives are rather ordinary. They faced their life as we all do, with moments of exhilaration, hours of satisfaction, and days of tedium. This book is a recounting of their lives, their stories about growing up gay or bisexual in our culture at this historic moment in time. I felt honored and privileged by their willingness to share some of the most memorable and painful aspects of their lives. I believe that the reader will be impressed by the detail and the emotional commitment to honesty that many of the youths provided. I trust that I have done some justice representing their lives.

I appreciate Philip Rappaport, the acquisition editor, for his faith, perseverance, and many helpful suggestions on an earlier version of this book. During a transitional period in management at Routledge, Heidi Freund maintained continuity and professionalism in bringing this manuscript to fruition. Once again, Deanna Johnson as copy editor smoothed the rough edges and graciously noted the errors I overlooked; she too must be thanked. Without their assistance and many others at Routledge this book would not today be in your hands.

I am also indebted to two of the best graduate students with whom I have ever had the pleasure to work—Lisa M. Diamond and Eric M. Dubé. We share ideas so frequently and so thoroughly that I can never be quite sure which ideas are whose. I ask for their forgiveness if I have unduly incorporated their ideas as my own.

During thoughts of shredding the manuscript, the computer, and our home, my partner Kenneth M. Cohen was always there for me. This manuscript is also his.

1.

Personal Stories and Sexuality

William James remarked that to best understand people one must first understand their stories. This book is about stories that are seldom told except in lurid, often pathetic tales of unbridled sexuality, prostitution, and suicide—those of gay and bisexual male youths.[1] Consequently, very little is known about the typical developmental histories and everyday experiences of gay youths. This distortion of their lives results from our cultural mythology which denies a sexual orientation other than heterosexual to children and adolescents. The limited attention given sexual-minority youths conveys the view that sexual orientation has little or no impact on one's developmental status prior to adulthood.

To correct these shortcomings, the young men interviewed for this book were asked to recall their developmental progression from first memories of being attracted to other males—which for some was as early as their first memories of life—to a subsequent integration of their sexual identity with their personal identity. This chain of feelings and events often included labeling feelings as "homosexual," first having sex with a male, first having heterosexual sex, labeling self as gay/bisexual, first disclosing this information to another, and first having a same-sex romantic relationship. Readily apparent throughout these narratives is the intense yet meaningful sexuality that many of the gay/bisexual youths felt during their childhood. Some not only felt *sexual,* they acted *sexually!*

Personal Stories

The personal narratives of sexual-minority youths reported in this book illustrate the normative experiences of growing up gay or bisexual during the present historic time and within North American culture. These narratives may also resonate with the lives of individuals with different personal histories living in previous generations or in other cultures. Thus, the stories may very well illuminate developmental processes that fundamentally characterize the human life course among sexual-minority individuals who, in their developmental trajectories, are both like and unlike heterosexuals and similar to and dissimilar to all other gays, bisexuals, and lesbians. This approach differs from the traditional method of simplistically portraying the apparent differences between sexual-minority individuals and their heterosexual counterparts as a "we" versus "them" dichotomy, resulting in the popularly accepted portrayal of a "gay lifestyle." Lost in that traditional approach are accounts that attest to the vast diversity *within* lesbian, gay, and bisexual populations.

Two examples elucidate these points. First, similar to some heterosexuals and disparate from many gay/bisexual youths, several of the interviewed youths were without sexual experiences with either sex yet claimed membership in the category *gay.* Their virginity has thus far exempted them from the subsequent impact that sexual experience has had on the lives of their sexually active gay/bisexual brothers, some of whom had "done" at least fifty males by high-school graduation. This exclusion from sexual acts does not imply, however, that the gay virgins were spared the ramifications also experienced by their sexually active peers when they disclosed their nonheterosexuality to friends and family, struggled to overcome peer ridicule, and survived growing up in an often homophobic and certainly heterosexist culture. Unknown is the extent to which these gay virgins share aspects of their lives with heterosexual male virgins—perhaps a religious or moral conviction not to engage in sexuality until one is committed to another, personality traits such as shyness or a desire for cleanliness, behavioral characteristics such as social awkwardness or intellectual pursuits, or simply bad (or good) luck.

A second example is the experiences of ethnic-minority youths who are also gay or bisexual. These youths are likely to be confronted with antigay attitudes and stereotypical beliefs that affect *all* gay/bisexual youths regardless of color, religion, or class. However, in addition to the pressure to be and act "straight" that they have in common with other sexual-minority youths, they are subject to mandates from the majority culture to act "White." Also unlike their White gay brothers but similar to other adolescents within their ethnic community, they must integrate their sense of self within the context of their ethnic reference group. That is, when developing their self-concept they cannot ignore the fact that they are Latino, African American, Asian/Pacific Islander, or Native American Indian. In many ethnic communities, for a complex set of religious and historic reasons, a clear and powerful assumption, even edict, of heterosexuality exists. To abrogate this community mandate may be especially threatening for some ethnic-minority youths. Facing the racism of gay/bisexual communities and the homophobia of their ethnic community, gay/bisexual youths of color often feel that they must choose which of two groups will be their primary identification—the gay or ethnic community. Their unique struggle is between who they are and what they feel they must be in order to avoid a stigmatizing identity as a gay/bisexual person of color.

The narratives reported in this book illustrate two very important points. First, the presence of sexuality during the childhood and adolescence of gay/bisexual boys is abundantly apparent. As children and adolescents they had sexual fantasies, and many engaged in same-sex behavior long before they understood the *meaning* of a gay or bisexual identity. Second, the youths reported with near unanimity that no one event "made" them gay or bisexual. Their same-sex attractions emerged early and forcefully, sometimes giving impetus to same-sex behaviors—the true expression of their desires. A gay or bisexual identity, which was usually not solidified until young adulthood, gave meaning to their attractions and behaviors. These conclusions are compatible with previous studies of gay youths.[2]

Before discussing these matters further, the distinction between sexual orientation and sexual identity must be clarified. *Sexual orientation* refers to the preponderance of sexual or erotic feelings, thoughts, fantasies, and/or behaviors one has for members of one sex or the other, both, or neither. It is present from an early age, perhaps by conception if caused by biological factors or by age five if caused by psychogenic factors, and is generally considered to be immutable, stable, and internally consonant, although the latter three are a matter of some contention among lesbian and bisexual women.[3] Sexual orientation is not thought to be subject to conscious control, can exist separately or independently from sexual conduct and sexual identity, and may be dimensional—where gay and heterosexual may be merely the ends of a continuum on which we all fall and in which many individuals possess degrees of homoerotic and heteroerotic attractions and feelings—or categorical, in which we are classified as *either* heterosexual, homosexual, or bisexual.

By contrast, *sexual identity* represents an enduring self-recognition of the *meanings* that sexual feelings, attractions, and behaviors have for one's sense of self. This self-labeling occurs within the pool of potential sexual identities that are defined and given meaning by the cultural and historic time in which one lives. It is symbolized by such statements as "I am gay" or "I am heterosexual" and is thus a matter of personal choice. For some individuals, sexual identity remains fluid during the life course, probably not on a day-to-day basis, and is not necessarily consistent with sexual orientation, fantasies, or behavior.

The contrast between these two constructs can perhaps be best understood as a distinction between an ever-present, invariant, biological and psychological truth (sexual orientation) and a historically and culturally located social construction (sexual identity). While this distinction oversimplifies both constructs, it is useful in clarifying developmental issues for children and adolescents with same-sex

attractions. For example, an individual with a gay sexual orientation need not recognize, self-identify, or publicly acknowledge a similar sexual identity. A teenage
boy may desire sex with other boys exclusively, engage in sex with both boys and
girls, and proclaim to others that he is heterosexual. Another adolescent boy may
be celibate, have a bisexual sexual orientation, and prefer to be gay-identified
because a local gay community offers him support for his homoerotic attractions.
The complexities of sexuality far exceed contemporary understandings embedded
in the question, "Are you gay or straight?"

The Book's Organization

The core of the book is organized around developmental milestones in the lives of
gay and bisexual male youths. These developmental transitions, or turning points,
are loosely sequenced based on the process whereby individuals navigate the
events that lead from a pregay neophyte who first becomes aware of feeling different from same-age male peers to a gay veteran who integrates and perhaps cele-
brates a same-sex identity and status. This process has previously been
conceptualized within the context of so-called "coming-out" models. These
models are cast in a somewhat orderly series of ideal or typical stages that profess
to characterize the ways in which individuals make sense, recognize, and give a
name to their emerging sexuality in a complex series of events, feelings, and
attractions. This process has been described as an "increasing acceptance of the
label *homosexual* as descriptive of self" (p. 146).[4] Later tasks include exploring the
implications of having and claiming the status of gay or bisexual.[5]

Although this sequence and the distinctions made are sources of some contention among scholars, they serve as a heuristic device for understanding the
lives of gay youths. However, the most basic assumption of coming-out stage
models—the uniformity of experiences—was set aside in the formulation of this
book, largely because relatively few youths followed the sequence of any one of the
numerous coming-out models that have been proposed. Invariant, inevitable, and
predictable did not characterize the majority of the youths who were interviewed.
For example, some youths had sex with other males before they labeled their feelings or self; others became fully accepting of their gay status but had not yet had
gay sex. Some youths were without heterosexual sex or romantic relationships;
others had many such encounters either before, during, or after disclosure to self
or others. Some youths simultaneously labeled their feelings and self as gay and
disclosed to best friends and family members; others separated and transposed
these "stages" by five to ten years. Some youths maintained that they have never
disclosed their sexual identity but are "happily gay"; others shout about their
sexual identity to anyone who will listen. It is within this developmental diversity
that a model for understanding the lives of young gay and bisexual males is

proposed in this chapter. This model is based on the ways in which individual lives have continuities and discontinuities with other youths, both heterosexual and not, and the turning points youths encounter that alter their life trajectories. This leads to an articulation of a *differential developmental trajectories* perspective that forms the guiding principle for this book.

The structure of the next eight chapters follows a general developmental progression.

Chapter Two	Memories of same-sex attractions
Chapter Three	Labeling feelings and attractions
Chapter Four	First gay sex
Chapter Five	First heterosexual sex
Chapter Six	Label self as gay or bisexual
Chapter Seven	Disclosure to others
Chapter Eight	First same-sex romance
Chapter Nine	Self-acceptance as gay or bisexual

In contrast to case studies, complete versions of the youths' sexual-identity histories from earliest memories to the present are not given in these developmental milestone chapters. To emphasize the developmental patterns that span individual lives, each story is divided topically and placed in different chapters. A premium was placed on ensuring anonymity, and thus potentially identifying details of stories have been altered. However, every attempt has been made to preserve the essential truths of the stories.[6]

Chapter Ten is devoted to the unique experiences of ethnic-minority youths. Reflections on the meaning of the life histories relative to issues of continuity, discontinuity, diversity, and a differential developmental trajectories perspective are provided in **Chapter Eleven.**

Developmental Themes: Similar or Unique?

If we assume that sexual orientation is an important context for understanding how individuals become the way they are, then the necessary corollary is that because of their sexuality, sexual-minority youths experience a life course substantially different from that of heterosexual adolescents. The counterargument is that development among sexual-minority youths requires no special attention because they are essentially similar to heterosexuals, differing only in whom they lust after, have sex with, and desire to love.

Both views appear to me to be *correct*—gays are both the same as everyone else *and* unique among all classes of individuals—yet also *wrong*, depending on the individual and her or his developmental trajectory. For example, in regard to sameness and difference, although some gay and lesbian individuals have a sex-atypical hypothalamus, in many other areas of neural anatomy they appear to be in-distinguishable from heterosexuals. Psychosocially, as a result of growing up in a culture that presumes and prescribes exclusive heterosexuality, same-sex oriented adolescents face unique challenges not encountered by their heterosexual peers in accepting and expressing their sexuality. Gay adolescents, however, also experience many of the same developmental issues experienced by heterosexual youths, including establishing a personal identity and resolving issues of individuation and attachment.

My further point, that both positions are wrong, is merely to assert that the "we are the same" versus "we are different" clichéd debate masks an enormous number of complex developmental issues, not the least of which is that significant and profound differences exist within sexual-minority populations. That is, not all gay people are the same! Subgroups sharing essential and defining characteristics do exist among gays.

Continuities and Discontinuities

From the personal life accounts of gay youths can be discerned two seemingly paradoxical characteristics. The experience of growing up gay in our society con-firms that individual lives are both distinct and common. This duality is of central importance to noted clinician and researcher Michael Rutter, who observes that a life history has many continuities with other lives and discontinuities—no other life such as one's own has ever been lived.[7] This does not negate the fact that an individual's life history also reveals basic developmental patterns that are shared with other sexual-minority youths.

The discontinuities perspective and its individualistic methodology are best exemplified in "coming-out" stories. These personal life histories are often insight-ful and provocative, and include individuals of diverse social classes, racial and ethnic identifications, and religious traditions.[8] The personal narratives usually stand alone, presented without structure, organization, context, or comment. Their strength is that the narrators, who may be adolescents at the time of the retelling or adults reflecting back on a life, describe and make sense of their devel-opment in their own terms, empowering them to speak without the aid of an external expert.

The continuities approach specifies common aspects of development among lesbians, bisexuals, and gays. Data are usually aggregate and mean scores on devel-opmental milestones are presented. The identity process has been detailed, staged, and universalized in coming-out theoretical models. These linear, orderly models propose that youths pass through a series of usually invariant steps or stages. One model frequently cited includes Identity Confusion (first awareness), Identity Comparison (possible gay identity), Identity Tolerance (probable gay identity),

Identity Acceptance, Identity Pride, and Identity Synthesis (integrated gay identity).[9] The strength of these models is that they collapse individual stories to identify common feelings, thoughts, or events that characterize gay lives, thus simplifying a very complicated process.

Coming-out models have been useful in describing the broad outlines by which *some* lesbians, bisexuals, and gays progress from an "assumed" heterosexual child or adolescent to a nonheterosexual adult. They are not, however, without value judgments. For example, healthy individuals are expected to move along a predetermined developmental sequence with advanced status or maturity marked by the author as the attainment of the final stage.[10] Provisions for alternative pathways that allow individuals to achieve the final endpoint of self-labeling and full disclosure are neither acknowledged nor discussed. However, some youths report never experiencing a coming-out process that consisted of temporal moments or events that culminated in a gestalt shift to a new identity. Rather, their sexual identity was a gradual, continuous endeavor, "a series of realignments in perception, evaluation, and commitment" (p. 75) that occurred before an ever-expanding "series of audiences."[11] Other sexual-minority individuals deny that a coming-out process characterized their adolescence because they were never in doubt about who and what they were and were thus never *not* out to self and others. It is also worth noting that coming-out stage models rarely explain the processes that bisexual individuals encounter in developing a bisexual identity or that heterosexuals experience in accepting their heterosexual status.

Although both the discontinuities and continuities approaches have merit, they are seldom used to complement or inform each other. The two genres, personal narratives and theoretical identity models, frequently exist in two disparate worlds, each intended for separate audiences that too rarely speak with each other. Audiences consisting of laypersons and health-care professionals who attend to individuals in medical, psychological, or social need too rarely interact with theoreticians and research scientists who revel in discerning group differences for professional conferences and publications and vice versa.

The approach adopted in this book attempts to balance these methodologies. By incorporating an idiographic approach, the youths' individuality is recognized through the narration of their life stories. Concurrently, an external voice is present—that of the interviewer—who attempts to discern similarities and patterns across the lives of the youths. What is apparent in both analyses is the persistence of notable events that alter the youths' life course.

Turning Points

The interviewed youths reported in their life narratives dramatic or unexpected events that transformed their life course. These life-altering events were usually particular to an individual and arose from his singular biology or life experiences in growing up in contemporary North American culture. Examples given by the youths included a chance sexual encounter with a best friend, a TV show or movie that portrayed homosexuality positively, a friend offering support or questioning the youth's sexuality, and an insight in which two seemingly disparate thoughts or feelings came together and assumed a new meaning.

Rutter refers to these experiences as "turning points," events that create changes in a life's trajectory and "alter our behavior instead of accentuating or perpetuating it" (p. 457).[12] Many of these life experiences do not occur randomly but are set in motion by previous experiences, decisions, circumstances, and even genetic codes. Because not all events or the same events affect everyone equally—to the same degree or in the same way—the consequences of turning points are often unpredictable.

Turning points are usually conceptualized in terms of the ways in which they affect individual lives rather than in general terms that apply to groups of individuals. However, if individuals share common experiences such as pubertal onset or first sex, or if they begin to decipher that they have a collective bond or an identity that is socially oppressed or deemed "minority" in their culture, then turning points can have communal aspects across individuals. Because individuals select, to some degree, their environments and hence experiences, by examining individual life histories and finding embedded in them patterns that cut across individuals we can better understand turning points beyond the individual level to encompass patterns among subpopulations of individuals.

The youths interviewed for this book provided narratives based on a select set of questions that attempted to elicit information from them on a number of critical developmental processes. Within these narratives a number of turning points emerged that affected identification of self as gay or bisexual and the communication of that revelation to others. Previous research has focused on the average *timing* of events, such as age of coming out to self and others; this essentially masks any attempt to discover the significance of these very same critical events for the life course of the individual. For example, age of self-identification informs us little regarding what is known about decisive events occurring prior to self-recognition and whether these are unique to an individual or shared by all or select subgroups of youths. The interviewed youths also speculated as to whether events in their lives "made" them gay or contributed to their gayness. These and other turning points are examined in the narratives of the gay and bisexual youths.

Differential Developmental Trajectories

Sexual-minority individuals have distinctive yet common life courses, a reasonable expectation given that the expression of sexuality is the result of a unique mix of biological, psychological, social, and cultural factors. In some domains of sexuality a gay youth may share experiences with other adolescents regardless of sexual orientation, with other gay youths, a subgroups of gay youths, or with no other adolescent who has ever lived or will ever live. Thus, the premise that not all individuals have identical pathways in the development of their sexuality becomes not only plausible but also particularly apparent once we listen to the candid and compelling life histories of sexual-minority youths.

One way to conceptualize this representation of the adolescent life course is through a differential developmental trajectories perspective. "Differential" names the variability within and across individuals, and "development" refers not only to specific events during particular moments of time but to the full range of milestones and processes that occur throughout the life course. "Trajectories" highlights forward movement and emphasizes that future development will be influenced by past and current maturational episodes and their aftermath. This approach to understanding individual lives forms the essential nucleus of the developmental perspective presented in this book.

Researcher Laurence Steinberg proposes that a developmental trajectory is a "probabilistic pathway through time and space" that is shaped by three sets of factors: "(a) characteristics of the developing adolescent, (b) influences of the immediate environment, and (c) opportunities and constraints inherent in the broader context" (pp. 248–249).[13] Adolescent behavior is thus influenced not only by internal processes, including biological makeup, but also by proximal forces such as friends and family and distal influences such as heterosexism and homophobia.

Steinberg further explains that adolescents are not passive objects controlled by forces beyond them but are:

> active, changing agents who select and affect the environments in which they participate. In this regard, developmental trajectories are not fixed paths that are charted for the adolescent by others or by society, but routes toward an endpoint that are chosen, or even created, by an active, self-directed organism. (p. 248)

In the same volume, Lisa Crockett argues that developmental trajectories imply a degree of adaptation over time to changing life circumstances—either in positive or negative directions.[14] Although I agree with these points, missing from their conceptualization of developmental trajectories is the full scope of its *differential* quality. That is, not only is a trajectory unique to an individual, as they maintain, but there are common developmental trajectories among individuals who share personal charcteristics. For example, in terms of sexual-minority development, subgroups of individuals exist, and these groupings are often fluid over time and are based on characteristics such as an individual's degree of femininity and masculinity, acceptance of a racial identity, willingness to accept or embrace familial social status, attitudes and beliefs about sexual orientation in the near and far environment, and age at which knowledge and acceptance of sexuality occur.

From my perspective, a differential developmental trajectories approach proposes that the task of developmental research is to investigate the ways in which sexual-minority youths are similar to *and* different from all other adolescents, as well as the ways in which they vary *among* themselves throughout the life course. It is my view that researchers have become too negligent with the vicissitudes in developmental processes and the outcomes within sexual-minority populations and have thus at times misled us regarding how sexual minorities lead their lives. Viewing development from a differential trajectories perspective heightens the focus on diversity within sexual-minority populations, recognizes continuities and discontinuities in development, and highlights the turning points in individual lives.

The life stories of the gay/bisexual adolescents and young adults interviewed for this book reveal a medley of life adventures and provide much needed information. Not infrequently, sexual recollections originated from first memories during early childhood, were exceedingly vivid and saturated with emotionality, and were subsequently interpreted to have had a range of consequential meanings during the evolution of their behavior and identity. But they are not all alike. One individual experienced his sexuality in a linear fashion, recalling a progression from early undefined feelings of being different from peers, to same-sex attractions, and to eventual self-identification and proclamation to others that he was gay. For another youth, the developmental interplay of these relationships in his life was more spiral, difficult if not impossible to separate. A significant number of youths identified themselves as bisexual during adolescence; a much smaller number identified themselves as bisexual during young adulthood. While this appears incongruent, the connection between the two for some youths was that it felt "safer" to identify during adolescence as bisexual, leaving some hope to self and others of a possible heterosexual lifestyle during adulthood; others mistook their early emotional attractions to girls as an indication that they had *sexual* attractions for girls.

If we misunderstand the lives of sexual-minority youths then we will likely misrepresent them. If we listen to their stories we discover that many are becoming proud to be gay and look forward to a prolific and energetic life as a gay adult. A differential developmental trajectories perspective is the most scientifically sound approach to understanding the lives of sexual-minority youths.

The Current Study

It is never easy to recruit "hidden populations" for participation in research projects, especially when the basis for the concealment is a very realistic fear of reprisals for membership in a marginal group. Yet without strategies to sample the diversity of the population under study, the very lives researchers seek to accurately depict may be misrepresented or distorted. When the intended participants are gay adolescents, the difficulty of finding "normal" representatives of this hidden population is especially problematic. Indeed, several of the earliest studies of gay youth were composed primarily of "marginal" teenagers such as male hustlers, streetwalkers, homeless youths, and draft dodgers.[15] Only at great peril could anyone attempt to generalize findings from these studies to current cohorts of sexual-minority youths.

Given this historic poverty of self-disclosing youths, previous generations of researchers were left with little choice except to rely on *retrospective* reports of adults to procure information about the experiences and developmental processes of sexual-minority children and adolescents and then try to generalize these reports to current cohorts of youths. This is necessarily problematic, resulting in a developmental psychology of the "remembered past."[16] The pitfalls of using this methodology are discussed by researchers Andy Boxer and Bert Cohler, who note that the "reconstructed past" may be dissimilar to how youths "experience their lives as they are living them, rather than as they are remembered" (p. 321).

Another problem is that even if these accounts are reported accurately by adults who grew up in the 1950s and 1960s, they may have limited relevance for youths growing up in the 1980s and 1990s. Contemporary researchers have a much easier time recruiting sexual-minority individuals; this can be largely attributed to the increased cultural visibility and decreased intolerance for lesbians, gays, and bisexuals. Cultural shifts in which sexual-minority issues have achieved eminence in mainstream newspapers, magazines, the Internet, and books and are portrayed in movies, television shows, and popular songs have allowed the emergence of a greater number of individuals who have declared their sexual status.

I first took advantage of this change in an anonymous questionnaire survey of 317 gay, lesbian, and bisexual youths between the ages of fourteen and twenty-three years.[18] After completion of that project, I undertook three more directed research projects. Two of these studies assumed a *narrative* or *interpretive interview* approach in which qualitative aspects of experiences were assessed. Considered ideal for exploratory studies of hidden populations and their life histories, the "remembered past" was narrowed by interviewing individuals relatively close in age to the events and processes they were reporting, thereby reducing the temporal limitations of memory. The youths were only several years or months removed from many of the developmental milestones considered critical in achieving their current sexual identity. Furthermore, requesting youths to ground their memories in specific details during face-to-face interviews and to tell "their own story" created an interview situation that was perceived to be safe and accepting by participants, thus further reducing memory distortion of life-history events. Previous methodologically oriented researchers have noted that these efforts increase the validity of collected data.[19]

The 180 gay/bisexual male youths who are included in this book were participants in one of these three research projects. Table 1.1 summarizes basic characteristics of the three samples. These youths were, for the most part, articulate, educated college men who elected to participate in research that was described to them as an attempt to understand the ways gay/bisexual young men come to recognize their sexual identity during childhood and adolescence. I want to be clear from the outset that these youths are not presented as representative of any

Table 1.1 Characteristics of the Three Samples of Gay/Bisexual Youths

Age	Sample 1	Sample 2	Sample 3	Total
Mean (SD)	21.0 (1.4)	21.3 (2.2)	18.4 (2.0)	20.4 (2.4)
Range	17–23	17–25	14–23	14–25
N	43	86	51	180
Ethnicity				
White (Non-Hispanic)	91%	72%	73%	77%
African American	2%	6%	24%	10%
Latino	2%	12%	2%	7%
Asian American	2%	7%	0%	4%
Native American Indian	0%	3%	0%	2%
International	2%	0%	2%	1%
Religion				
Protestant	27%	13%	44%	24%
Jewish	22%	21%	5%	24%
Catholic	17%	24%	32%	7%
Eastern	0%	2%	0%	1%
Personal	0%	2%	0%	1%
None	34%	37%	20%	32%
Sexual Orientation (Kinsey Ratings)				
6	70%	66%	46%	61%
5	16%	19%	36%	23%
4	9%	10%	10%	10%
3	2%	3%	8%	4%
2	2%	1%	0%	1%
Community				
Farm/Rural	14%	15%	10%	13%
Small Town	33%	20%	8%	20%
Medium Town/Suburb	26%	21%	6%	18%
Small City/Large Suburb	12%	15%	60%	27%
Urban	16%	29%	16%	22%
Parents				
Married	58%	62%	53%	58%
Divorced/Separated	40%	30%	41%	37%
One Parent Deceased	2%	7%	2%	6%

larger population of gay/bisexual youths. The reader should not assume that the interviewed youths speak for those who did not volunteer their life histories. The sample is further biased in that few youths of color or those closeted to themselves or to others volunteered their services; neither were those of diverse educational, socioeconomic, and geographical backgrounds adequately sampled. Nonverbally oriented and shy youths probably decided not to participate in the face-to-face interview studies. Finally, the reader should not assume that the lives of lesbian and bisexual female youths are necessarily similar to these male youths.[21]

To participate in one of the three studies, a volunteer merely had to identify himself as either gay or bisexual. How he conceptualized those categories and his subsequent membership in one of them was left to his own discretion. To verify this membership, each youth rated himself on the the Kinsey Scale, from zero, exclusively heterosexual, to six, exclusively homosexual. Given the focus of this book, it is not the Kinsey categories that are of paramount importance but rather the story of how each youth got to this point in his sexual identification.[22]

An age ceiling of twenty-five years was set to limit the time lag between the experience of developmental events and their recall during the close of adolescence and the beginning of young adulthood. Because such memories are susceptible to becoming blurred or misconstrued by later life events, the key to eliciting this internal representation was to encourage the youths to remember specific details of their lives. To help youths recall their momentous turning points, specific cues and probes were provided. At appropriate moments during the narratives I asked for *specific* memories. For example, regarding first gay sex I queried:

> How old were both of you? Who was this person to you? Where did you meet? Who initiated the interaction? Where did this occur? What happened, sexually? How did you feel afterwards? How did this affect your sense of being gay? Were there further contacts?

Indeed, all youths remembered exact markers; these details enhance the stories' readability and credibility.

Youths were interviewed at a time and place of their choice and convenience. They appeared to feel comfortable and safe during the interview. In fact, the youths were often reluctant to end the interview, reporting that they greatly enjoyed talking about their past. Several volunteered to be interviewed again if I ever needed them. Their readiness to refer friends to the study further demonstrates their feelings of safety and comfort.

The Researcher

The youths' stories were often so emotionally laden that it was difficult to hear them. Others were so funny or moving that it was difficult not to respond. Especially poignant was the anguish of gender-atypical youths, many of whom experienced a traumatic childhood and adolescence coping with peer ridicule and abuse. I frequently added some measure of support and appropriate response, and encouraged further reflections on their identity development. At times I felt voyeuristic and feared that I was intruding on sacred territory. I occasionally questioned my right to know this information. I left each interview feeling that the story told was an authentic one, not a contrived snapshot, and that the specific life history was shared unedited.

I felt a sense of privilege and responsibility receiving the youths' stories, a point echoed in another study of a hidden population. After interviewing working-class lesbians and gay men, historian Alan Berubé in his lecture "Class Dismissed" noted that disenfranchised populations often use the researcher in a triangular conversation. The interviewees communicate their concerns and struggles to a researcher who in turn represents them to a larger audience.[23] The researcher thus exchanges the privilege of gathering data that enhance her or his career or prestige for the responsibility of presenting and interpreting the lives of often powerless populations. When interviewing merchant marines and stewards, Berubé discovered:

> They teach me as their student. They expect me to get it right and then use my power to take their histories where they have little access. "Tell them what we did! Tell them what our lives were about! Use your power to help us get it back."

This book is thus a partial fulfillment of my responsibility, my payback if you will, to the youths who so freely and openly disclosed the most intimate secrets about their lives. Their agreement to do this was with the understanding that I would use my access to other researchers, educators, clinicians, policy makers, and even other youths to communicate their lives growing up gay in the 1980s and 1990s. They trusted that I would accurately represent their lives and that some good would come of their narratives. I have tried to fulfill my triangular role and to reliably "speak for" the youths. If the youths' power is to be realized, we must depend on each reader of this volume to enhance the lives of sexual-minority youths, either through direct contact with them or through changing the private and public conditions under which they live.

Summary of Group Findings

Sample means, range of ages, and presence of various developmental milestones, averaged across the three samples used, are presented in Table 1.2. Although the focus of this book is on subgroup differences and diversity of experiences, averages of developmental transitional points provide an overall portrait of the sampled youths and how they compare with previously sampled populations of sexual-minority youths.

Table 1.2 Identity Milestones for Gay/Bisexual Youths

Variable	Age Mean (SD)	Age Range	Percent Who Had Not Experienced	N
Awareness of Same-Sex Attractions	7.97 (3.3)	3–17	0%	177
Knew Meaning of "Homosexuality"	10.06 (3.0)	4–19	0%	96
Applied "Homosexual" to Attractions	13.12 (2.8)	5–20	0%	127
First Gay Sex	14.11 (4.1)	5–24	7%	180
First Heterosexual Sex	15.14 (3.1)	5–22	48%	180
Recognized Self as Gay/Bisexual	16.87 (3.0)	8–24	0%	126
First Disclosed to Other	17.89 (2.5)	13–25	0%	102
First Same-Sex Romance	18.33 (2.7)	11–25	29%	115
First Disclosed to:				
Sibling	18.72 (2.5)	13–25	38%	93
Father	18.88 (2.4)	13–25	44%	94
Mother	18.91 (2.4)	13–25	31%	103
Developed Positive Sexual Identity	19.15 (2.5)	10–25	23%	105

From a developmental perspective, an average of five years elapsed from the time the youths first became aware of their same-sex attractions to the point at which they labeled these attractions as "homosexual." It took another three and one-half years before they identified themselves as gay or bisexual. Within a year of labeling their desires they usually had their first gay sex; one year after that, their first heterosexual sex. First romantic relationship usually came four years after first gay sex. Prior to this, however, they recognized themselves as gay or bisexual. Thus, two years after their first sexual encounter with a girl and three years after first having sex with a boy, the youths self-identified as gay or bisexual. They disclosed this information to another person, usually a best friend or a girl they were dating, one year after they first knew; another year elapsed before family members were told that they had a gay/bisexual son or brother. Two-thirds of the sons disclosed to their mother, but just over one-half told their father or sibling. Thus, ten years after becoming aware of their same-sex attractions, the average gay/bisexual youth in the current samples first disclosed his sexual identity to parents. Two years after self-labeling, the average youth finally placed a positive spin on his sexual identity—*eleven* years after he first experienced same-sex attractions.

The ages at which these milestones were reached by youths in other research studies with a substantial number of gay/bisexual males are presented in Table 1.3.[24] A comparison of the two tables reveals changes over time in developmental outcomes. Most pronounced are the ages at which these developmental milestones are reached: They have been steadily declining from the 1970s to current cohorts of youths. For example, awareness of same-sex attractions has dropped from the onset of junior high school to an average of third grade. Although few other researchers have assessed age at which youths label feelings but not self as gay, the same temporal trend is apparent—dropping from high-school graduation to the beginning of junior high school.

Incompatible with this earlier-onset trend, however, is the age at which youths first engage in sex with another boy or man. This has been fairly constant across the twenty years, occurring during the fourteenth or fifteenth year. Two reports, however, are inconsistent with this finding. The Herdt/Boxer and Rosario studies, both of which sampled urban youths attending support groups in Chicago or New York, report a much earlier age of first same-sex experience. These youths

Table 1.3   Mean Age of Developmental Milestones in Other Studies[1]

	Kooden et al. (1979) N=138	Troiden (1979) N=150	McDonald (1982) N=199	Rodriguez (1988) N=251	D'Augelli (1991) N=61	Herdt & Boxer (1993) N=147	D'Augelli & Hershberger (1993) N=142	Rosario et al. (1996) N=81
First same-sex attractions	12.8		13	11.1	10.8	9.6	9.8	10.9
Label feelings but not self as homosexual		19.7		16.2				12.3
First homosexual sex	14.9	14.9	15		15.6	13.1	14.9	13.3
First heterosexual sex						13.7	15.0 (approx)	11.9
Label self as gay/lesbian	21.1	21.3	19	20.6	17	16.0	14.8	14.7
First disclosure to other	28[2]		23[2]	23.6[2]	19	16.8	16.7	
First disclosed to parent							17.6	
First relationship	21.9	23.9	21	22.8	18.8		17.6	
Positive gay identity	28.5	22	24					

1 Exact wording of milestones varies somewhat across studies.
2 To significant nongay other

may represent a highly select population, one with many accessible sexual outlets. Ninety-three percent of the youths interviewed for the current book reported that they had had sex with another male; in other studies the proportion of youths with at least one same-sex experience ranged from 91 to 98 percent. Age at which youths first had sex with a girl or woman is seldom asked by researchers cited in Table 1.3. Just over one-half of my population of youths and of Rosario's gay/bisexual males have had heterosexual sex—somewhat lower than the 63 percent reported by D'Augelli/Hershberger.

The earlier temporal trend is again operative when youths are asked when they labeled themselves as gay or bisexual. Current cohorts of urban youths appear to recognize this aspect of themselves at younger ages than earlier cohorts of youths. The age at which they first disclosed their sexual identity as gay/bisexual to others has also sharply declined since the 1970s. The present youths reflect this trend, although not as dramatically as samples of urban youths.

Finally, the age at which youths begin their first same-sex romantic relationship has also declined during the last twenty years. Studies conducted during the 1980s and 1990s, including the present one, indicate that the first relationship usually commences during the seventeenth or eighteenth year. Over 70 percent of the youths in the current samples have had at least one romantic relationship with another male.

The applicability of the life histories of youths in Samples One and Two to more ethnically and socioeconomically diverse youths remains to be demonstrated. Indeed, some differences are readily apparent. For example, the Detroit-area youths (Sample Three) reported a slightly older age of awareness of their same-sex attractions and had their first gay and heterosexual sexual experience about a year before youths in Samples One and Two (Table 1.4). In this regard they are similar to the samples of urban support-group youths in the Chicago and New York studies. Detroit youths were no more likely than the other youths to have disclosed to their parents and siblings their sexual orientation.

While it is seductive to consider developmental averages—after all, they afford an easy way to grasp the big picture—they obscure the richness of the youths' lives. For example, some youths in the three samples reported that they could never remember a time when they were not aware of their same-sex attractions; others did not identify their attractions until they were ready to graduate from high school. First gay and heterosexual sexual activity occurred as young as five years old for one of the boys and as old as twenty-five years for another youth. One youth disclosed to his mother, father, and sibling when he entered junior high school; another, near completion of his Ph.D., has yet to disclose to parents. One youth had a positive image of his sexual identity at age ten and a romantic relationship with another boy one year later; another youth has yet to achieve either milestone and believes he never will.

Table 1.4   Comparisons of Identity Milestones for Two Samples of Gay/Bisexual Youths

Variable	Sample Two			Sample Three		
	Age Mean	(SD)	Age Range	Age Mean	(SD)	Age Range
Awareness of Same-Sex Attractions	7.7	(3.0)	3–17	8.8	(3.4)	3–15
First Gay Sex	14.3	(4.6)	5–24	13.8	(3.8)	6–21
First Heterosexual Sex	15.7	(3.5)	5–22	14.3	(2.6)	9–19
		Percent			Percent	
Disclosed to Mother		63%			67%	
Disclosed to Father		45%			58%	
Disclosed to Sibling		51%			64%	
Sexual Orientation (Kinsey Ratings)						
6		66%			46%	
5		19%			36%	
4		10%			10%	
3		3%			8%	
2		1%			0%	
	Mean	(SD)	Range	Mean	(SD)	Range
Self-Esteem Level	21.8	(5.2)	6–30	20.6	(5.4)	9–30

It is this diversity that is the focus of this book. Although patterns of experiences among the youths are highlighted, most impressive are the variations illustrated through their personal narratives.

A Final Reflection

Telling one's story can be both threatening and self-validating. Although a youth may want to reminisce about his early sexual feelings, the recounting necessitates sharing with others aspects of an often hidden inner self. A youth may fear that his personal story will have little correspondence with the stories of other adolescents, that it is too strange, and that he will consequently embarrass himself if he is truly honest. I believe that in most cases these apprehensions were overcome. In fact, many youths expressed amusement as they shared their stories and it often appeared as if they were acting as a third person or as a spectator as they recounted important developmental events in their lives. For example, one youth recalled, "I noticed that I would fall for these distant male guys" and observed that whenever he leafed through his yearbook, "I would always pick out the cutest guy.

So I *must* have been attracted to other guys." By telling their stories they made connections that better helped them understand their own history. The interviews stimulated snapshots of their lives that the youths then interpreted like "mini-scientists." Promising anonymity, stressing the uniqueness of all life histories, and highlighting their potential contribution to the liberation of other youths appeared to act as catalysts for honest self-revelation. One can never be assured of this, of course, and you the reader will ultimately be the best judge of the youths' honesty.

Although several narratives in this book are painful to read, the stories are not censored. The language is often explicit, and at times people are treated as objects. Regarding the latter, I am referring primarily to reports of girls and women being used by the male youths to prove their heterosexuality to peers, to lash out at a lost or prohibited same-sex love, or to hide from themselves their same-sex orientation. To censor or alter the narratives would be unfair to the youths and, ultimately, disrespectful if not insulting to the reader. Among the interviewed youths, however, misogyny is neither pervasive nor normative. Most of the youths loved women, treated them with respect, and treasured their friendship and support. Frequently their relationships with girls and women were absolutely critical for their developmental well-being. Without them many would not have survived their childhood and adolescence, certainly emotionally and perhaps physically.

The youths' narratives express the complications, adversities, and satisfactions of being a sexual outsider in North American culture in the 1980s and 1990s. It is my hope that aspects of those youths' lives parallel the experiences and feelings of the reader. If true, then the stories possess additional power to inform, entertain, and heal. If they increase an understanding of our culture and time and the subsequent impact that they have on sexual minorities, then the stories will have taken on universal and political meanings.

2.

Childhood:
Memories of Same-Sex Attractions

Recalling their childhood, gay/bisexual youths often report the pervasiveness of distinct, early memories of same-sex attractions. They remember particular feelings or incidents from as young as four or five years of age that, in retrospect, reflect the first manifestations of sexual orientation. These memories often comprise some of the youths' earliest recollections of their lives, present in some rudimentary form for many years before the ability to label sexual feelings and attractions emerges, usually after pubertal onset.[1]

Indeed, over 80 percent of the interviewed youths reported same-sex attractions prior to the physical manifestations of puberty. By the completion of puberty, all youths recalled attractions that they later labeled as "homosexual." Nearly half noted that their feelings for other males were some of their very first memories, present prior to beginning elementary school. Revelation for one youth came through his kindergarten naps: "Dreams of naked men and curious about them. Really wanting to look at them." Another youth was acting on his sexually charged feelings at age four: "I particularly remember an incident with a cousin in the bathroom and we both having hard-ons and feeling a tingling sensation when we rubbed against each other. I wanted to repeat it, and did!"

The origins of these feelings and their meanings are difficult to discern because prepubertal children are seldom asked if they have sexual attractions for other boys or girls. Thus, clinicians, educators, researchers, and other interested professionals must rely on retrospective data from adolescents and young adults. Although these later recollections may be distorted by an awareness of current sexual identity, they provide an invaluable source of information.

Gay/bisexual youths often recall a vague but distinct sense of *being different* from other boys. Indeed, characterizing most developmental models of sexual identity is an introductory stage in which an individual has an unequivocal cognitive and/or emotional realization that he or she is "different" from others. An individual may feel alienated from others with very little awareness that homosexuality is the relevant issue.[2] For example, sociologist and sex educator Richard Troiden proposes a coming-out model that begins with an initial sense that one is marginalized in conjunction with perceptions of being different from peers.[3] This undeniable feeling may be the first internal, emotional revelation of sexual orientation, although it is not likely to be perceived initially as sexual but rather as a strongly experienced sense of not fitting in or of not having the same interests as other boys/girls.

The existence of these early feelings implies that youths have both an awareness of a normative standard of how boys are supposed to act, feel, and behave and a belief that they violate this ideal. Troiden describes this conflation of feeling different and gender inappropriate:

> It is not surprising that "prehomosexuals" used gender metaphors, rather than sexual metaphors, to interpret and explain their childhood feelings of difference. . . . Children do not appear to define their sexual experimentation in heterosexual or homosexual terms. The socially created categories of homosexual, heterosexual, and bisexual hold little or no significance for them. (p. 52)

Retrospectively, the gay/bisexual youths interviewed for this book reported three somewhat overlapping sources as a basis for their initial awareness of differentness:

- a pervasive and emotional captivation with other boys that felt passionate, exotic, consuming, and mysterious;
- a strongly felt desire to engage in play activities and to possess traits usually characteristic of girls;
- disinterest or, in more extreme cases, a revulsion in typical boys' activities, especially team sports and rough-and-tumble physical play.[4]

These three sources are not mutually exclusive—many youths recalled instances of all three during their childhood. For example, one youth who felt apart and isolated during his childhood was obsessed with wanting to be around adult men, frequently developed crushes on male teachers, and spent considerable time with neighborhood girls, particularly enjoying their games of hopscotch and jump rope. He was called "sissy" and "girly" by other boys, and he detested team sports and all things athletic, especially locker rooms.

The prevalence of these three is difficult to determine because few researchers have systematically asked boys the relevant questions that probe these issues. It also bears noting that not all gay or bisexual individuals recall this sense of being different during childhood and adolescence and that these feelings and attractions are not solely the domain of sexual-minority youths. Heterosexual boys may also feel different, have same-sex attractions or desires, enjoy feminine activities, and avoid aggressive pursuits.

Youths interviewed for this book easily and at times graphically remembered these same-sex attractions that emanated from their earliest childhood memories. Despite the dramatic significance that these early homoerotic attractions would have, at the time they felt natural, omnipresent. Many recalled these attractions to other males by identifying concrete, distinct memories prior to first grade. Without great fanfare, with no clashing of cymbals, and with no abiding shock, later homoerotic attractions were felt to be contiguous with these early feelings.

Captivation with Masculinity

Of the three sources for feeling different, the vast majority of the gay/bisexual youths interviewed for this book attributed to themselves an early sense that in some fundamental way they differed from other boys. This difference was an obsession of always wanting to be near other males. Most boys did not at the time believe that these attractions were sexually motivated; they were just overwhelmed with an all-consuming desire to be with other males. Some became flushed or excited when they made contact, especially physical, with other boys or men; some arranged their lives so as to increase time spent with males, while others avoided males because they were frightened by the male aura. Above all else, their obsession with males was mysterious and pervasive. It was also present from an early age, from first memories.

One youth's childhood was one massive memory of men. He decided that the death of his father ten years earlier was the reason that he would always need guys in his life.

> I can remember wanting the men who visited us to hug me when I was real little, maybe three or four. I've always wanted to touch and be touched by guys, and I was a lot. Guys loved to manhandle me. They would throw me up in the air and I'd touch the ceiling and I'd scream and would love it and would do anything to make it happen more and more. It never was enough and I'd tire them out or I'd go to someone else who would toss me. Sometimes I would be teased for the "little points" [erections] in my pants, but no one, including myself, made much of it.
>
> I think I spent my childhood fantasizing about men, not sexually of course, but just being close to them and having them hold me or hug me. I'd feel safe and warm. My dad gave me this and my older brother Mitchell gave me this but all of this was never enough. With the other men I'd feel flushed, almost hot. Maybe those were hot flashes like what women get! Those were good days.

Although he may have been an extreme case, other youths also recalled distinct attractions to men that a decade or more later were still vivid, emotional, and construed as significant. This obsession with males remained at the time nameless for the following three youths.

> I was seven at the time and Will, who was working for us doing yard work, was twenty-one and a college student/athlete. One night when my parents went to a hotel for their anniversary dinner and whatever, they asked Will to stay the night to watch over me. He was in a sleeping bag on the floor and I knew he was nude and he was next to my bed and I kept wondering what was in the sleeping bag. I just knew that I wanted to get in with him but I didn't know why or that I could because I didn't want to bother him. I didn't sleep the whole night.

> Maybe it was the third grade and there was an ad in the paper about an all-male cast for a movie. This confused me but fascinated—intrigued—me so I asked the librarian and she looked all flustered, even mortified, and mumbled that I ought to ask my parents.

> It was very clear to me around six years of age. There was a TV beer commercial which featured several soccer players without shirts on. I mentioned to my brother how much I liked this TV show because the guys didn't have shirts on. I remember this but I'm sure I had thoughts before this.

Those who monopolized their attention were occasionally same-age boys, but were more often older teenagers and adults—male teachers, coaches, cousins, or friends of the family. Public male figures were also sources of fantasies—Superman, Scott Baio, Duran Duran, John Ritter, Bobby Ewing, and Hulk Hogan. Others turned pages in magazines and catalogs to find male models in various stages of undress; especially popular were underwear advertisements. The captivation with men had a familiar tone—a drive for male contact or the male image from an early age with little understanding of what it meant—and a common emotional quality—excitement, euphoria, mystery.

These same-sex attractions were not limited to gay boys. Bisexual youths recalled similar early homoerotic captivation with men.

> Technically it could be either male or female, no matter. I just was into naked bodies. I had access and took, without him knowing it, dad's *Penthouse* magazines. Such a big fuss, but actually in them and whatever else I could find, turned on by both the girls and the men. The men I recall most vividly. It was the hairless, feminine guys with big penises and made-up faces. I loved make-up on my guys, the eyelashes and the eyes, blue shadow, but mostly it was the look. Tight jeans, lean bodies.

Homoerotic desires were often interpreted as natural and hence characteristic of all boys. Many youths articulated that their desire for the "male touch" was deeply embodied in their natural self. By this they implied that their attractions to boys were not a matter of choice or free will but were of early and perhaps, they speculated, genetic origins. For example, one youth never felt that he had a choice regarding his intense attractions to adult males.

> My infatuation with my day camp counselor I didn't choose. Why him and not his girlfriend? I never chose my love objects but I was always attracted to guys. In all of my early dreams and fantasies I always centered on guys whether they were sexual or not. What I wanted to do was to get close to them and I knew that innately, perhaps even by the age of six or seven. I felt it was okay because God said it was okay.

Similarly, many other youths noted that their homoerotic desires were never a matter of choice but "just were." Most believed that they were gay or bisexual in large part because of genetic factors or the "way the cards were dealt—luck of the draw, like something in the neuro-structure or hormonal."

> I'd dream of my uncle and wake up all euphoric and sweaty and eroticized. Another dream that I had at six was of my [boy] classmates playing around in their underwear with these big cocks sticking out. It just happened. How could I choose these things to dream about, to check out the cocks in my mom's *Playgirl*, and to cut out pictures of guys from movie magazines? I was very intrigued by all of this and knew somehow it related to me.

> Maybe my child sex play taught me how to be gay but then maybe it only reinforced what already was. I know that I've been gay for a long time, probably I was born with it. I assumed when I was young that all people had a pee pee. It doesn't have to be genetic but then it could happen during the first year of life. I think I was born being gay, leaning toward homosexuality, and development just sort of pushed it further.

> My brother is gay, my uncle is gay, my father acts like he is gay sometimes, and my mother is hanging out with feminist support groups and really butch-looking women. Did I really have a choice?!

> I can't stand the smell of women. Who really cares? I could have gone straight but it would have been torture. I am what I am, from birth.

Some youths simply assumed, based on the egocentric principle that their thoughts and feelings were shared by others, that all boys must feel as they do but were simply not talking about their desires. With age, however, they came to realize that perhaps they were more "into it."

I guess I was pretty touchable—and I still am based on what guys I know or am with tell me. I didn't understand why because I thought all kids liked it. Others have told me that they liked it too but somehow I think I liked it more. I craved and adored it and my day would not be a good one unless I had this contact. Only later did I find out why I liked being touched by guys.

Another youth decided that he would simply "outgrow" his obsession with males. He was not, however, going to let this future keep him from enjoying this wonderful pleasure at the moment.

As a child I knew I was attracted to males. I was caught by my mother looking at nude photographs of men in her magazines and I heard my father say to her that, "He'll grow out of it," and so I thought and hoped I would. But until then I just settled back and enjoyed my keen curiosity to see male bodies.

You see, it did not feel threatening because (a) it felt great, and (b) father said I would grow out of it, and he was always right. So why not enjoy it until it went away?

Other youths, however, recognized that these undeniably homoerotic attractions were not typical of other boys. They knew they were extreme cases but they "could not help it."

Even at eight I could tell that my interest in guys was way beyond normal. Like this time that we were out with my friend Chad's big brother catching fireflies and he took off his shirt and I forgot about the fireflies and just stared at his chest. Chad got really irritated and called out, "Hey homo give me the jar!" I'm sure I blushed.

When we played truth-or-dare I always wanted to be dared to kiss one of the guys. No one ever dared me to do that, probably because they knew that I'd like it. And I would have! I knew it was strange of me and that they didn't want to kiss boys. They all knew that too but I really didn't care.

Eventually, most youths understood that these undeniable attractions were the wrong ones to have. Despite the belief that they had no choice in matters of their attractions, most inevitably came to appreciate that they should hide their attractions. Snide remarks made by peers, prohibitions taught by parents, and the silence imposed by religion and by teachers all contributed to this realization. Thus, although early obsessions with males were experienced as instinctive, most of the gay/bisexual youths acknowledged from an early age that their impulses were somehow "wrong" but not necessarily "bad."

Despite the presence of an older gay brother, one youth was vulnerable to society's negative messages about homosexuality. His concern centered on being "strike two" for his mother.

Well, I knew enough to hide Sean's *Jock* after I looked at it. It was not guilt—it was too much fun!—but fear that I felt. I was afraid if mother found out that she would feel bad that she had two failures and that Sean would kill me for getting into his stockpile.

Very few youths made the connection during their childhood that these attractions that felt so natural and significant placed them in the stigmatized category of "homosexual." Although most had a passing acquaintance with the concept and had seen "homosexuals" displayed in the media, relatively few would have situated themselves in this category at this point in their lives. One youth believed that "it" was something to be outgrown: "I thought maybe that it was just a stage that I was going through. But if it wasn't a stage then it was probably no problem for me to worry about now." Other youths, however, were worried.

Something was different about me. I knew that. I was afraid of what it meant, and I prayed to God that whatever it was that He would take it away. It was a burden but I liked it, and so I felt guilty about liking it.

It was not until many years later, with the onset of sexual maturations that these attractions would be fully linked with sexuality and perhaps a sexual identity. Homosensuality for these youths was not foreign but natural, a lifelong intrigue with men's bodies. However, as the societal wrongness of their intuitive obsession with masculinity became increasingly apparent, many youths hoped that their attractions were a phase to be outgrown or that their feelings would make sense in some distant future.

The feared repercussions from family members and peers if they were known to have gay traits served as a powerful reason for the boys to feel that their same-sex desires and acts were improper and should not be shared with others. Acting on them was thought to be wrong because if caught, punishment would likely ensue. Balancing desire and fear became a significant dilemma. Eventually, many of the youths recognized that others rarely shared or understood their same-sex desires. This pact of secrecy with themselves was a major theme for many of the youths. It did not, however, always inhibit their sexual behavior; a significant number of the boys acted on their sexual desires during childhood, as is apparent in Chapter Four.

Acting Like a Girl

A second source of feeling different, not explicitly linked with same-sex attractions, involved cultural definitions of gender—how a boy should *not* act, think, and feel. Characteristics deemed not appropriate for boys included observable behaviors such as play with girl-typed toys, especially dolls; involvement in female activities and games; cross-dressing; sex-role motor behavior including limp wrists, high-pitched voices, and dramatic gestures; and stated interests such as wishing to be a girl, imagining self as dancer or model, and preferring for female friends and being around older women. These boys did not wonder, "Why am I gay?" but "Why do I act like a girl?"[5] For example, one youth recalled his childhood in the following way:

I knew that a boy wasn't supposed to kiss other boys, although I did. I knew it was wrong, so this must be some indication that I knew. I also knew that I wasn't supposed to cross my legs at the knees, but I wouldn't like quickly uncross my legs whenever that was the case. So this is certainly at a young age that I noticed this. I think I knew that it was sort of a female thing, sort of an odd thing, and I knew that boys weren't supposed to do that.

Many boys who fit the category of gender bending were at once erotically drawn to boys and men (the first source) but were repelled by their behavior, their standard of dress and cleanliness, and their barbarian nature. They felt ambivalent regarding their attractions to males; intrigued by male bodies and the masculinity mystique, these youths saw men as enigmatic and unapproachable.

Psychotherapist Richard Isay characterizes this sense of gender atypicality in some pregay boys: "They saw themselves as more sensitive than other boys; they cried more easily, had their feelings more readily hurt, had more aesthetic interests, enjoyed nature, art, and music, and were drawn to other 'sensitive' boys, girls, and adults" (p. 23).[6] Indeed, research amply demonstrates that gender nonconformity is one of the best childhood predictors of adult homosexuality in men.[7] Findings from prospective studies are fairly straightforward: The proportion of *extremely* feminine boys who eventually profess a same-sex sexual orientation approaches 100 percent. However, the fraction of these gender-nonconforming boys in the total population remains considerably below that of gay men. Thus, while the vast majority of extremely feminine boys eventually adopt a gay or bisexual identity in adulthood, so do an unknown number of boys who are not particularly feminine.

Feeling more similar to girls than to boys, one youth described his experience "as if I was from a different planet than other boys." He was not alone; a substantial proportion of the gay/bisexual youths recalled that this "girl-like syndrome" was the basis of how they differed from their male peers. Of all boys interviewed, over one-third described their self-image as being more similar to that of girls than boys, and nearly all of these boys reported that this sense of themselves permeated areas of their lives.

One consequence of having more culturally defined feminine than masculine interests was that many boys with gender-atypical characteristics felt most comfortable in the company of girls and women or preferred spending time alone. Two youths described their gender nonconformity during their childhood years.

> I had mostly friends who were girls and I can remember playing jump rope, dolls, and hopscotch with them, and I can remember being very interested in hairstyling and practicing on dolls. I got into sewing and knitting. I played make-believe, read spy and adventure stories, house with my sisters. I had a purse and dolls that they gave me. We did everything together. I was never close with my brother and we never did anything together. I was always accepted by girls and few other boys were.

> Thinking back I did play with girls in the neighborhood a lot. I loved actually to kiss girls and I was always wanting to kiss girls and I thought this might be a little strange or weird because I liked girls so much at such a young age. I just felt very comfortable with them. I felt more self-conscious around boys because I always wondered what they were thinking about.

The extent to which such behavior could produce a gender-bender who is accepted by girls as one of them is illustrated by a third youth.

> I was even invited to slumber parties and I always went. They were so much fun! Just the five of us in our gowns, with lace and bows that my mom had made for my sister and I "borrowed," laughing, sneaking cigarettes, and gossiping about other girls.

Thus, almost without exception boys who displayed early gender-atypical behavior strongly preferred hanging out with girls rather than with boys. Girls were far less likely to reject the "feminine" boys, a reaction that has been confirmed by research studies.[8] If such youths had male friends it was usually one best friend, perhaps a neighbor who also disliked masculine activities.

> I have always been gay although I did not know what that meant at the time. But I knew that I always felt queer, out of place in my hometown. . . . Mostly I spent my time alone in the house or with girls at school. We ate lunch together and talked in between classes. I always felt that girls received the short end of the stick. I really did not have many friends because I lived in a rural area. I felt rejected and I feared being rejected.

> I have usually had one best male friend, who might change every other year or so but who always was like me in hating sports. Like Tim who was one of my best friends because he lived across the street and was handy, someone so I would not be alone. We spent time together but I am not sure what else we ever did. Otherwise I hung with girls.

Not uncommonly, boys who displayed interest in gender-atypical pursuits fervently expressed strong preferences for solo activities such as reading and make-believe games, or for artistic endeavors.

> But my major activity during childhood was drawing and I was sort of known as "The Artist," even as early as third and fourth grades. Today I can see some very gay themes in my drawings! Whenever anyone in the class wanted anything drawn then they asked me. No matter how much they had ridiculed me I agreed to do it.

A second youth made up plays for the neighborhood, role-played TV characters, and cartooned.

> I took part in dance, ballet, singing, and had good manners. I liked Broadway musicals, Barbra, Bette, Joan, Liz, Judy, and Greta . . . I did drama, lots and lots of drama! Anything pretend. I did lots of skits for the Mickey Mouse Club, play writing, and office decorating.

Unclear from these accounts is whether the decision to spend time alone was one freely chosen by the gay/bisexual youths or was a consequence of exclusion dictated by others. That is, were they loners by choice or by circumstance? Although most evidence supports the banishment hypothesis, time alone may have been desired and pursued for creative reasons; time alone may have enhanced their creative efforts. One youth found that he spent a lot of time "doing nothing, just being alone, playing the violin, planting flowers, and arranging flowers." Another youth loved "building and creating things like castles and bridges and rivers in the backyard. Maybe it was because I was an only child but I was into any kind of art and I also composed on the piano." When asked about his childhood activities, a third youth was merely succinct: "Shopped. Homework. Masturbated. Read."

Most difficult for many gender-atypical gay/bisexual boys was the almost universal harassment they received from their peers. As a consequence of associating with girls and not boys, spending considerable time alone, and appreciating female activities, they faced almost daily harassment from peers, usually boys but sometimes girls, teachers, parents, and siblings. Perhaps most insufferable to their male peers was the gay/bisexual boys' feminine gross and fine motor behavior. Their hand gestures, standing and sitting posture, leg and hip movement, voice pitch and cadence, and head tilt conveyed to others that these boys were girllike and hence weak and deplorable. The reactions they received from peers went beyond mere teasing, which most youths receive during childhood and adolescence as a mechanism for social bonding, to outright verbal abuse that was harassing and sometimes extremely destructive to a sense of self. The abuse was occasionally physically expressed and always had emotional and self-image consequences.

Below is a list of names that boys with gender-atypical characteristics reported that they were called by age mates. Not all youths recalled or wanted to remember the exact names.

• sissy	• clumsy	• bitchy	• fag
• queer	• little girl	• cry baby	• fem
• gayson	• faggot	• super fem	• queer bait
• fruitcake	• wimpy	• fruit	• gay
• schoolboy	• pansy	• gaylord	• Janus
• fairy	• softy	• girl	• fag boy
• girly	• homo	• cocksucker	• lisp
• wimp	• gay guy	• Avon Lady	• Safety Girl
• Tinkerbell	• flamer	• mommy's boy	

One youth reported that in grammar school he was voted "The Person Most Likely to Own a Gay Bar."

The specific provocation that elicited these names during school, on the bus, and in the neighborhood varied, but several patterns are discernible. The abuse usually occurred because a boy was perceived as a misfit, as acting too much "like a girl." Three youths provided testimonies from their lives:

Because I was somewhat effeminate in my behavior and because I wore "girly" shoes. Some said that I was a little girl because I couldn't play baseball. I played the clarinet in school and this was defined as a female instrument so I got some teasing for that. I thought I could control my behavior but it got so bad that my family decided to pull me out of the public school to go to a private Catholic school where the teasing receded.

Because I was weak and a cry baby. I was not in the "in" crowd. Also because of the way I dressed and that I got good grades. I was very thin and got every disease that came around. I had all sorts of allergies and was always using all sorts of drugs. I was told I looked like a girl. I played with Barbies and taught her how to sit up and later how to fly. I just wasn't masculine enough I guess.

People thought that perhaps I might be gay because they thought I was just way too nice and also because I was flamboyant. They really didn't think I was like homosexually gay. It was just a term that they used for me because it seemed to fit my personality. People said I'm gay because of my mannerisms, also because I slur my s's and I'm so flamboyant. I think it's the way that I walked, the way I talked, the way I carried myself. I had a soft voice. Lots of boys blew me kisses. My voice is just not masculine. Also I tended to be very giggly and flighty and flaky and silly at times.

One youth believed that "most kids were just looking for a laugh" and that he was the easiest target, because of his femininity, they could find. He was their "amusement for the day."

In no story were girls the only ones who verbally abused a youth for being gender nonconforming. On many occasions, however, boys acted alone. Perhaps the most usual pattern was for boys, or a subset of boys, to be the persistent ridiculers with a few girls chiming in when present.

> Some of the jocks really bothered me but mostly it was these three guys every day making my life miserable. Always done by males who really had this pecking order. Real bullies!

> This was mostly males—this one guy seemed to have it out for me. But some of the girls who hung out with him also did it. The girls thought I was bitchy and called me "fag" and "homo."

Although reactions to being victimized by peer ridicule were diverse, the most common responses, illustrated by three youths, were to ignore, withdraw, or cry.

> I took it without saying anything back. I'd pretend that I didn't hear them or hide my feelings. I hated it but didn't say anything back. Guess I was benign to it. Just sat there and took it. I did that for protection. I was so much of a misfit that bullies did it to me. I offended them in some way. Just a horrible, wrenching experience.

> I became more withdrawn and thus more of an outcast. I'd cower and keep my distance, keeping it inside myself. I did nothing or remained silent or said "leave me alone." Once I fought back and lost, which made me withdraw even more.

> I was very, very sensitive and would cry very easily. I had very little emotional control at the time. Cry, yell at them, cry some more. I would tell my mother and cry and she'd try to comfort me or she'd just dismiss it all. I would tell the guys that I had told my mother and they would make more fun of me.

Not all boys reacted so passively to the verbal assault. Several developed innovative, self-enhancing ways to cope with peer harassment. For example, one youth noted an unusual situation:

> All my boyfriends, the jock types, always protected me and punished those who teased me. I would just turn away as if I never gave notice because I knew that I would be protected by all the guys, the jocks, that I was having sex with. I never did try to get back at them [the harassers]. Once they realized this then they kept quiet.

Another used his intelligence and experience as strategies for coping with peer harassment.

I think it was because I was so flamboyant and I was not so sports-oriented. If they said it to my face then I would say "get out of my face!" Or I would point out their stupidity. I considered them to be rather stupid, so immature. I'd been around the world and I knew I could say things that would damage them because I was smarter than them and because I had so many female friends. I tried to ignore it because I knew that I was better than them. I sort of got respect for not fighting back or sometimes I would say, "I like girls! What's *your* problem?"

It is difficult to ascertain the true impact on a youth of this constant bombardment of negative peer review. Few of the boys thought it was anything but negative. Most felt that the most significant effect of the verbal harassment was what it did to their personality: They became increasingly withdrawn from social interactions, despondent, and self-absorbed. The aftermath for the four youths below was a decrease in their self-image and self-worth.

I felt very conscious about my voice and somewhat shameful that I wasn't masculine enough. I actually just sort of retreated more and became more introverted. I felt rejected and it hurt my self-esteem. I took the ridicule to heart and I blamed myself.

Because I knew that indeed I had the attractions to guys I knew that they were right and that I was a disgusting human being. I just spent a lot more time alone to avoid the pain. I just sort of blocked it all internally because it hurt so much. I just sort of erased all my memories of my childhood so I can't give you much detail.

A real nightmare! I really felt like I had no friends. It really did lower my self-esteem and it made me focus on sort of my outer appearance and ignore the inner. It devastated me because I felt everything they said was true. I was quiet and kept it inside.

Heightened my sense of being different. Caused me to withdraw and not feel good about myself. Cut off from people and become shy. Became introverted, guilty. I hated that time. Childhood was supposed to be happy times but it was not. Later, I dropped out of school, thought about suicide, and ran away from home.

Although none of the boys felt that the labeling made him gay, many believed that the name-calling contributed to their negative image of homosexuality. Hence, the ridicule became a central factor in who they are. The abuse also kept them in the closet for a considerably longer period of time. These effects are apparent in the two narratives below:

It just sort of reinforced that men are scum. I viewed being a fag as so negative that it hurt my self-image for them to call me that. I didn't like myself, so being gay is bad and what they're saying I knew it to be true because I am bad and being gay is bad and I'm gay. It's made me think of males only as sex objects because I wanted to be hated by men because I didn't like myself. I started back in elementary school to believe it was true.

I had such a hostile view towards homosexuality, so it was hard to come out as a result of this stigma because I had really low self-esteem. It affected me by not having a positive attitude about homosexuality in general. I needed at least a positive or even neutral point of view and that would have made my gay life so much easier. I continue to suppress things.

It was the rare youth for whom anything positive emerged from the verbal ridicule. One youth noted that "teasing sort of helped me to deal with my gay identity at a very early age because everyone was calling my attention to it." He was proud to be effeminate; he reported that the teasing made him stronger and was thus beneficial.

I wore stylish clothes and was my own individual self. My teachers appreciated this but not the slobs. Because of this a lot of them said that I was gay and so I thought I must be, although I did not know what this meant except that it meant I would not be shoveling cow shit!

Unfortunately, few youths could recall such positive aspects to their gender atypicality. More often, the consequences of being true to their nature were that other boys viewed them as undesirable playmates and as "weird." Labeled sissy or effeminate, they were rejected by boys, and, equally important, they had little desire to fraternize with their male peers. Because other boys did not constitute an enjoyable or safe context for play or socializing, the youths often turned to girls for activities and consolation. They preferred to dance rather than shovel shit, to sing rather than yell "hike," and to draw rather than bash heads. Thus, childhood was usually experienced as a traumatizing time by youths who did not conform to cultural sex roles. The fortunate ones sought and found girls for solace and support. Girls became their saviors, offering sources of emotional sustenance as the male world of childhood became increasingly distasteful. It was to these girls that many gay/bisexual males subsequently disclosed their sexual affiliations during middle or late adolescence (see Chapter Seven).

Not Acting Like a Boy

A third source of feeling different among the interviewed youths originated from a disinterest or abhorrence of typical masculine activities, which may or may not have occurred in the presence of a captivation with masculinity (first source) or of high levels of femininity (second source). Thus, a lack of masculinity did not necessarily imply that such youths were fond of female activities or were drawn to or hung out with girls. Many reported never playing house, dressing up as a girl, or having a passing acquaintance with Barbie. In the absence of typical expressions of femininity, boys without masculine interests were usually loners or spent time with one or several best male friends.

Compared with what is known about gender-atypical boys, considerably less is known concerning those who during childhood do not fit cultural images of how a boy should act, think, and feel. Characteristics labeled as unmasculine or as failure to conform to gender expectations include observable behaviors such as avoidance of rough-and-tumble play, typical boys' games, and athletic activities; no imagining of oneself as a sports figure; and no desire to grow up to be like one's father. These boys did not wonder, "Why am I gay?" but "Why don't I act like a boy?"[9]

Childhood activities that constitute "unmasculine" all share the characteristic of being gender neutral by North American standards, suitable for both boys and girls. Within this gender nonpartisanship, active and passive patterns were evident in the interviews. Some boys were as active as masculine-inclined peers but in nonmasculine, nonathletic—at least in a team sports sense—activities.

> My friend and me made roads and gardens. I liked to sort of build cities and bridges outside and in the garden. Played in the woods, hiked in the woods, camped out, and hide and seek. Ted and I were almost inseparable for a couple of years. I also biked, swam a lot, jumped on the trampoline. Biking was my way of dealing with stress. I was into matchbox cars.

> I enjoyed playing office, playing grow-up, walking around the city basically looking at other people. Mind games and chess with my brothers. Creative imaginative play. Discovering and enjoying spending a lot of time on bike trips, going to new places. Getting out of the house and being outside, just wandering off by myself.

More common were boys who spent considerable time alone pursuing passive activities. This passivity should not be equated, however, with having a bad time or having a bad childhood. Many recalled an enjoyable if unconventional life during childhood.

> At school I hung out with myself but on weekends it was primarily guys in the neighborhood and we would like watch TV and videos. They were like my best friends and we were not really into moving sports. We were more into passive activities like music and cards. I've always been in the band. Hanging out at the mall. A couple of us guys would do this.

> Very quiet pursuits, stamps, cooking, which my mother liked. Guess I played verbal games, board games with the family, Risk and Candyland, and crossword puz-

zles. Did a lot with my family, like family vacations, visiting historical things. I read, played with Lincoln Logs, fantasizing, spending time by myself, drawing, and swinging. I loved the freedom of the swing and I'd do it for hours. Oh yes, I loved croquet!

I read a lot—like the encyclopedia, the phone book, science fiction, science, mystery, and gothic novels. I had a comic book collection and Star Wars cards. I spent most of my other time drawing maps. I was really into getting any information anywhere I could, even from the atlas or an almanac. I can remember actually setting out to read the dictionary, although I don't think I got very far. Almost every book in the public library later on.

Most explicitly, unmasculine youths felt particularly ill at ease with archetypal male sports, especially loathing team sports such as baseball, basketball, and football. If they became involved in competitive, aggressive sports it was in response to family or peer pressure. Perhaps forced by a father or coach to participate in sports as a right fielder, a defensive back, or a bench warmer, they deeply resented such coercion and their inevitable failure. Severely repulsed by many typical masculine pursuits, this source of trauma was to be avoided at all costs, even at the price of disappointing parents. Unmasculine youths often shared with the following very gender-atypical youth his rejection of masculine activities and hence of masculinity.

I did not play basketball or wrestle and I was not a farmer nor a slob nor did I shovel cow shit like my classmates. Girl, they would come in smelling like they looked and you can be sure it was not a number Chanel ever heard of! There was no way that I was going to let this be a part of what I wanted for my life.

Well they [parents] wanted me to try at least one sport but I was always sort of the last chosen. I knew I was effeminate and clumsy and my father ridiculed me for it. So I avoided sports and I did this by going home for lunch and visiting my female friends rather than playing sports with the other guys during recess.

For one youth, the appeal or even logic of sports baffled and befuddled him.

I really did not care about most sports and I still do not. I liked more intellectual than physical things. I enjoyed more talking philosophy, writing poetry, and drawing than spending time throwing stupid balls away, then running after the stupid balls, trying to find the stupid balls, and then throwing the stupid balls back to the same person so that he could throw it away again and have somebody run after it, find it, and throw it back to him again. Sounds real intelligent does it not?! Doing these stupid ball tricks made Bill [twin brother] real popular and me really unpopular. Where is the fairness in that?

> I only played sports during recess when I had to. I hated little boy games such as basketball, kickball, football, baseball, or anything that had a ball or a peck order. It was very aggressive and used all of the wrong parts of my anatomy and my personality.

The most aversive aspect of sports was its aggressive, dominant, physical nature. One youth remarked that in sports someone always has to lose—"and it was usually me!" This reflected not only his own personal experience of losing but also an antipathy to his life philosophy of peace, harmony, cooperation. Another youth astutely recognized another reason not to become involved in sports—his true nature might emerge and become figuratively and physically visible.

> I was not on any team sport because I was so self-conscious about being around other males. I was afraid of how I might be looked upon by them and what I might do or say or look at if I was around them a lot. What would I do in the locker room? What would happen to "George," who has a mind of his own? Maybe my feelings might come out and then where would I be?

Other youths reported that they wanted to participate in sports but could not because of physical problems. One noted, "I could never much be a sports person because I had a coordination problem because of my vision that caused me to be physically awkward." Another compensated by reading about sports: "Well, I read the sports pages and sports books! I hated gym because I was overweight. I could not do sports because I felt so evil watching men strip naked in the locker room and I couldn't take it." A third youth was on the swim team before getting pneumonia, forcing him to quit. His restitution was to remain active: "I hung out at the beach (yes, looking at the guys!), played Atari, skateboarded, and played Pogo."

Those who became involved in sports almost always preferred individual to team sports. These "jocks" included the two youths below.

> Some track, cross-country, swimming. I never liked the team sports. I had to do soccer in fourth grade because my best friends were into it but I disliked it immensely. Guess I was mid-level in ability and lower than that in interest but it gave me something to do and kept me around guys. I lived in a very sex-segregated rural area. I gave all of these up in junior high, except swimming in the Scout pool.

> I was really into sports. Let's see. Gymnastics in fourth to sixth grades; bowling in third; darts in third; ping pong whenever; dodge the ball in second to fourth; volleyball in sixth.

Perhaps because of their paltry athleticism and low levels of masculine interests, these boys were not immune to peer ridicule and teasing. They were not, however, ridiculed nearly to the degree that gender-nonconforming boys were. They were often teased for non-gender-related characteristics or for individualized perceived deficits in physical features ("fatty"), in normative masculine behavior ("wimp"), or in desirable kinds of intelligence ("nerd"). Some were also called names more typical of effeminate youths ("fag") without, they almost universally acknowledged, the connotation of sexuality. One youth defended himself by asserting, "Being called a fag really was not a sexual thing. It was more that it reflected on my low self-esteem and that I was so wimpy."

The most common name callers were same-age, same-sex peers, although occasionally girls also participated. One youth had an unusual experience. Called "nerd" by three girls who were making his life miserable, "several boys seemed to go out of their way to protect me and shield me from this kind of teasing. Of course I was giving them answers on their exams!" Otherwise he simply withdrew. Because ridicule was seemingly random and seldom daily, it was sometimes difficult for unmasculine youths to understand what provoked the name calling.

One youth reported that he enjoyed his life as a loner and that others seemed more upset than he was that he was spending so much time alone. With his involvement in computers, the complaints lessened, perhaps, he guessed, because others envied his knowledge and saw it as a means to earn a good living. He was subject, however, to the taunts of male peers. Occasionally he was ridiculed by several boys on the school bus and during recess for reasons that were beyond his control.

> At first I didn't understand why they were on my case, but since I didn't fit in in a lot of ways, they had their way. It was just the usual thing. Probably because I wasn't good at sports but I can't remember what I was called. In gym classes primarily by macho males. Nothing I didn't want to remember. I really can't remember too much of it or certainly not the names. It just seemed like I was teased about as much as anyone else was. Not every day, maybe once a month, and I just sort of reacted passively. Never really a major thing or very threatening, just sort of stupid kids' stuff. Just sort of let it go away.
>
> I didn't fit in because I was against the intellectualism of the smart kids and I wasn't a jock. Hence I was not respected. I have no real memories of the exact names but I think they weren't happy ones because I was thin and, oh yes, my ears stuck out so I was called "monkey face."

The name-calling message might be that the boy was too feminine or not masculine enough, but more commonly it was because he was simply different or had undesirable characteristics. Very few felt that being gay was a cause of the verbal abuse. The following youths recounted the reasons they believed they suffered at the hands of their peers.

I was awkward and wore glasses. I had a speech impediment and a birthmark. I was ostracized, sort of left out because I wasn't conforming and I was very shy. I was sort of known as an only child and thus a spoiled brat with very little social skills. I was never teased about being gay.

For being fat and overweight. Maybe I was teased more than average. It did hurt. I reacted by just crying because I really couldn't ignore it. It was a weight issue and not a sexual identity issue.

Because I was quiet, shy, and geekish. For being physically awkward, being different, bookish. As a kid I was teased for having cow eyes because my eyes were large. For not going to church. Very low-class assholes, mostly males. Then I went to a school for gifted children and it stopped.

I was ridiculed about being a softy and brain box because I was so intellectual or consumed in the books. They said I got good grades because I was kissing teachers' asses. I think I was just different from all of them and the teachers liked me because I liked learning. Perhaps it happened because I went to an all-male Catholic school.

I was shy and I got called Spock a lot because of my eyes which were real dark. They thought I was wearing eye shadow.

The most common response of the youths was to remain silent. One youth felt scared and frightened but "later it just got to be an annoyance. My response was to remain rather stoic." Another hated gym because he was not "graceful" and because of a particular nemesis.

A classic case of one guy on my case which I usually ignored. But one day he threw me to the gym floor but a guy came to my rescue. He was bigger than me so my reaction was basically to brave it, to try to show that it did not affect me by just walking away. I would usually not talk back and I would not cry.

A second common response was to simply avoid situations where one might be ridiculed. This was not always an easy task.

Being not good at sports, I tried to avoid all sporting situations if at all possible. I just felt like I was left out of everything. I sort of internalized it but I can't really remember how I reacted. I dreaded going to the gym. I was afraid and felt that I was bullied. I was not verbally equipped to deal with this kind of teasing. I really didn't fight back until high school.

A third response, somewhat less prevalent, was to feel extremely hurt and cry, either publicly or in private. One youth grew to hate and fear school. "It was very painful and I was upset by it and I cried. In fact, so much so I didn't want to go to school." Another cried in private.

> I was teased for being very heavy and for being slow. I reacted by being very hurt; I couldn't accept it. I cried a lot, not in front of them but in the bathroom or my room. My out was always, "Well, I'm smart."

Finally, several youths reported that they surprised their tormentors by behaving in a very masculine way, fighting back against the name-calling.

> I rode the bus. I felt singled out and ridiculed. Initially what I did was simply relax and ignore it but then at one point I actually fought back, physically and verbally attacking sort of the main person who was ridiculing me the most. If I did fight back, which was the case occasionally, I would usually win. Because it was a small school, the word got out and after that I had no problems. I gained in popularity and the teasing tapered off to almost nothing.

> There were rumors about me being gay. I got teasing when my friend told others that we had slept together. I confronted these people but it didn't help. I ended up going back at others or attacking them. I confronted them, "Why are you so interested in my sexuality?" After awhile they left me alone. I denied being gay but I knew I was. I wasn't ashamed but I wanted the ridiculing to stop. I was very wicked to others.

The immediate effects of the ridicule are difficult to determine. However, based on their reports, consequences appear far less severe than they were for youths who enacted femininity, perhaps because the ridicule was not as frequent and did not focus on a central aspect of their sexuality. For example, one youth noted that the name-calling had no repercussion on his sexuality because he did not interpret the ridicule as emanating from his unconventional sexuality. He did not feel that the abuse made him gay or caused him to delay self-identifying as gay. He felt, however, that the ridicule contributed to his tendency to withdraw from social settings, causing him to be more introverted and self-effacing.

> It had no real implications for my sexual identification. Everybody in my school was teased; everyone was called faggot, so I really didn't feel like I was singled out. But it made me trust people less. Hurt my self-esteem. I still need to be liked by others and if not, it upsets me. Maybe why I spent so much time alone. People hurt you. On the good side, I developed good sarcastic skills and a dry wit.

Including those who had many feminine characteristics during childhood, as many as three-quarters of the gay/bisexual youths interviewed had few interests or characteristics usually attributed to men in North American culture. Being *neither* particularly masculine *nor* feminine resulted in youths occupying the middle rung of the peer-group status hierarchy. When not alone, they were usually with a best buddy or a small group of male friends with whom they spent considerable time. Although they were seldom as frequently ridiculed by peers as were youths who were gender atypical in their lifestyle, such youths still faced verbal abuse, usually from same-age boys. The personal characteristics that became targets of abuse were notably analogous to those that heterosexual boys also receive teasing about if they are "unconventional": physical features, personality characteristics, and intelligence. Similar to other gay/bisexual youths, however, most recalled early, intense, natural attractions to other boys and men.

Acting Like A Boy

Not all of the gay/bisexual boys felt different from peers, acted in gender-atypical ways, expressed effeminate gestures and postures, or disliked team sports during their childhood. One in ten was masculine in appearance, behavior, and interests—nearly indistinguishable from their childhood masculine heterosexual peers. Although these relatively rare boys recalled, in retrospect, that they might have had "nonsexual" attractions to males during early childhood, they had few memories of *sexual* attractions to girls, boys, or anything else. Now, however, they believe that their same-sex attractions have always been a natural part of who they are.

Many of these youths reminisced that as children they chased girls, but this was more of a game that they joined with other boys than a statement about their sexuality or their true sexual interests. As adolescents they were simply disinterested in sexual relations with girls, in being emotionally intimate with girls, or in developing romantic relationships with girls. Most never fantasized about girls. The gay youths with masculine characteristics often had difficulty articulating precisely what it was about sexuality that excited them. Many failed to recall any prepubertal sexual or erotic attractions; thus, in some respects, they appeared to be asexual, especially during the years preceding adolescence. One youth reported "a vague sense that although I did not desire intimate relations with girls, I was not sure what I wanted." Unsure of how they "became gay," the youths characterized their life before puberty as "sexless" and as deeply invested in masculine activities, especially sports.

One youth, who would later run track and play high-school baseball and football, remembered his childhood as his "glory years." Girls were not an integral part of his life.

> As a child I used to run a lot, just everywhere I could, and play tag, swimming, kickball, and softball. Loved making forts. Building blocks, Legos, war games. Just like my best buddy, which changed from time to time, well at least every year I

would develop a best buddy, and it was always the best looking guy in my class who was my best friend—always an athlete. I hung around totally guys.

Maybe I just did not have time but I was not into sex. I would have to say that I was sexless because I cannot remember any sexual thoughts. I was not interested in girls even though I had several girlfriends. In general I felt left out of what my teammates said they were going through.

When asked during the interview to elaborate *any* aspect of his childhood sexuality, he drew a blank. He had many stories of athletic exploits but no sexual ones. Years after pubertal onset he discovered his sexuality and expressed wonderment regarding the location of his sexual desires during childhood.

Similar to this youth, others appeared in most respects to be the traditional, heterosexual boy next door. This was especially evident in their play activities and partners. They enjoyed their popularity with other boys, and they often developed a best friendship with another boy, usually a teammate on a sports team. One swimmer noted that the time he spent "with Jared and the other guys on the swim team was the happiest time of my life."

The sports acumen of these youths was equal or superior to many of their heterosexual peers. However, a distinct bias existed in terms of liking and participating in individual rather than team sports. While many played competitive team sports, their participation appeared more obligatory as an important aspect of male culture than a real choice. Their true love was more apparent in individual sports, especially swimming, track, tennis, and wrestling. Similar to other gay/bisexual youths, many disliked the aggressive, competitive nature of team sports.

For Dad I did baseball—and it wasn't that I was bad, because I made the team and started—but I just couldn't get into it. Like I refused to slide because I was afraid I'd hurt the other guy, and I was just not going to go crashing into fences to catch a ball! I didn't like being challenged at sports because I was afraid I wasn't good enough so I went into individual sports like tennis, track, and swimming. Dad and I reached a compromise with my track, especially when I won the state 1000M.

As a child I really liked horseplay, tag, and wrestling. I have to admit that I hated the Little League but as a kid I played Little League for five years, usually at second base. Later tennis, two years of which were on varsity and I lettered. Also track and lifted weights. I was accepted by everyone, but the baseball guys who were so cutthroat; every game was the end of the universe for them!

As a result of their peer status, few of these boys were teased by others. When they were, it was usually within the context of normative male bonding—teasing in good humor. Although relatively few heard references to being gay, they nonetheless dreaded such accusations. One youth feared that his friends would notice his head turning when a good-looking guy passed by.

In contrast to the gay/bisexual youths previously discussed, masculine youths by disposition looked and acted like other boys their age, participated in typical masculine pursuits, and "fooled" peers into believing that they were heterosexual. They claimed no memories of homoerotic or even sexual attractions during childhood, perhaps, one might speculate, because the realization that the true objects of their sexual desires were boys would have caused them considerable grief and confusion. They were often perceived to be social butterflies and they actively engaged in male-male competitive sports, although their preference was for individual sports. Their male friendships were critical to maintain; they wanted and needed to be members of the "male crowd." From all appearances they succeeded in creating a facade of heterosexuality, in being accepted as "one of the guys."

Reflections on the Childhood of Gay/Bisexual Youths

From an early age, the vast majority of the gay/bisexual youths believed that they were different from other boys their age and that regardless of the source of this feeling, it was a natural, instinctual, and omnipresent aspect of themselves. The pattern that most characterized the youths' awareness, interpretation, and affective responses to childhood attractions consisted of an overwhelming desire to be in the company of men. They wanted to touch, smell, see, and hear masculinity. This awareness originated from earliest childhood memories; in this sense, they "always felt gay."

Most ultimately recognized, however, that these feelings were not typical of other boys and that it would be wrong or unwise to express them because of family and peer prohibitions. Others simply assumed that all boys felt as they did and could not understand why their friends were not as preoccupied as they were with homoerotic desires. Although these attractions may have felt natural, the youths were told by parents, friends, religious leaders, teachers, and dogma that such desires were evil and sinful. Many knew that their homosensuality was ill-advised, but they did not thus conclude that it made them sick or immoral.

Beyond this common pattern, two other sources of "feeling different" characterized the vast majority of the gay/bisexual youths. Many were dominated by an overwhelming sense that their difference was attributed to their feminine appearance, behavior, and interests. In many respects these characteristics typify the stereotype that many, gay and nongay alike, have of gay males. Youths so feminized felt natural and true to self, despite the fact that their gender nonconformity was frequently and severely punished with ostracism. Most of these youths detested cultural definitions of masculinity and felt at odds with other boys because they did not share their peers' interest in team sports, competition, and aggressive pursuits. Being an outcast in the world of male peers was usually felt to be unfair and unnecessary, but also inevitable. To avoid becoming expatriated, these boys developed friendships with girls, perhaps because of common interests such as attractions to boys and appreciation of the arts, creativity, clothing, and manners. They felt more comfortable and had greater comraderie with girls than with boys. Few wanted to change either their genitalia or their behavior; they did not view themselves as women in disguise—they were simply repulsed by the "grossness" of masculinity and attracted to the sensitivities of femininity.

Other youths failed to duplicate standard masculine characteristics without necessarily assuming feminine traits. In this they may well have resembled heterosexual peers who were also neither particularly masculine nor feminine in behavior. They differed, however, in the direction of their sexual attractions. Being disinterested in team sports and other typical aggressive and competitive pursuits caused them to feel unmasculine, but they did not thus necessarily construe themselves as feminine. Relatively few spent time with girls or participated in girl games. Rather, their activities can be characterized as "appropriate" for either girls or boys.

Many of these youths felt that they simply faded into the background when with peers. Most were loners for a considerable period during their childhood; when they socialized with peers they were usually with one or two male friends. Although they were spared the vicious, pervasive verbal abuse that their effeminate counterparts received during childhood, they were not immune from harassment. Boys still ridiculed them for their physical features, lack of ability in athletic pursuits, and unconventional behavior or intelligence.

In contrast to these gay/bisexual youths was a much smaller group of youths who were nearly indistinguishable from masculine heterosexual boys their age. Constituting at least one of every ten youths interviewed, their participation in typical masculine pursuits, especially individual and team sports, blended them into the fabric of male culture. Many were socially active and one might speculate that their male friendships were an enjoyable sublimation of homoerotic attractions that they only later, often during adolescence or young adulthood, recognized. Their failure to recognize any sexual feelings during childhood could be attributed to the direction their sexual attractions might take if they were allowed into consciousness. In this respect, their psychic investment was to conceal this secret from themselves and others.

Unknown is the etiology of these patterns and their long-term effects on other aspects of development, including participation in sexual activities, self-recognition of a sexual identity, disclosure of that identity to others, romantic relationships with other males, and developing a positive sense of self.

Although several of the interviewed youths experienced same-sex attractions as arising abruptly and unexpectedly, for the vast majority these feelings emerged as gradual, inevitable, and not particularly surprising. In this sense, these findings are at odds with the theme of this book—diversity in developmental patterns. Few if any youths believed that they could control the direction of their sexual feelings and no youth believed that he ultimately chose his sexual orientation or sexual attractions. The incorporation of the various masculine and feminine behavioral patterns was felt by youths to be less a matter of choice than an experienced naturalness that was derived from their biological heritage and, less commonly, from early socialization processes beyond their control. On his emerging sexuality, one youth reflected, "It was like being visited by an old friend." This awareness may have emerged early or late, surfaced gradually or arrived instantaneously, felt normal or wrong, motivated sexual activity or abstinence—but it was one aspect of the self that was present without invitation. Future development, discussed in the following chapters, was simply an unfolding of that which was already present, with puberty playing a crucial turning point for many youths in clarifying for them that their homosensuality had a sexual component. From this awareness often loomed first sexual encounters, which occurred during the earliest years of childhood or waited until young adulthood. They too were interpreted by the youths in diverse ways, thus having a differential impact on the eventual incorporation of a gay or bisexual identity.

3.

Labeling Feelings and Attractions

After feeling an early sense of being different from peers, youths typically report, usually following pubertal onset, an awareness of the sexual nature of their attractions. This milestone involves *labeling* same-sex attractions as "homosexual" without necessarily understanding the logical extension of this discovery—that one is gay or bisexual. The interval between feeling different and labeling attractions as homoerotic is occasionally nonexistent, as when they occur simultaneously, but typically stretches to several years, sometimes a decade, or, for some individuals, a lifetime. That is, it is possible that a boy will immediately connect his feelings of difference with his homoerotic feelings, or he may never recognize the sexual component of his attractions.

The time frame between the two milestones may have been especially elongated among previous generations of men raised during times of severe stereotypes and oppressive invisibility. This is illustrated in Table 1.3 by the older ages of "labeling feelings and self as homosexual" in studies conducted in the 1970s. Many men now in their fifties, sixties, and beyond perceived what a "homosexual" must be based on the caricatures personified in the media, such as the 1970 movie "The Boys in the Band" and the 1968 book by Martin Hoffman titled *The Gay World: Male Homosexuality and the Social Creation of Evil*—and thus could not identify with such images. Other men in these generations never had available to them a concept of homosexuality that would have helped them make sense of their internal feelings of difference and of same-sex attractions. In many pre–1970, nonurban locales in the United States, homosexuality was never spoken of or described in the media, including newspapers, television, movies, and the radio.

For contemporary gay/bisexual youths, however, the ultimate resolution of these initially vague but compelling desires for other males often takes place during adolescence or young adulthood.[1] This abbreviation of time within modern cohorts of youths is especially understandable now that same-sex attractions has garnered extensive national and international media attention. Youths face daily reminders of homosexuality on the playground and in the media, and they have available to them a diversity of gay images. Promoting this awareness has been AIDS, which "has meant talking about gay people in the most human terms—as sons and daughters, lovers and caretakers" (p. 2D).[2]

The accelerated process of labeling attractions as "homosexual" can pave the way to further developments, such as labeling oneself gay or bisexual, having gay sex, and disclosing to others before the conclusion of adolescence. This is a remarkable timetable given previous cohorts of gay/bisexual men who often internalized without question negative cultural values and beliefs regarding homosexuality and thus postponed or totally avoided healthy sexual development.[3]

Puberty and Its Effects

The spiraling realization of homoerotic desires usually appears with the onset of puberty and thereafter increases exponentially. For many youths, puberty is a critical turning point at which time *preexisting* thoughts and feelings become associated with sexuality. It is as if the hormonal changes and cognitive shifts that are secondary to puberty *stamp in* the sexual nature of a youth's attractions, adding (sometimes) unwanted clarity that defines heretofore poorly understood feelings. Regardless of previous childhood sexual activities and labels, with the onset of puberty the elusive same-sex desires of the to-be gay/bisexual-identified youth are frequently demystified.

Little consensus exists regarding what it is about puberty that renders it such a convincing context for labeling and understanding. Perhaps the critical instigator is the biologically induced increase in sexual libido that is linked with a dramatic escalation in hormone production. These hormones, in turn, sexualize the physical appearance of the body and the youth's cognitions, emotions, and behaviors. Furthermore, because a youth now looks, acts, thinks, and emotes sexuality, others treat him accordingly, as a sexual being. These biological and social changes elicit within him an increased perception of himself as someone with a sexuality.

Indeed, many of the gay/bisexual youths who were interviewed reported that shortly following pubertal onset, sexuality intruded into every thought, feeling, and behavior. This alternately frightened and energized them. Although the ways in which youths responded to the onset of puberty and the accompanying increase in sexual libido were not uniform, the heretofore unknown sexual universe now open to them often provided the context for self-reflection and interpretation. This interplay between biology and the environment is consistent with modern developmental perspectives on sexuality during adolescence—that all behavior is a function of the person and the environment and that the arrow of cause and effect points in both directions.

Although the growing cognizance and intensity of same-sex attractions are often electrifying, they can also create immense complications and obstacles for a youth. In either case, they raise the stakes for the naming of a sexual identity and bring some clarification of previously misunderstood feelings. In this regard they are a source of great relief and perhaps exhilaration. For relatively few youths, however, do puberty and its accompanying consequences induce sufficient clarity regarding the meaning of these strongly felt homoerotic sexual lusts and desires that a declaration of homosexuality or bisexuality becomes imminent.

One example of such a youth is a sixteen-year-old who recalled his reaction at the age of twelve when he learned the meaning of his sexual interests: "It was a shock to discover that my impassioned, if unarticulated, love affairs with fellow schoolboys which had held so much poignant beauty carried that weighty word *homosexual.*"[4] The application of a sexual label provides not only an explanation for formerly vague feelings, but it also affords a context in which future thoughts, emotions, and identities can be understood.

Not all youths came to realize their "homosexual" attractions at pubertal onset. Indeed, some youths became cognizant of their desires prior to puberty; others, during the later years of puberty or years after completion of sexual and physical growth. Explanations for these atypical departures are not always decipherable from the youths' stories, but they will be proposed when appropriate.

Prepubertal Awareness

Despite the critical role puberty plays in providing the context or the motivating force for many gay/bisexual youths to recognize their same-sex attractions, not all boys "wait" until puberty. Some other factor(s) instigated the awareness among 10 percent of those interviewed for this book. These youths acknowledged to themselves prior to puberty that their attractions were "homosexual," but they did not consequently thus label themselves a gay or bisexual person. That is, they knew they had homoerotic feelings but that realization did not, from their perspective, make them gay.

One youth's homoerotic revelations forced their way into childhood consciousness through his dreams. They did not, however, mean that he was like his gay brother or his gay friends.

Around eight I had two dreams that told me what I liked. The first was a repulsive dream of a girl that I was supposed to date but didn't want to. The second was of a man chasing me wanting to have sex. I was not sure what to think about these dreams and so I really didn't, even though I remembered them and told my shrink. But she just asked me what I thought they meant and I said, "I guess I hate girls and I don't want to have sex with old men." That's not what she wanted to hear.

By nine I knew the same-sex attractions were there, but I wasn't gay. I had this image of what gay was, like Joe and his friends, queening it up, talking about cock all the time, measuring each other with this ruler and prancing around the house. I heard the words they were called and I knew that it was not me.

Other youths erroneously normalized their homoerotic feelings as characteristic of all boys and so attributed no personal significance to them. One youth believed that all boys shared his desire to be touched by males and that, as a result, they had the same attractions to men. These were his childhood needs and he thought that once he "grew up" he would outgrow these desires. "I didn't think there was anything unusual in my need for the male touch. Everybody, including me, figured I'd outgrow these needs eventually and be like everybody else."

Still others had difficulty making the association because they did not have the concept of homosexuality or a gay person. As a result, by default one youth considered himself heterosexual even though he later recognized that he was experiencing "homosexual" feelings during this time. Despite his voracious reading and television watching, he never read about nor saw overt displays of homosexuality. Thus, "I'd watch dancers, especially skaters, on TV and I felt a vague, emotional— or was it sexual?—attraction to their bodies showing through their tights."

Other youths simply pushed the meanings aside to be interpreted at another time and place. One seven-year-old watched "boys more than girls and I recognized that this was important in some part of my awareness." Perhaps it was just a "homosexual stage" that he was going through; if not, "then it was probably still no problem." Another youth felt "something was different" in an elementary health-education class when he heard the word *homosexual.* Although it described his fantasies about his male babysitters, he had no reason to believe that it *was* him. During day camp a six-year-old found it "very interesting and attractive" when male counselors changed clothes. By age eight he labeled his feelings as gay and at age eleven he bought male pornography, "supposedly for my female friend but, of course, I always kept it at my house 'for her,' although it meant nothing about me."

Youths who recognized their same-sex attractions prior to puberty experienced these feelings as a protracted and natural aspect of themselves. They did not, however, immediately leap to the apparent conclusion that it meant they must be gay. These youths either did not have the concept of gayness, could not identify themselves with the social stereotype of a gay person, universalized their feelings to all other boys, or intentionally suppressed the meaning until a later age.

It is not feasible based on the testimony given by these youths to decipher why they, of all gay/bisexual youths, named their homoerotic feelings prior to pubertal onset. Biological factors may be important. For example, perhaps youths with an unusually strong sex drive or those who had a temperament that was not rigid and inflexible but open and receptive to new ideas were most willing to entertain the possibility that they had "homosexual" attractions. Other youths may have understood their attractions at an early age as having sexual and personal consequences because they had persistent, personal exposure to homosexuality that was *positive,* thus helping to negate disapproving cultural images of same-sex attractions. Several youths with an early awareness had gay family members such as a brother or aunt or close friends who were gay; others lived in a positive gay environment such as lesbian/bisexual communities in Northampton, MA, or Ithaca, NY.

More common than the experiences of these youths are the experiences of those who became aware shortly after pubertal onset that their attractions were defined by the weighty word *homosexual.* For some this revelation was sudden; for others, gradual. For some the apocalypse was a welcome relief; for others, devastating.

Pubertal Onset Awareness

The majority of youths first became aware of the sexual nature of their affections during early and middle adolescence. The sexual feelings accompanying puberty were often experienced as threatening their childhood homeostasis with meanings and repercussions that frightened them.

The gay/bisexual youths seldom had the experience or the language to make sense of what they were feeling. Many were simply puzzled by a sexual libido that intensified between the ages of twelve and fourteen years; they had no context in which to make sense of it. While growing up, one youth felt "peculiar, strange, as if something was not quite right." The answer came to him shortly after pubertal onset while watching a talk show about gay men married to straight women. He noticed that he "took a real interest in it, and I began to label my attractions as gay." For another youth the turning point occurred at age thirteen during a sex-education class when he heard the word *homosexual.* "Well I looked up the word as soon as I got home for its meaning and I felt it definitely had big meaning for me. It had a connection with me." A third reached clarity when he observed during junior high school that he would always pick out the cutest guys in his yearbook. "I thought my feelings might be abnormal."

This sexualization of attractions but not of an identity could have a positive aspect to it, clarifying many formerly vague feelings. Once he turned thirteen, one youth better understood his sex play with neighborhood boys, his interest in *Gen-*

tleman's Quarterly, and the fascination he had with male nude photographs in his mother's magazines and his father's medical books.

> I noticed that I would fall for these distant male guys, like substitute teachers, people on TV, athletes, actually anyone with great legs. I often feared gym classes and showers because my attractions might become a little bit too obvious, if you know what I mean. I certainly knew that those attractions were not acceptable. By then I had begun to label them as homosexual but I told no one, not even myself, that I was homosexual.

More typically, however, the awareness accompanying pubertal changes was seldom welcomed or positive. The boys' desires were not discussed in school or at home, except in a denigrating fashion. If they were to accept or even articulate their same-sex attractions, they feared that they would be committing social or emotional suicide. Thus, the deepness of the valley between labeling *feelings* as gay and labeling *identity* as gay may be partially perpetuated by successful attempts to suppress, deny, rationalize, intellectualize, or sublimate same-sex attractions. An example is one youth's response to the realization that his interest in other guys *might* have implications for his identity.

> I always seemed to be attracted to sports guys and what I did was to develop these very deep, intense friendships with male athletes. These were never of course sexual except in my mind, or I should say in my jeans, and I never really wanted them to be sexual in actuality because it would seem somehow inappropriate or dirty or awkward or disgusting—you know, not right.
>
> I knew I was attracted to boys but that did not say I had to be gay. I just felt everyone was attracted like I was, but just no one talked about it because no one wanted to admit that they were immature. It was a phase that all of us would grow out of. But until then it felt important to keep it a secret, especially from my family because I wanted them to think highly of me because I was the oldest child and all. But I still sat back and enjoyed it and waited for nature to do its self-correction.

Another youth decided not to wait for nature's self-correction but turned to his religious beliefs in order to overcome his "horrible fantasies." While prayer was effective for the short term, it was not the ultimate solution.

> When I was in the eighth grade I realized what all the male fantasies that I had were about and that they were sticking and that I had to deal with them. I was terrified. I was going to a very evangelical Christian school and they gave me clear negative messages. I was horrified when the imagery was not going away but in fact increasing. Through my daily prayer rituals I survived, shoving the meaning to nonawareness and putting everything on God's shoulders. Well, it worked until I took a hard look into the mirror two years later.

The negative connotations of being gay were so intense for some youths, including this last, that they blocked the possibility of recognizing the logical consequence of having gay feelings—that of being gay. One youth became aware of his attractions and immediately "knew they were very bad, awful, a side of me that I was trying to block out. To myself I never tackled it. I didn't define it. I wanted to be straight so I told myself that I was straight."

Common strategies used to alleviate the emotionality of acknowledging same-sex attractions included denying the existence of the potential meaning of their desires, suppressing an awareness of the sexual component of the attractions until later, and committing oneself to changing the attractions in adulthood. One youth tried to disavow the sexual aspect of his attractions for personal as well as for social reasons.

> In grade seven, god, I was suddenly bombarded with the reality of being attracted to men's bodies, which really floored me. I felt it had to be normal because the feelings were so intense. Although I now know these were sexual and emotional, at the time I tried not to link it with sexuality, just with being different. I was okay with it in the seventh grade because it was me.

A second youth hoped that his attractions would "wear off, that I could make the decision as an adult not to be gay." A third strategized that he would outgrow it because, "It was only a phase. I wasn't really comfortable with it. I kept asking myself questions, like why wasn't I attracted to females?" A bisexual adolescent who felt very much alone convinced himself that he could change with sufficient willpower and discipline.

> My initial response was I've got to change my reactions because this can't be the way I am. I didn't want to be this and probably the only one within a two thousand mile radius. I felt very much alone because I was in a rural school. I could do anything if I only wanted to bad enough.

Perhaps counterintuitively, boys who had sex with other boys during childhood and early adolescence were not necessarily the same boys who readily recognized the meaning of their sexual behavior. Having sex with boys was not the same as being gay.

> It was early, perhaps when I was eleven. I remember a friend with whom I'd been best friends and he was looking at men and women nude pictures in a *Hustler* magazine. Something vaguely I remember, something about discussing the issue about these men in these pictures, and I knew I was attracted to them and not sure about him and about discussing how I was attracted to them. I guess I tried to think this was temporary because I really enjoyed screwing him and his friends. There was a sense of denial to justify this relationship. We looked at it as simply fun, but I

couldn't help but notice even then that this was the kind of fun that we didn't tell anyone else about.

The paradox of having sexual attractions and behavior that were discordant with sexual identity was compounded for bisexual youths who possessed sincere erotic interests for both girls and boys. Simultaneously having girlfriends and homoerotic desires could be an impediment to self-recognition. Though he was voted "most popular" student in his junior high school and had an impressive history of girlfriends, one bisexual youth feared that his attractions to boys would destroy his popularity. He had too many "heterosexual things" going for him.

> In junior high I knew that what I was doing with boys might be called homosexual sex, but because I found girls really attractive and was also having sex with them then I knew that I could not be gay because fags didn't have sex with girls, didn't wrestle, didn't like sports, and didn't like guy things, which was all of what I was.

One youth, who currently characterizes himself as an "unlabeled person with bisexual interests," reflected on his dilemma during the sexual deliberations he undertook during his early adolescent years.

> I fantasized about males in my masturbations but it is also true that I had the same with females. They really shared equal time in my fantasy. It was when the physical feelings became emotional feelings with emotional situations that scared the shit out of me. Well, maybe I knew what it was but I did not have the words for it. I led a straight lifestyle with homosexual tendencies. Homosexuality was not really a deep part of my life. It just simply was not an issue.

A very different conclusion was reached by a youth who assumed that if he were truly attracted to men, then it would logically follow that he must really be a female. "I fantasized about men so I thought I might be a straight female." He, like his junior-high group of female friends, wanted a boyfriend: "I was attracted to the guy sitting next to me in science, which all the girls swooned over. I wanted *him* as a boyfriend. The girls said, 'Go for it!' but I remember my parents saying, 'No, it's not possible.'"

Although the onset of puberty clarified the nature and direction of sexual attractions, it did not necessarily lead to an identification, especially for those boys who in their appearance, behavior, and interests were gender atypical. The cost to them for liking boys could be unbearably high; in addition to the problems they faced by their femininity, they now had one more hurdle to surmount. Their understanding that they had the hated, despised "fag" desires that their nemeses verbally and physically harassed them about only made their lives more distressing. A long history of failing to conform with social definitions of masculinity would only be prolonged if they were also to have an "inappropriate" sexuality.

Although ostracized and harassed by peers, their homoerotic sexual feelings were simply not disappearing.

> I knew that no one was interested in what interested me—other guys—and I knew enough to say nothing because no one would listen. I knew it would not be a good situation. But I knew what I liked, and I liked boys.
>
> I was ostracized by the farm boys as a faggot because I was effeminate and hung out with the girls. I just did not like homosexuality because I was hit over the head with it. I never asked for it. It was never cool. I never labeled liking men as gay because it just seemed a part of me. I was most scared because here was one more thing that I knew I would get teased about and one more thing that my family would have to put up with. It would embarrass Tom [older brother] and make it more difficult on Dicky [younger brother] coming into junior high next year, and it would be my fault because I like to look at boys.

If the onset of puberty brought homoerotic attractions to consciousness for youths who were typically masculine in appearance and behavior, it was only momentary. Unlike other youths, these boys ignored or delayed awareness of their sexual urges, maintaining a prepubertal "blank slate." Several, however, experienced a peripubertal crack in their armor of psychological invincibility—they reported an initial inkling of sexual impulses and homoerotic attractions. Those who were aware of their attractions believed that they had little control over either the onset or the content of these attractions. Their potential meaning threatened an established equilibrium. The youths' responses were consistent with their past defense against sexuality—suppress, resist, or deny.

One such youth described his junior-high years as "pretty much of a vague feeling." He dated, but "I was not really much interested in it. I really went with the girls sort of as best friends." He had only one memory that might have indicated an early adolescent interest in other boys.

> I can recall an incident in which I was playing hockey in a seventh-grade PE class. I can always remember the seniors going into the showers and that I would suddenly decide it was time to go to the bathroom. Of course I now know why I was in there, and I always have this fear that they knew as well. I was afraid that they could tell what I was feeling because of the way I looked. In fact, once a guy asked me what I was looking at and I said "nothing." He didn't say to stop looking!

Once he recognized his homoerotic attractions during high school, "It helped me actually to make sense of all the crushes and feelings that I had had in the past. I was not ready, however, yet to say to myself that I am gay."

Pubertal onset was the time at which the majority of the gay/bisexual youths interviewed declared that they first affixed the label *homosexual* to their attractions, but not to their identity. The meaning of these attractions for their sexual identity, however, would have to wait until a later time. Many boys were frightened by yet another thing for which they would be ridiculed and abused; others feared losing their peer group status if the nature of their true desires were to be known.

Awareness during Puberty and Beyond

Almost one-third of the youths did not acknowledge their homoerotic attractions to themselves until pubescence was well under way or completed. For them, the cognitive process of naming sexual desires appeared to reverberate relatively little with pubertal processes. Rather, the critical factor in instigating self-awareness was living in a facilitative environment such as a college that had an active student gay group, or in a larger culture that if not celebrating homosexuality certainly made it visible, allowing these youths to finally place a sexual label to their sexual feelings. Within this environment, the defenses that prevented self-recognition—including denial of homoeroticism, repression of sexual feelings, and rationalizations that all youths must feel as they did—could be overcome by idiosyncratic, at times chance, occurrences.

Slightly less than one-half of these youths did not acknowledge their homosexuality until after pubescence was completed, usually several years following high-school graduation. In these cases it is difficult to decipher any significant impact puberty had on labeling same-sex attractions as "homosexual"—except as a necessary but not sufficient causal agent. That is, similar to all other boys except the less than 10 percent who were cognizant of their sexual interests prior to pubertal onset, puberty may have engraved homoeroticism into the minds of these youths, but they "chose" to defend against such knowledge until a later time. Indeed, many of the youths gave hints that they "may have had" an episodic thought or feeling at pubertal onset that they possessed gay feelings, but they quickly called on their defensive abilities to drive out or reject the thought. Thus, puberty may have exacerbated the homoerotic nature of their feelings, making them harder to ignore. For many years, however, the youths were successful; though inevitably, unique experiences ended their charade.

The majority of these youths developed both simple and elaborate defenses to avoid the realization of what their feelings meant. One youth said that he "simply avoided sexuality altogether." His self-deception or naiveté was expressed as a "feeling that all guys felt the same way that I did and that we were just all playing the heterosexual game."

> I was really into learning all about sex—and I'd heard that one-third of all males had homosexual sex—so for me I figured I was one of those one-third who was attracted to males, so I figured it was just a phase. I felt like those feelings that I had

were okay because a lot of other males had them and furthermore, every time I thought about it, it seemed like it was the first time I'd thought about it. That is, I repressed everything absolutely totally I thought about before.

Another youth knew that he could not be gay because there were so many "negative, gross, immoral things about it that I was not."

This does not imply, however, that these youths never felt attracted to other boys. Indeed, some acknowledged that they simply were attracted to male bodies yet did not interpret this appreciation to mean that they had homosexual feelings. One youth bought "tons of physique and weight-lifting type of magazines." His excuse to himself was that he just wanted to look like the guys in the pictures.

> I was an art major and I just figured that my artwork was just art, not this homoeroticism that I can now see pervades everything I have ever done. Art majors are supposed to enjoy the male nude models, incorporate penis-type things into their work, and you know. I finally gave up this belief about a year ago when I met Jose.

Another had dreams of boys urinating, rubbing against each other, and being swallowed up by big giant men—none of which meant anything to him at the time.

In retrospect, many youths believed that they *should* have known that these attractions were homoerotic, in large part because same-sex bonds commonly became quite potent.

> I had a crush on my best friend in high school and it felt really weird. I knew I couldn't tell anyone, but yet I didn't feel that it was wrong; but I still didn't feel that the word had anything at all to do with me. I idolized him, especially his exuberance. It was all that I wanted to be. I liked hearing his sexual stories and I know I made many sexual overtures to him. I was just very curious.

Youths who played the "heterosexual game" of girlfriends, fraternities, and athleticism were those most likely to delay naming their attractions as same-sex desires until puberty was well under way or completed. Although homoeroticism was conspicuous in their developmental histories, a profound obstruction was frequently apparent that required considerable "data" or a traumatic event to overcome. Fear of personal and social stigma and disbelief were impediments that prevented them from christening their feelings "homosexual." Their defenses were truly impressive, so intact that they drove the youths to date girls, suffer incomprehensible jealousy toward their male friends, and, in some cases, become one of the most homophobic members of their peer group.

One fraternity brother who was also a first-class athlete did not want to jeopardize his status by being indiscreet regarding the nature of his sexuality. On reflection, however, he recalled many "gay" moments in his life.

I can recall vague signs of awareness. Like the time my family went to Ft. Lauderdale. I saw all of the guys holding hands and I felt an excitement. I was thirteen or fourteen. Then I saw a Bloomingdale ad for Calvin Klein underwear that I could not take my eyes off of. Then another fleeting moment was when there was this guy, a runner, I fell over.

Gee, I guess I must have been pretty gay, huh? But somehow I blocked the meaning of these things from my mind. And the time when I was sixteen and saw two senior football teammates going at it in the second-floor school bathroom. I had not remembered that for a long time!

Another youth, a former football star at an all-Catholic high school in Boston, considered only momentarily during junior high school that he might have gay feelings. His response to the possibility was a resounding "No!"

In the locker room I loved to go in early and stay late until everyone had left and just stare. I'd have this cute blond freshman trainer wrap my leg, even when I didn't need it, all the way up my thigh. Only my cup hid my hard-on. Still I just never labeled what was going on for me as gay.

The later the age of reckoning, the greater the probability that the acknowledgement of same-sex attractions and labeling of self as gay would occur simultaneously. One youth noted, "There was never a time when I recognized my attractions as homosexual and not myself as gay." Another could never remember a time when he separated his feelings from the label *homosexual*. A third youth admitted that he "never put it all together" until he came out as gay.

If not the biological aspects of puberty that sexualize same-sex attractions to become homoeroticism, then what else could have instigated self-awareness? Within the context of a facilitative environment, the youths frequently alluded to relatively idiosyncratic, chance incidents that provoked self-awareness. Without these events the youths doubted that they would ever have acknowledged the reality of their attractions. This defining moment varied from media presentations of homosexuality—such as television programs on gay issues, newspapers accounts of AIDS, magazine features on gay life, and gay characters in movies—to personal experiences that became an impetus for lifting the blinds of self-duplicity.

Watching *Philadelphia* and during the slow-dance scene I began to sob. Really uncontrollably and really embarrassing but I didn't really care. Like I was being brave for the first time in my life. I didn't know why but I had to find out. But I still wasn't gay; that came later.

I think it was *Newsweek*—or was it *Time*?—that had the front page story on being gay. I read it and knew I was born with homosexual lust.

I kept noticing all the "Gaypril" signs on campus and that made me nervous. Then my best friend in the dorm came out to me as lesbian and I shared with her—and actually with myself for the first time—that I too had attractions to gay people.

A defining moment occurred in the one place that one youth least expected it. He served as a junior deacon in his family's Assembly of God church and had preached during youth services for the past four years. He became aware of his attractions after his minister came on to him.

I was forced to face the issue when I was approached by my minister. Before this the whole thing of homosexuality was a very vague, strange thing, a sort of a perversion I felt like. This individual responded to me and I responded favorably toward him. All of a sudden then something clicked for me and I understood. Of course, this was after we had been drinking.

Even though I had an inkling before of what I might be, I was not willing to say that made me gay. I feared coming out for fear that I would then not be accepted by Mom, Dad, my brothers, and church people.

Another youth's critical personal incident occurred when he returned to his dorm room one night during his sophomore year of college. He had always suspected that his roommate might be gay. That night his suspicions were confirmed and the self-crisis that he had been dodging was now upon him.

I walked in on a situation when he [roommate] was with someone and he was actually poking it into this guy, but with a condom, and I felt like a really weird third wheel. I left real quietly, like I had not really seen anything, but I felt jealous—or was it envy?—but certainly livid. Why had he done this to me? Why did I have to see this? When I came back he was drunk and puking and crying. He begged me to forgive him, to punish him. So I entered him as he did the other guy, only with no condom and no lubrication. I figured what would it mean for me to try it out just once? The rest is history; I haven't stopped since!

Most gay/bisexual males who did not acknowledge gay feelings until midadolescence or later simply denied to themselves and to others that what they felt had any allegiance to homosexuality. These youths may well have recognized earlier in their life, usually after pubertal onset, that they had same-sex attractions; however, they were labeled as similar to those that other youths experienced and hence normal and of no significance. The majority simply avoided the topic of sexuality. Although these youths eventually defined themselves as gay or bisexual, they reported that scores of similar youths existed whose closet doors would remain tightly nailed shut until they too experienced a moment of self-revelation. The "out" youths were not optimistic that their "brothers in hiding" would ever emerge, at least not unscathed.

Girls and Girlfriends

In recounting their adolescent narratives, youths noted the highly significant, often unsought and unrewarded, roles that girls played in their lives. Similar to their heterosexual male peers, some youths, especially the bisexual ones, felt an honest, sincere emotional and sexual attraction to girls. As a result, they courted, dated, and developed romantic relationships with girls; however, they also desired sexual relations with males—although they seldom courted, dated, or romanced them. They dated girls, not boys; understood their feelings toward girls but not boys; and received widespread support for their relations with girls but not boys. Attractions to both girls and boys felt natural, an expression of their bisexual orientation.

Other youths felt strong *emotional* attractions toward girls but little or no *sexual* desire. These emotional, affectionate feelings shielded some youths from self-awareness; they reasoned that if they had such strong feelings, "I can't be gay." In their adolescent understanding about sexuality, being gay meant they would have no interest in girls. Because they had heterosexual emotional attractions, they could justify denying the *significance* of their sexual attractions toward males. Thus, they did not so much deny their same-sex attractions—which were for the most part too intense to disavow—as repudiate the *meaning* of their interest in males. The effect of this was noted by a youth who reported that he knew what his feelings were but "to say I was gay would be too much of an assault on my self-esteem and I'd risk total abandonment if I came out."

Another youth concluded that this mix of heterosexual emotional attractions and homosexual sexual attractions must mean he was bisexual.

> I developed a crush on this guy and yet I was still seeing a girl, this being my junior year. I knew what my feelings for him were and that was what I was supposed to feel for her. I think this is sort of the beginning of my realization. I concluded that I must be bisexual because I had an emotional bond to women and I never really had that with a guy, which was just sexual.

In a less sincere and more self-serving mode, some youths consciously used girlfriends to enact a deliberate charade, the purpose of which was to protect them from family, religion, and other coercive forces determined to make them heterosexual, as well as to screen them from the accusatory eyes of peers, especially other boys. Thus, it was permissible for boys to have sex with each other as long as they talked about their girlfriends during sex. Girlfriends became usable material, but not sexual objects.

> I slept with this same guy for seven years. We just kept fooling around. If someone had asked me I would have said that I was straight because I dated girls during

high school. I had to date and so I did, for myself, my family, my church, and my country!

Other youths dated, not so much to conceal a gay sexuality, but to secure positive interactions with someone they really liked and with whom they shared many similar interests and perspectives. These "friendship dates" were important because they provided emotional support.

It was not so much that as a child I liked boys rather than girls, because I did like girls, but I now realize more as friends. I did date but was not really much sexually interested in it. A lot of the girls refused to date me because I was tagged early on as gay. They said I was too good of a friend and they didn't want to jeopardize it. So we'd go out, as friends.

Perhaps the most negative reactions toward girls were those of boys who also reported an abnormally zealous desire to constantly be with their male friends and to exclude girls from their "boy things." Excessive jealousy, disdain, contempt, and even rage could be roused when their teammates and friends expressed sexual interest in girls; the gay youths seldom understood the basis of their anxiety or hostility toward girls. Several pursued girls for self-serving reasons, occasionally dating simply to appease social pressure to be "normal" or to "get even" with the real objects of their sexual desires—their best male friends.

For many gay/bisexual boys, as will become apparent throughout this book, girls were an integral part of their child and adolescent emotional and social world. For bisexual youths, girls were usually pursued for sexual as well as emotional gratification, while other youths used girls as a psychological and social cover—both at the subliminal and manifest level.

Verbal Ridicule during Adolescence

Over 90 percent of the youths reported a gradual reduction in peer-initiated verbal abuse from childhood through high-school graduation. Although the vast majority recalled childhood as the worst years of name-calling, the sharpest drop occurred during the transition from junior to senior high school. Youths who experienced little or no diminution of verbal abuse during this time frame were usually extremely effeminate boys.

In contrast to ridicule received during the childhood years, that encountered in adolescence was less likely to be direct, in-your-face harassment. One youth reported hearing boys call him names "under their breath." Another found graffiti written on his locker; a third "felt people might still say 'fag,' but I never actually heard it even though it just felt like they were saying it." A fourth noted that he was "rarely ridiculed, though at one point I found a piece of paper in my locker with the word 'faggot' on it."

Reasons for this adolescent abatement in verbal abuse were attributed to external factors such as the greater maturity of peers, a move to another school where the youth's reputation was unknown, and the greater anonymity of the high school. More common, however, were reported changes in the gay youths themselves. They began dating and having sex with girls, raising doubts among their peers that they were "homosexual"; many felt more comfortable fighting back when their peers became abusive or aggressive; some became more adept at being invisible and thus avoiding those most likely to harass them; and several established a unique niche or cultivated other avenues for success and popularity—such as academics, a dry wit or sarcastic humor, theater, and individual sports. Two youths illustrate these adaptations.

> I never put myself into a situation where I could be teased or where someone might think that I was a fag. I was not teased as much because I carved out my own niche. I still wasn't "in" with the guys. I was different. I think it happened primarily because I went to an all-male Catholic high school and began dating beautiful girls.

> In high school it wasn't nearly as much, in large part because I was very popular, and I didn't hang out with the jocks and those who were most likely to make jokes. Occasionally I would react by ragging back at them. Because I had a wit, this was my defense. I was also very flamboyant and very funny and a lot of the girls liked that. Once a nun asked me in class about whether or not I was homosexual. I said, "I'm like the priests and His Holiness." It got me applause and howls of laughter.

Another explanation for the decline in peer ridicule involves both changes within the individual and the environment and proposes that many male adolescents become less feminine and more masculine over the course of adolescence. Two explanations for this development of greater gender typicality have been proposed by the biologist, community activist, and educator Simon LeVay:

- Increases in levels of androgens and estrogens at puberty stimulate the development of sex-typical traits that had been dormant.
- The relentless pressures exerted by society on adolescents may force them to conform more closely to what is expected of their sex.[5]

The result of these developmental processes may be an individual who conforms more closely to peer expectations of how an adolescent male ought to look and act. Furthermore, the establishment of an identity by an abused youth in other spheres of expertise helps protect him from peer ridicule and strengthens his self-image, thus decreasing the likelihood of further abuse. It becomes less fun to ridicule someone who has an enhanced popularity status, does not react as passively as in previous years, and has an attack weaponry of wit and sarcasm. Finally, the inclination of peers to act more maturely and to reduce their level of abusiveness also plays an important role in the abatement of peer ridicule.

The youths also undermined a popular theory about the cause of homosexuality. Contrary to labeling theory's assertion that an individual becomes gay because he accepts the labels attached to his behavior by significant others in his environment, such as peers,[6] no verbally abused youth believed that the "homosexual" name-calling he received during childhood and adolescence made him gay. The ridicule was not of etiological significance but had its effect on a youth's *self-acceptance* as a gay person—silencing a youth and reinforcing negative attitudes and stereotypes. One youth noted, "The teasing limited the extent to which I would speak about being gay. I would have barely mentioned it in school."

Other than the quantity of exchanges, only slight fluctuations in ridicule from childhood to adolescence could be noted. The youths were called the same names, with perhaps proportionally fewer nongay-related names, and the primary perpetrators remained the same, although fewer youths reported the participation of girls. Finally, most youths felt that the negative consequences of the abuse decreased in significance as adolescence progressed. Perhaps they had adapted after being harassed for so many years, or perhaps they felt that no further damage to their self-image and self-confidence could be inflicted.

Reflections on Labeling Attractions as Homoerotic

The onset of puberty served as an important and necessary motivator in the lives of most gay/bisexual youths, linking early feelings of being different with the understanding that these same-sex desires were "homosexual" in nature. That is, it appears that puberty *eroticized* early same-sex attractions, converting them to homoerotic sexual desires. One youth noted, "Well, if I had the feelings, I didn't have the words for it." This intensification of the sexual component of prepubertal attractions raised the possibility for youths that their seemingly innocent, universalized same-sex attractions had more ominous repercussions. Although many youths originally expressed hope that the sexual implications would evaporate in time, they had lingering but persistent doubts that they were similar to other boys in their sexual attractions as puberty progressed.

It should also be noted that relatively few youths responded in a positive way to this realization. In part, their hesitancy to recognize their sexuality was the result of having an image of what a "homosexual" was, and it was not they. The cultural images presented to them were of extremely effeminate, poodle-strolling, swishy gay men who talked with a lisp and wore tight leather pants with dual holes in the back. They were sick and perverse cultural deviants—images the youths could not identify as themselves.

Although most youths recognized the "homosexual" nature of their sexuality during their early teenage years, two other developmental trajectories were discernable. Approximately 10 percent of the youths became aware that their same-sex attractions had a sexual component prior to pubertal onset, and another sizable minority named their sexual desires during the waning years of puberty or after pubertal processes were completed. For many in this latter group, pubertal onset expedited the labeling of erotic feelings. However, after only a momentary biologically induced awareness, psychological defenses such as denial and rationalization blocked a conscious awareness of the homoerotic meaning of the attractions. After all, they reasoned, these feelings might be "just a phase," "all boys experience these desires," or "I won't deal with it now." Their homoeroticism would play itself out, once high school, the family, and the community were safely left behind. For these youths, puberty was a necessary but not sufficient motivator; a cumulative effect was necessary.

The growing consciousness and acceptance of same-sex attractions appeared particularly onerous for youths with masculine characteristics. Immersion in male culture during childhood and adolescence, active participation in masculine sports and activities, and heterosexual dating for social purposes served as deterrents to naming same-sex attractions. These boys felt extreme internal and external pressure to conform and to *be* heterosexual. Their ability to suppress, deny, or repress the onslaught of their homoerotic libido shortly after pubertal onset is a testament to the power of peer and family pressures to conform. Progress toward a gay or bisexual identity was problematic and prolonged, perhaps a lifelong process.

Recognizing the sexual nature of attractions was also difficult for youths with feminine characteristics. After a childhood characterized by taunts and verbal/physical abuse, especially from boys who were angered or amused by the gay boys' dearth of masculine traits and preponderance of feminine traits, many felt that their realization foreshadowed *one more way* they would be ridiculed and made to feel destitute. Whether the pressures of being gender conforming or noncompliant delays or enhances the self-disclosure process is a topic reviewed in Chapter Six.

Regardless of the youths' pattern of awareness and interpretation, pubertal onset did not lead many of the youths to immediately embrace their homosexuality and disclose to themselves or others their newly found sexual identity. A significant number eliminated from consciousness homoerotic attractions, allowing them to surface only gradually over an extended period of time during puberty and beyond. Most youths, especially those who recognized the sexual nature of their desires during early and middle adolescence, paid their homoerotic feelings little heed, postponing the consequences for their identity until the future.

The dual tasks of *labeling feelings* as "homosexual," the focus of this chapter, and *labeling self* as gay, bisexual, or some other socially constructed label (Chapter Six), are often interdependent but distinct developments. The interval between when a youth comes to realize that his feelings are homoerotic and when he understands that the attractions mean he is "other than heterosexual" can be a matter of seconds or of decades. Both milestones, however, usually precede *disclosure to others*, the topic explored in Chapter Seven. Sexual behavior with other males (Chapter Four) and with females (Chapter Five) may ensue at any point during this process or be essentially independent of it, as in the case of virgins.

4.

First Gay Sex

Parents of the youths who were interviewed grew up in the 1940s and 1950s when books such as Frances Bruce Strain's *The Normal Sex Interests of Children* were published.[1] On its meritorious side, Strain recognizes, at least to a limited degree, the sexual fantasies and behaviors of children.

> The love forces within boys and girls awaken regardless of each other's presence, and regardless of parental desire, or circumstance. If the natural, legitimate love objects are at hand, they will find each other, but if they are not, love will find a way, some way. (pp. 179–180)

Her inclusion of "legitimate love objects" did not, however, extend beyond a heterosexual object choice.

Strain portrays same-sex attachments as merely transitional, longings that evaporate once members of the other sex are available. Children and adolescents are to avoid prolonged exposure to same-sex settings (e.g., boarding schools) and places where the opposite sex is denigrated. She further notes that "confirmed homosexuals ... frequently exist in organized groups and work to recruit adolescents to their ranks [and] recognize these laws of sexual development and time their approaches accordingly" (p. 180).

Despite these warnings, parents are frequently unable to deny their son's same-sex outlets during childhood and adolescence. Motivations to satisfy homoerotic desires are often stronger than prohibitions against such behavior. One study conducted with over one thousand men in the mid-1970s inquired as to the age of first same-sex encounter.[2] Although early adolescence was the favorite time for initial exposure, the range was from three to over twenty-four years of age. First sexual activities were playful, usually with friends or relatives of the same age. A clear pattern emerged:

> An individual's first sexual experience is recalled by him as a beautiful awakening, a reaching out, a culmination of sexual desires. It is most often characterized as an unpleasant experience only when outside forces (parents, society) condemn it. (p. 31)

One man recounted with extreme fondness his first sexual experience with a same-age, same-sex, six-year-old friend:

> We were walking home from the store when suddenly we walked over to a patch of grass in front of a home and got down on our knees and pulled out our penises and started rubbing them together. I remember we asked each other why are our penises so hard and veiny. That was definitely one of the purest experiences I have ever had. There was no guilt feeling or shame at all. (p. 31)

Although subsequent research documents the mean age of first sexual experiences, usually in conjunction with other "coming-out" events,[3] missing from these reports are the *details* of the first sexual experience and the *meanings* that it has for the individual and his evolving sexual identity. The stories recounted below address these shortcomings.[4]

First Gay Sex

Of all developmental milestones assessed, none varied as widely among the interviewed gay/bisexual youths as did the age of first same-sex experience—as early as five years of age or as late as the oldest of the youths, twenty-five years of age. The partner could also be as young as five years or, as was true in one case, as old as forty-five years. He was most often a best friend, but he could also be a complete stranger; contact with him could be made within the family, the friendship network, a gay bar, a shopping mall, a Boy Scouts' meeting, or a church. Orgasms were optional; either partner could have initiated the interaction or it could have been mutually determined. Sex with a first partner was occasionally a singular event but it could also be an act that would be repeated many times over a number of years. The initial encounter was occasionally anonymous, in a public restroom or an adult theater, or it could be with a boyfriend in one's bedroom with parents downstairs. The sex was often labeled "fantastic," "erotic," "the best"; other times it was "horrible," "seedy," "devastating." Born of lust or disinterest, carefully orchestrated or a chance encounter, life-altering or forgettable, the first sexual act was perceived as diversely as having no effect on the youth's sexual orientation, as causing him to be gay, as reaffirming his heterosexuality, as constituting his sex education, as helping him disclose his homosexuality to others, and as confirming that which he already knew—his gayness or bisexuality. This vast diversity permeates the sex narratives in this chapter.

One initial problem emerged when asking the youths to recount their first sexual experience—defining what constitutes first sex. The youths were encouraged to use their own definition, but if their story was, as was true on several occasions, one of desire rather than of action, I suggested that they tell me their next encounter. In all circumstances this elicited a story with genital activity.

In this chapter the narratives are divided among the 25 percent who first had sex with another male during childhood (prior to pubertal onset), the slightly more than 20 percent whose initial encounter was during early adolescence, the 33 percent who first had gay sex during their high-school years, and the 10 percent who "waited" until young adulthood. The others, gay virgins at the time of the interview, were still waiting for the right moment.

For a majority of the youths, the first partner was a same-age male friend with whom they interacted during daily life—a friend or best buddy. Three-quarters of these peers were assumed to be heterosexual; in other cases the youth suspected at the time or later discovered the friend was gay or bisexual.

Twenty-five percent of the initial partners were people the gay/bisexual youth had not met prior to their sexual activities. These strangers were often considerably older than the youths. The third and fourth categories of first-time sex partners were of two sorts. Ten percent were a date, and, in 60 percent of these cases, the men were considerably older than the youth. The remainder of first-time sex partners were family members, usually a cousin, but also a brother, a brother-in-law, and a father.

Other than the neighborhood or friendship network, first sex partners were met in a range of settings, most usually at a gay organization, club, support group, or bar. Other meeting places included shopping malls (especially for older strangers), bathrooms, Boy Scouts, personal ads, dormitories, boarding schools, theaters, adult movies, church youth groups, Science Clubs, music camps, and athletic locker rooms.

Under most circumstances (66 percent), gay/bisexual youths were within two years of age of their first partner. However, in all but 10 percent of pairings, the first partner was older than the interviewed youth. Over 40 percent had their initial sexual experience with a boy or man at least one year older than them; 25 percent with some one at least five years older; and 10 percent with a man ten or more years older. The largest age difference was one pairing in which more than thirty years separated the two.

The premiere sexual encounter was usually initiated by the partner or was mutually initiated. When the age difference between the pair was greater than five years, the initiator was almost always the older partner. The location of the first sexual rendezvous was usually, with some notable exceptions, in the home of one of the two individuals.

An orgasm was achieved in less than one-third of the initial encounters. This poor showing was due in large part to the young, prepubertal age of the youth or to the somewhat awkward or nervous conditions of the initial sexual encounter. In nearly two-thirds of the situations, the two boys or men came together again for multiple sexual encounters. That is, the initial encounter was more likely than not to be the first of several sexual situations for the pair. This was less likely to be the case when a large age difference separated the two partners, perhaps because these encounters were most likely to occur when the older partner was a stranger to the youth.

The overwhelming emotional response of gay/bisexual youths to the initial sexual encounter was positive—even ecstatic. Despite this normative positive experience of first gay sex, a significant number of youths reported that the first encounter was unpleasant, largely because it occurred under less than ideal circumstances—fear of getting caught, of getting AIDS, of the possible meaning of the sex act. Other youths felt guilty or ashamed, believing that they should not be having gay sex because it was forbidden by their religion, parents, or morality. Others wanted the first sexual experience to be something "special," and the seedy, anonymous circumstances of the setting or the person negated this idealized dream.

Perhaps counter to public images, in less than 5 percent of the cases was either partner drunk, and in only a few cases did a youth volunteer that he was madly in love or lust with his partner. One youth worried about the legal implications of his activities; several of the partners expressed the same concern.

When first sex was with an older individual—such as an adolescent for a child, a young adult for an adolescent, or a man for a young adult—then the younger youth, with only a few exceptions, welcomed and enjoyed the sexual relationship and wanted it to continue. When, however, a youth was *considerably* younger than his partner negative personal reactions to first sex with a male were most likely to ensue. Also in this situation, youths were more frequently fearful of the *consequences* or *meaning* of their behavior. These reflections do not imply, however, that having a considerably older partner was necessarily negative, although the ratio of positive to negative experience dropped to 50/50 when the partner was more than five years older than the youth. Thus, having an older partner was not necessarily distressing or disturbing to a youth—for some perhaps, but for many others it was not.

The most frequent consequence of the initial sexual encounter was a confirmation of the youth's gay or bisexual sexual orientation. The gay sex served as the necessary "acid test" that corroborated what the youth already suspected or knew.

The second most frequent response was that the sexual encounter had "no effect" because the youth already knew that he was gay or bisexual. The sex was merely fun—something that he had wanted to do for some time. Other positive consequences included helping youths disclose to others, serving as sex education for the world of gay affairs, and making contact with gay communities.

Less than 15 percent of the youths reported that the sexual encounter upset them because it meant that they would have to admit to themselves that they were gay or bisexual. The same number, however, concluded on the basis of their first sexual encounter that they were *not* gay. All would later renege on that conviction. Only a single youth believed that the initial same-sex encounter made him gay; he was still happy being gay, and, if given a choice, he would choose the same outcome in his next life. A significant age difference between partners did not alter the effects of the initial encounter. Such pairings also produced "no effect" or "helped confirm my gay identity" consequences.

First Gay Sex during Childhood

One-quarter of the gay/bisexual boys acted on their homoerotic attractions and engaged in same-sex activities prior to pubertal onset. These sexual experiences were nearly always with same-age, same-sex buddies or cousins and were occasions of gaiety and playfulness. The youths were usually enthralled by their sexual encounters, committed to continuing the sex, and saw little significance to it except as a rollicking diversion during childhood. Some youths continued sex with their friend(s) throughout childhood, at least until puberty; other pairings lasted only for a day.

In no case was the partner of the prepubertal gay/bisexual boy someone more than four years older than him. A prepubertal/pubertal difference characterized only several cases. One pairing that constituted this biological difference was recounted in the following way.

> My twelve-year-old cousin initiated sex with me while we were showering. We had been out playing and afterwards I was showering and he came in to piss, saw me in the shower, and came in. I was eight and we were at my grandma's house. It was quick. He rubbed soap on his cock and then rubbed against my backside. Only took thirty seconds. He came. I'm not sure I could have, but he did.

In nearly all other cases the other boy was the same age or one year younger/older than the interviewed youth.

The boys usually discovered their mutual interest and desire for pleasure during normal boyhood play. In the next account, a ten-year-old and his best friend were fortunate, from their perspective, to have had a role model who helped them initiate several glorious years of sexual experimentation and fun. They used the advantage of the outdoors during the heat of summer and boyhood passion to begin a pattern of sex play that brought great pleasure and memories.

> One day while we were fishing we saw this good-lookin' guy downstream watch us fish, and I guess he saw us lookin' at him because he pulled his peter out and started makin' rubbing motions. He ask if we wanted to help and we said "no" out of fear. Afterwards I told Jamie that it looked like fun, so we unzipped, pulled our peters out, and touched each other. It was fun. Later we put it in our mouths and up the rear. We did this off and on for two years. It was easy, fun, and felt great. It had no significance other than that.

Occasionally these friends or cousins were construed to be gay or bisexual themselves. The sexuality of first partners was a matter of considerable speculation for many of the youths. Most were individuals who now identify as heterosexual, although many of the gay/bisexual youths expressed some doubt that this was really their true sexual orientation. In the following evolution of a relationship that began when the boys were both eleven years old, one youth eventually identified as gay, but he continues to wonder about his boyhood partner.

> We sort of spent time sleeping over at each other's houses and on this one occasion we slept in tents in his backyard. We were talking about girls, as we usually do, and then at some point we began to play strip poker and we would take flashlights and look at each other, very discreetly at first. That then evolved to we would lie on top of each other and read sort of racy kinds of things to each other. This is all, of course, heterosexual stuff. Then the next step was that we began to sort of rub together, you know, sort of rub each other's back while on top of each other naked. We never kissed.
>
> At some point we didn't know what else to do and we had heard from other boys about sucking. We didn't know exactly what was supposed to happen or what we were supposed to do, but we did have a rule that we agreed that neither one of us would pee in the other's mouth.
>
> I know that he did not like it as much as I did. This one time that we got most active, neither one of us came. It was just that we did it for fun and neither one of us was particularly upset with it. We both knew that we still liked girls and we just assumed that all boys liked to do what we were doing. We sort of believed that what we were doing only existed in our minds. Kind of strange in a way because last week I was in this boy's wedding and I sort of felt like saying to everyone, "I remember when we did it; I had him first!"

In several situations the first partner was a family member, usually a cousin. In nearly all of these occasions, both boys were prepubertal.

We were six and he was my cousin. We were playing doctor with hard-ons and we took every chance to feel each other. Started basically by petting each other, fondling each other's genitals. I was fascinated by the event. He initiated and I just went along. I had no idea about how he felt about the situation. I really didn't think it had any significance because we were just playing.

These prepubertal encounters were initiated by either partner, rarely resulted in an orgasm, and were usually the start of multiple encounters. Almost without exception the initial prepubertal sexual activities were reported by the youth to be fun and enjoyable.

I was in a Christmas play and afterwards he wanted to play truth-or-dare. He kept showing me more and more of himself until he was finally naked. He finally said he dared me to touch him and I said "don't be a faggot," but I eventually did. I wished I had done more! Eventually I did because we did this every chance we got during the next two years.

All youths whose first sexual activity took place prior to pubertal onset reported it to be a positive experience. Although enjoying the sex, some also expressed fear—frightened that they would be caught and punished for their activity. These anxious feelings emerged only when the youth felt guilty that what he was doing was wrong or would be discovered by his parents. One youth was part of a gang of neighborhood kids who discovered during the hot days of summer how to enjoy not being in school. But it also brought misgivings.

Maybe eight or nine of us, usually in a garage at this guy's place or in his family's car. We would put towels over the windows and then we would take our clothes off. We would masturbate each other as sort of play and we would get erections. I certainly remember having a lot of interest in this activity, but I also remember that I didn't want to get caught with this kind of fun and play.

Another youth felt "guilty because I let him show me sex techniques. I guess I enjoyed it and I felt more gay, so I felt more guilty."

Other settings for first sex were school and summer camp. Although "everyone was doing it," some youths remembered that they were more "into" the sexual experiences than were their male partners.

In the fourth grade we boys would ask the teacher to use the bathroom and we'd go to the bathroom and jerk each other off. We'd go two by two. Everyone was doing it. I had my favorites. Tom was best because he was biggest. She never caught on!

I remember that I really enjoyed it. It was really basically just sort of manual, jerking each other off. This was before either one of us could even ejaculate and I remember that he kept on pulling on my penis and that it hurt. I told him it hurt but I wanted him to continue. And it did for the whole summer.

Then when we got home he lost interest because he didn't want to do it anymore, but I did. It was clearly more than just an experiment for me. He got me to promise that "let's never talk about it," but I wanted to and I knew that I wasn't supposed to.

Almost without exception, youths, including the one below, reported that these early encounters had no effect on their sexual orientation.

My first experience was when I had a cousin and we whacked off together in the same room under the sheets, but we didn't touch each other. We had fooled around before as something that was fun and just something that we did but this wasn't gay. The first time that we did it [touched each other] we were watching a heterosexual porn movie, and then we did it when we were alone at his house and I massaged him while both of us were nude.

Childhood sex could, however, be a confirmation of a youth's growing awareness of his sexual orientation. Between the ages of ten and twelve, one youth had sex with a neighborhood boy who was a year older. By this age he knew what he wanted; the sex made tangible his sexual reality.

I knew that I wanted a dick and I knew that two guys could do it and so we did it. First up his ass and then up mine, at my house. At times we said to each other that we were just doing this because there were no girls, and other times I said I knew that I was doing it because I really liked guys. At first he initiated a lot of it and then it became much more mutual. We would do it every day if we had the chance. Both of us came, but not initially because I wasn't mature enough. This didn't make me gay because I already was, but it did make my sexual identity more concrete.

At age eleven another youth heard neighborhood rumors that excited him and began the process from which he would later emerge with a solid gay identity.

The bunch of us who were about the same age and I heard several of the guys were sort of really into showing off their bodies. I found out about this, so on a camp out I made sure that we sort of always ran around naked, and it was a particular boy. We had regular sexual contact and this is before puberty. It would involve some fondling and kissing, and it would never go to orgasm. I knew I loved it but I had no name for it, and this is sort of how I got to know all about sex education.

This went on for like a couple of years and it became, eventually with puberty, that we reached orgasm with each other. I knew that this was on the path that I wanted and I knew that I was on it. I knew that others could sort of experience what I was and I knew that other people would think of it as being disgusting. I knew also that I always wanted to do more than other guys wanted to do except, of course, for this one guy. We never really talked about it though. By the time we were in junior high we basically went our own way.

Occasionally, sexual experiences became more than merely sex and evolved into a love relationship. One youth was quite certain that he and his partner fell madly in love with each other, beginning at age ten.

> We both felt that we were never close enough to each other. We always felt that we loved each other and wanted to get closer and closer. I was very comfortable with nudity because actually my parents were as well. He stayed over one night and we went camping. It was sort of initiated by both of us. I really wanted to please him. I had no sense at that time that what we were doing was wrong. It just felt like I was getting closer and closer to someone that I really loved, and it really felt good. I was never really that close to my parents and so in some ways this helped to make up for that. This was pre-puberty. I remember that my body really tingled and his touch felt really good because I missed that from my parents.
>   At this point my friend does not know what he is, whether gay or straight, but I think that he is probably gay. We sort of continued our physical sexual relations for another five years, not every day of course. We eventually became just friends and I was not so much in love with him, but it was really hard for him when I had to leave to go to college. He cried and cried, but I was glad to be free.

In summary, although early sexual activities were initially construed to be merely enjoyable, playful experiences with neighborhood buddies, cousins, and friends, perhaps at some level of awareness the boys knew that these sexual encounters were not merely capricious, random events that their partners enjoyed as much as they did. It would be several years, sometimes many years, before these prepubertal youths associated their early sex-play experiences with their sexual orientation. Early sexual activities did not make these youths gay, according to all but one of them, but were simply an expression of personal pleasure and excitement. Little did they know that one of the best predictors of adult homosexuality is child and adolescent same-sex sexual activity.[5]

The circumstances for halting childhood sex varied, obstructed for some by the onset of puberty of either partner or terminated after one encounter by a frightened, but willing, partner. Perhaps the effect of puberty was to intensify for biological or social reasons sexual feelings present during childhood, fashioning implications for the youth's sexuality that were too glaring to ignore or excuse as curious play. The onset of puberty appeared to do two contrary things—bring into sharp relief for the gay/bisexual youth and his partner societal naysaying of such activities and motivate their sexual activities.

First Gay Sex during Early Adolescence

Early adolescence was often an extremely erotic time for gay/bisexual youths. Slightly over 20 percent launched their sexual careers within two years of beginning pubertal maturation. Although most of these youths reported enjoying their often furtive sexual escapades, few understood their behavior as indicative of their sexuality's future direction.

The narratives in this section vary in details—such as the age and identity of the sex partner, the type of sexual acts, and the frequency of encounters—but they share many themes with those who had their first gay sex during childhood. Similar to their earlier onset colleagues, the first sex partner was usually a same-age peer, usually a best friend from the neighborhood or from school, who was seldom perceived at the time or later as gay or bisexual.

> We were both thirteen and he was my best friend. We were sitting on my bed reading comic books and I started playing with his foot and he reciprocated. Neither of us came the first time, but he did the second. I masturbated to orgasm right after, however. So, just playing around having fun but there was some sense that what we were doing we were not supposed to do, but it was just so much fun. We did it a couple of more times that summer and from then on once or twice a year, and the last time that we did it we were seniors in high school. He is now married.

A few youths were fairly certain that their first partner not was entirely heterosexual. For example, one youth reflected that although his early partner was now married, "Over time he grew to be far more closeted and I think that he's a closet bisexual man." Another youth noted, "People have said that he became very feminine and there is a distinct possibility that he, in fact, was gay. I know that he committed suicide last year and I often wonder what about."

Similar with those whose first gay sex occurred during childhood, the best-friend network and the neighborhood were prime settings for finding the early adolescent's first same-sex partner. Together, these included nearly 90 percent of all initial sexual encounters. Other settings included a boarding school and a Boy Scout meeting.

> I was thirteen years of age when my first homosexual sexual experience occurred at boarding school, with a friend in my class. It began by all of us playing around, that is, horseplay. Also there were jokes between us about being homosexual and everyone was screwing everyone else at night, mostly the big guys fucking the asses of the younger kids. Since I was new I got it up the ass by this guy who was in charge of my class. I loved it but could not say it of course; it didn't hurt because he wasn't that big and I had been masturbating myself for some time by sticking things up my ass, usually coke bottles—the real thing! After that I got to do it to

others, although I really wanted it done to me, but could not because that was not acceptable, for a class member doing it to another or a younger one doing it to an older one. You know, the rules, the tradition!

We were thirteen, Boy Scouts, and we'd been friends since grammar school. While peeing side-by-side after a meeting in the church basement we both caught each other looking at each other get harder and harder. Right there. Very mutual, oral and anal. We both ejaculated. We were exploring each other's bodies very closely. It was a good feeling and was the first of many. After each Boy Scout meeting we'd head down to the basement.

Only rarely, about 10 percent of the time, was an adult stranger the first partner. At that time the encounter was not construed by the early adolescent as abusive but as serving a very important function.

I was thirteen and he was in his early thirties. At a shopping mall and he asked me for a light. I said I had to go to the bathroom. He followed me into the bathroom. He came and I think I did. He initiated the fondling in the stall but it was honestly mutually wanted. I was curious but a little nervous that someone would walk in. He asked me to come back to his place but I was afraid something would happen to me, like kidnap me. I was pleased, glad, and scared. I wanted to explore more. I wanted a man in my life who was accepting, there, and caring. I told no one and I didn't want to. Society said "bad!" so I didn't talk about it. I wanted it to repeat so I returned to the mall, but I never saw him again.

Even more rare were circumstances in which the adult sexual partner was known by the early adolescent. One youth was quite intimate with his first partner, his older brother. The brother was openly gay but their first sexual encounter was unexpected.

With my brother at age thirteen and he was twenty-two, after a friend's wedding. We spent the night in a double bed in a hotel room. Just after my shower, he gave me a whole body massage, which was something we always did for each other. This time, however, I got a little hard and then he noted I had grown so much since he last saw me naked. He asked me jokingly if he could suck my dick. I said "yes" so we got off on each other. He me and then I did him. He came all over me but I did not. This lasted for a month until he headed back to work. I do miss him as a friend and a brother. Was nothing romantic. I also miss the people I met through him.

Only later did he realize that society would label their interactions as incestuous. But, "I liked it, felt good. I wanted to do it again and again. I already knew my brother was gay and that I was attracted to men so this did not prove or disprove that I was gay."

The initiator of sex during early adolescence was as likely to be the interviewed youth as his partner. In many cases the agreement to engage in sex was mutually initiated. Also similar to a common childhood pattern, most sexual encounters were not singular events but became ongoing affairs, sometimes for years. Several of the narratives already reported indicate the longevity of the sexual relationships that were begun during early adolescence. The youth cited below, however, had only a one-time sexual encounter; he later regretted his decision.

> I was twelve years old and my best friend at the time was eleven. He initiated it. We tried anal sex but it wasn't successful because we didn't know how. We were both in the same private school system and it's only when he moved into my neighborhood that we became close friends. At the time I washed over it as much as I could, making little of it as much as I could. At the time I avoided seeing it as being gay. As I look back on it I felt I missed out because it could have continued much longer and I missed that.

Unlike his prepubertal brothers, an early adolescent was far more likely to report that both he and his partner had an orgasm during the initial encounter. Despite this considerable increase, over one-half did not have an orgasm during the first sexual experience.

Although two-thirds of the youths reported enjoying their maiden gay experience, this percentage is less than for those who began their sexual activities during childhood. The negative consequences of sex began to intervene in their fun, causing some early adolescents to feel guilty, ashamed, and fearful after their initiation into same-sex activity. No other age group reported such a high level of guilt, which could make a nonreligious youth religious.

> My first time started in the dormitory when the older guys built a fort and membership was we had to masturbate in front of them. I dropped my pants and came in a couple of strokes. They clapped, gave me a card, and taught me the motto. I should have felt great but I was extremely guilty about it after it happened. I prayed all night, confessed the next morning, and went to mass. I wasn't really religious before that.

The most usual response—and in this they were unique among the four age groups discussed in this chapter—was to claim that the sexual activity meant nothing about their sexual orientation because they remained "heterosexual." For example, one pair of early adolescents discovered their own unique way of having fun without having to recognize its potential meaning.

> I was thirteen and I had this friend. We sort of began to explore each other sexually, not real emotional but just sort of curiosity. He was about twelve years old. It was sort of a projective thing, that is we would say to the other, "If you were a

woman I would do this to you." Then we'd try to put it up the other's butt or suck on the other's nipple. Neither one of us really came because we didn't know what we were doing.

After narrating his first time, one youth noted, "This had no real impact on my sexual identity because whatever caused me to be the way I am happened before this time."

Only rarely did an early adolescent believe that his first gay sex helped him develop a positive view about being gay. Equally uncommon were reports that the sex was upsetting because it might mean that he was gay. Most had psychological defense mechanisms that disallowed such thoughts into awareness. Being "homosexual" was not a reality that a youth could bear to be burdened with at this point in his life.

Only one youth that I interviewed believed that his initial sexual experience made him gay. Although he very much enjoyed being gay, the youth wondered if he would now be heterosexual had the partner been a girl.

We were fourteen, classmates, and we were talking on the phone and the conversation just sort of led to sex. I finally initiated the sex talk and just said why don't we do it and he agreed very readily. So, I went to his house and I was very shy. I didn't take off any of my clothes. He on the other hand came to the door naked. We hugged and kissed and felt each other. There was no orgasm the first time but he did teach me later how to masturbate.

I liked the feeling and I wanted to do it again and he said okay as soon as possible. Maybe this was the experience that made me gay. Maybe if the first person had been a female I would be straight today. Maybe I just wanted sex and because the first one was with a guy, this made me gay. It's what I thought then and sometimes I still think that now. It's not a problem because I like being gay and in the next life I'd like to be gay again.

In summary, when youths whose first same-sex act succeeded pubertal onset by less than two years are combined with those who first had sex prior to pubertal onset, nearly one-half of the interviewed youths experienced gay sex before beginning high school. This is nearly two years earlier than that reported by heterosexual boys for their first sex with a girl.[6] For the most part, first sex was with a same-age friend, usually perceived to be heterosexual—as the gay/bisexual youth also generally understood himself at the time—and only rarely with someone over four years older than him. Sexual contact was typically made during the everyday world of the youths—in their homes and backyards, on the playground, in public and private schools, at social and religious events, and at any other place where children and early adolescents congregate. Furthermore, once started with a particular boy, sexual activities often continued for weeks, months, and sometimes years. Termination could be induced by one partner moving away or, more commonly, when one or the other tired of their sexual adventures.

The unique dimensions for those who began their sexual careers during early adolescence rather than childhood were that orgasms became more central to the interactions and cousins were less likely to be a sex partner. Although most experienced sex with other boys positively, regardless of when it began, the physical expression of their homoeroticism appeared somewhat more troublesome for early adolescent beginners. Their pleasure was enhanced if they could void from their mind the possible implications of their sexual activities. Only several youths reported that the initial sexual encounter helped them affirm a gay identity or disclose to themselves or others.

First Gay Sex during Middle Adolescence

The largest percentage of youths initiated same-sex contact during their high-school years in middle adolescence. Some were unaware of their sexuality before this time; others simply lacked the right opportunity. To alleviate the problem of their virginity, some youths made special efforts to place themselves in appropriate situations. They may or may not have known their sexual orientation prior to first same-sex activity, although all were aware of earlier same-sex attractions.

Best friends still constituted the largest category of first-time sex partners for high-school students, although this number (less than one-half) is considerably less than those who first had sex before or just after pubertal onset. Special circumstances were necessary to loosen the asexual bonds of two best friends. In the two examples below, one had a positive consequence while the second had negative fallout.

> We were both sixteen, my best friend. We had met in Cub Scouts when we were nine. I had been in a bike accident on a camp out and I remember crying, crying and he put his arm around me. One thing led to another and five hours later the event. Mainly foreplay, genital contact, no orgasms. I remember being nervous. Couldn't stop shaking, excited, but scared to death. Odd sensation feeling someone else. Never thought what it would be like. Took me by surprise. I was aware of my attractions before this but never acted on them.

> At high-school graduation party. Was drunk and my best friend was drunk as well. I initiated it and he responded. He says he is straight but I wonder if he is not bisexual. We did it after that point several times. We just did not talk about it and then we did not speak for a month after it stopped. I was so angry at myself and very suicidal that I would risk a friendship for the sex. We just talked about it last year when I came out to him. I said to myself that it is okay to be bisexual but I can't hurt

my friends. I always knew that I was attracted to him. I did not try to explain anything to myself but just denied the significance of it.

In terms of partner selection, one new phenomenon emerged during this time period. Ranking as the second most common category, nearly one in five first encounters transpired within a same-sex dating context. Few of the youths, however, waited beyond the first date before having sex. One youth who practiced delayed gratification believed that this was the only way that he could have his first same-sex experience.

Two summers ago toward the tail end of my senior year in high school was my first sexual experience. I was eighteen and he was twenty-five. It developed gradually because he knew that I had not ever had any sex at all. We began by holding hands and touching and then sort of progressing. Both of us were really nervous. I felt I might hit a wall so to speak, in my thinking and feeling—that I shouldn't be doing this.

Over the course of several weeks we eventually got to the point where we slept together and made out but didn't have sex. Then several days later we were in bed with just our underwear. This was sexual but once again we didn't "have sex." So it was very gradual. Then the moment came in his bedroom. At first it was just a lot of heavy kissing and eventually our shirts came off and then our pants and then our underwear. When his underwear came off I just broke out in a great big grin.

It was not a shock. It was very, very comfortable. This was around three weeks after we met. We had oral sex to orgasm. I initiated it because by doing this it conveyed to him that I was feeling comfortable and this was what I was wanting to do. This had no effect on my sexual identity because I already knew that I was gay.

Similar to early adolescents, only rarely was the first sex partner a biological relative. Once, however, the first partner was an unrelated family member.

I was eighteen and he was in his late twenties. He was actually my brother-in-law. He was in academics and was very impressed by my high-school record and that I was going to Cornell. He came to town one day and while watching TV I asked if he wanted a massage. He first showered, then came into my bedroom with only a towel on, and then I massaged him. He was very passive and I did what I wanted to do with him. So I did a lot, gently at first, feeling my way. He is straight but seems to have had bisexual curiosity. I enjoyed it more than I have anything else since then. I worried that I was attracted to someone who was my sister's husband!

In marked contrast to their earlier-onset peers, finding the appropriate sexual experience increasingly meant searching beyond neighborhoods and friendship networks to more anonymous situations and people. High-school students found their first sex partners not only among known associates but also among strangers (nearly one-third) whom they encountered in a variety of contexts, such as school clubs, shopping malls, movie theaters, and summer camp.

> I guess actually my first time was when I was fifteen and at music camp. I'm not sure what this other guy is even today and he writes to me and said that he's had no sex at all since that time, but I think he must be leaning towards the gay side. Both of us were very curious. There was a hetero porn magazine that had been passed around from room to room and finally we had it. I think that maybe my gaydar was working even then because I somehow felt that he would be open to suggestion. So I suggested that we masturbate together. He didn't really want to but I did and he watched. The next night we did it together, both of us masturbating separately. Then by the third night we began to fondle each other and then we had oral sex, which we did for the next three weeks, every night.

Nearly one-half of first sex partners were individuals more than four years older than the youths. This age differential seldom characterized the sexual experiences of those who began sexual activity during childhood and early adolescence. In these cases, the partner was usually a stranger who picked up the youth or seduced him in an anonymous but consensual situation.

> He was married, around thirty-five, and I was seventeen. He worked in my apartment building and we made eye contact during lunch one day. He was very nice looking and it was very obvious that he was attracted to me. He initiated all of the contact. I was very nervous and yet very excited. We had lunch a couple of times and then he invited me over to his penthouse after work one day. I definitely wanted to go; I went on my own free will. It was a very positive experience. He was the right person for me for the first time. I knew I liked him and I knew that I wanted to do something, but I didn't know what to do. So I let him take the lead. The first time there was no anal intercourse but we had full sex. I was also nervous because I was late for home after school. I already knew that I was gay long before this. We had several more experiences.

Perhaps related to having sex with anonymous strangers, high schoolers were least likely of all age groups to follow up their maiden sexual experience with more of the same. Two-thirds of all such encounters remained singular events with no future sexual activities between the pair. The sex act itself was considerably more likely to be initiated by the older adult than by the adolescent. In relatively few cases did the first encounter result in an orgasm for either partner, perhaps because of the anonymous, furtive nature of the act.

Unlike the lightness and frivolity of the first sexual activity initiated during childhood, first gay sex during middle adolescence appeared heavy, rife with meaning beyond the sex act itself. One youth worried and was emotionally upset because, "This meant I was gay and thus I would become a fit target for all those gay jokes." Nearly as many youths rated the first sexual experience negatively as positively—very much unlike the glowing evaluation given by their earlier-starting cohorts. It was not that the high-school students felt guilty about their sexual activities or that they feared getting caught but that gay sex confirmed that which they could not imagine during childhood, feared but suppressed during early adolescence, and came to accept during late adolescence and young adulthood—that they were gay or bisexual.

> Fifteen years old and he was forty-five. Oral sex. I met him at a gay theater. I came out thinking, finally I did it! I did it! I guess this is what is supposed to happen. I was nervous but I had a fake ID to get in. Looking back it made me feel really cheap. I didn't like it because of the circumstances. Not dirty but it made it difficult to accept the whole gay thing until I fell in love in college.

Not uncommonly, the meaning of these initial adolescent sexual experiences was highlighted when they progressed to the point that youths were confronted with the possibility that sex with other males was more than experimentation or physiological release and expressed a romantic involvement. Once this occurred, the implications of same-sex attractions became overwhelmingly potent—an underlying gay predisposition. In the following account an expression of sexual attraction for best buddy threatened the friendship and plunged the narrator into a deep depression.

> Well, when I was sixteen I was going to boarding school. There was much homo-eroticism there. The kids were playing, but I took it very seriously. I was madly in love with a male friend across the hallway. We would stick to each other like glue. One time, as usual, we were watching movies in his room, and we leaned on each other as was the custom. But this time I kissed him a little bit like a schoolgirl. This was the first time I had ever channeled my fantasies to a real person. We didn't do anything other than that. He did participate. It was for five minutes, open-mouth kissing. We never talked about it after that and he avoided me for a week. As far as I know he is straight, but it was definitely a love attachment that I felt. When he didn't talk to me, I was crushed and devastated and sought counseling. I was very depressed.

These vague feelings of attachment and possession are difficult for any adolescent to understand. If combined with the prohibition that guys are not supposed to fall in love with other guys, they can become debilitating.

Rather than being upset by this sexual revelation, many youths felt relieved. Their speculation and confusion were now over. The first sexual experience clarified and confirmed their sexual orientation. One youth traveled to one of the nation's gay meccas to discover the truth about himself.

The first sexual occasion occurred when I went to San Francisco. This was when I was fifteen years old. I was still very closeted. I saw advertised a gay film festival. And so I went with the purpose of trying to find other gay people. There was this one guy who was my age, so I went over to him and initiated a conversation. We went back to his place and we did mutual masturbation. This over the summer of my sophomore year in high-school. He was also fifteen. He had been adopted by a lesbian couple, so he was very out. This felt like I could do it because it would be very anonymous and away from my home. We still actually have contact with each other. It felt very good. Later some guilt would set in. But he showed me the gay discos and the gay clubs.

Another youth reported that "by doing it with him I was saying goodbye forever to being straight, sort of a rite of passage. I was very nervous, but I knew it was the right thing."

This need to have a "rite of passage" might explain, in part, why many of the adolescents had their first sex with strangers and older adults outside of their friendship network. In these settings youths could test their sexuality, not among friends who might turn on them or not appreciate their struggles, but among strangers in a one-time act. If it did not work out, they could always return without friends or family ever knowing about their experiment. The purpose of the first sexual experience was not so much to engage in multiple experiences of fun and lust or to find a life partner, but to test a sexuality, best done in the relative anonymity of singular events. The older age of the recipient of these experiments may also have served a purpose—someone more experienced and sure of his sexuality might better serve as the acid test for a youth's uncertain gay sexuality: "It was a really wonderful experience because he was so patient and gentle. I discovered it really was a confirmation, a solidification of who I am."

Another youth wanted to know if he was really bisexual. He had dated several girls during high school and had sex with all of them. He was uncertain, however, as to his "homosexual tendencies." Finding no one at his suburban high school whom he trusted or felt would understand, he searched an alternative newspaper in a nearby city to discover where gay men hung out. He then arranged to be away from home for an afternoon and sought an anonymous experience with a mature man. "I knew I wasn't as sexually attracted to females as I wanted to be, but I loved being with them. And I knew how they made me feel, but they didn't make me feel what I wanted to feel when I was having sex with this guy."

Many of these youths reported that the purpose of the initial sexual experience was also to learn about gay sexuality and to feel more comfortable disclosing to others. As adolescents they longed to be categorized as "sexually active men." One youth reflected that sex with men did not so much affect his "sense of being gay, but it did in the sense that now I felt more like an adult." Thus, of all age groups, youths who began sex during their high-school years were least likely to claim that these sexual activities had "no effect" on their sexuality. After gay sex, relatively few youths continued to profess to themselves that they were heterosexual.

First Gay Sex during Young Adulthood

A relatively small number of the gay/bisexual youths had no sexual encounters with other males until they graduated from high school. Given the high educational status of the sample, most of these post-high-school experiences occurred in college after they left their hometown community. This group constituted about 10 percent of the total sample.

Unlike all other age groups, these individuals seldom had their first gay experience with someone within their friendship network or with a family member. Rather, at the time of the encounter the sex partner was most likely to be a stranger: someone they had been dating for less than two weeks or someone they had met at work or school or in public places such as a bathroom, a bar, or the street. These experiences could restrain a young adult's coming to terms with his sexuality.

> Well, the first experience was kind of gross. I mean seedy. This guy followed me home on the bus. He asked me if I was gay and I said I liked both. So we went into a back alley. There was no anal intercourse, just oral sex and a mutual jack-off. It felt very dirty. In fact, I scrubbed my teeth for a hour afterwards. I guess I was lucky I didn't get oral herpes. I was twenty and he was, I guess, the same age. What this did was push me further into the closet.

Of all age groups, young gay/bisexual adults were most likely to have their initial sexual experience with an adult at least five years older than them. The split was nearly 50/50 between older adults and same-age peers. Some met the older man at a gay club or social event, through a personal ad, in other public spaces, or in class. "I was twenty-two and he was thirty, a graduate in the same department. I just remember at the time feeling I was a very asexual being. I said it just wouldn't work. As I look back on it, I chalk it up to experience."

Young adults rarely had only a single sexual act with their first partner. Having several encounters with the same person, however, was unexpected for some young adults, such as the following one.

> I was about nineteen and this man was the first person I told that I am gay. He wasn't interested in a relationship and I was not interested in him really except to have sex with him once and only once. I initiated the moves at a fraternity party. I didn't think much of him at the time. It evolved from kissing to oral sex. I wanted

never to see him again, but the next morning he called me and we got together several more times. This was affirming to me because I could express myself sexually to someone I liked. Gay wasn't just anonymous sex.

In most other cases, the first sexual contact was initiated by the partner rather than the interviewed youth.

Although the first sexual experience for young adults was as likely to be pleasurable as negative, it was more likely to be upsetting than in any other age group. Young adults seldom reported that they felt guilty or ashamed over their sexual activities, but neither did they often affirm their sexuality, for reasons noted in several narratives.

One youth met, quite by accident, the man of his dreams. Unfortunately, the other man did not share this vision and the first sexual experience became an upsetting one because it was wasted, relegated to a singular event.

Well while I was in Germany and I was helping a female friend move into her apartment and her brother was helping us as well. He was an incredible hunk, a real beefcake, the man of my many many dreams. She left (finally!) and we were left alone. We ate dinner and watched TV and then one thing led to another, as I was hoping.

I know that I liked it a lot, but somehow I felt empty afterwards because there was no follow-up. It was just a one-night stand; he never returned my calls and I've never seen him since. He definitely initiated it by putting his hand on my thigh while watching TV. I was very excited and very thrilled about the possibilities. It was the aftertaste that was negative.

My plan was to fall in love with a guy like this and I had been saving my first time for him. I thought it was him; I wasted it on him. I can never be a virgin again. How could he not call? How could he not be decent enough to tell me it was over? I should have saved it. I should have known him better. I was just blown away by the physical presence.

Another youth also realized that he made a mistake. In retrospect he came to believe that if he had developed a more positive image of himself as a gay person he would have been strong enough to have backed out of a bad situation.

Beginning my college freshman year and he was in his late thirties or early forties. It was a very negative experience. I found his phone number in a personal ad and I called this stranger and I went to his apartment. I didn't want to do it and I wanted to get out but what I did was just put up sort of a psychological wall around me. I felt good about myself because of this psychological wall and that I really just wasn't there. There was no further contact. I defined myself prior to this, although not in a positive way, so it really had no impact on my identity.

Because sex often took place within the context of a gay bar, alcohol became a problem for several youths. Sex and alcohol did not mix well for most of them, resulting in a dubious beginning for their sexual careers. One youth was devastated when he compared the fantasy of what his first sexual experience would be like and the reality of the evening. The night did not go as planned.

So we went back to my apartment and got drunk, but then I froze. I was anticipating this event for a long time and so I was really looking forward to my first time, but I can't even remember it! It turned out to be a bad experience because I couldn't even get an erection. Afterwards I was so mad at myself that I sort of laughed hysterically at myself for getting so worked up for the first sexual experience.

Several young adults who had a negative experience enjoyed the actual sex act but soon thereafter worried excessively about the possibility of acquiring AIDS. Against his better judgment, one youth had unprotected sex during his first encounter.

It was stupid of me because here I was having unprotected sex at nineteen and I was supposed to be a sex educator! I felt really awful afterwards, like I really wanted to throw up. I think that was because of all the fear and the worrying that I had. The fear was of catching AIDS. Here I knew everything that one was supposed to do and I didn't do it. I know it was irrational but what I did was I gave him a blow job without a condom, and this just seemed so stupid to me.

Despite these narratives, half of the young adults reported a positive first experience. It was evaluated as positive in retrospect largely because it fulfilled particular needs. The following youth knew that what he wanted was not so much sex as affection.

My first encounter I was twenty and he was twenty-nine. I was in a bar and he was a stranger to me. He was cruising me and came over. I was certainly willing, very excited that he found me attractive. I wanted his affection so we went to his place. I didn't climax, but I think maybe he did. He was not real pushy, like he didn't force me to have sex, but I don't think that I was best prepared for it. Later I thought that I was in love with him. In fact, I think I was probably obsessed with him. By that point, of course, I already knew I was gay. I was sort of slightly turned off by the whole sexual thing, even though I was attracted to him. Now, on the other hand, I'm certainly against, you know, anonymous sex. Then it was not so much that I wanted sex as I wanted the affection that he offered me.

One youth, notable for his wavering reflections, typified the feelings of many young adults in the sample regarding their first sexual experience—it had both positive and negative aspects.

I was twenty-one and he was twenty-nine, strangers. We met at a gay bar. I had just come out and I was so excited and I wanted to talk about it, but I noticed that it seemed like I was losing my sexual attraction to males so I wondered if in fact I really was gay. So I felt I needed to do something about being gay, so I went to the bar several times and made some eye contact. He came on to me and I was certainly attracted to him. So it was the first time.

He invited me home and I told him I didn't know if I wanted to have sex, but I did tell him that I definitely didn't want to sleep over. I regretted it almost immediately and I lost interest but I went to his house anyway. But I felt like it really wasn't me that was going. I did come, but I'm not really sure if he did or not. I was sort of really removed from the whole thing, sort of an out-of-the-body experience.

I really didn't enjoy it all that much and I was certainly glad to leave. I took a taxi home. It was bad because he was a stranger, and I didn't like having one-night stands because I'd always looked down on that and now I would have to look down on myself. But it did relieve pressure because it did confirm, in fact, that I was gay. Afterwards, thinking about it, I felt much better because it was a confidence builder.

Not one of the young adults considered himself to be heterosexual after his initial sexual experience with another man. For most, gay sex was a confirmation of themselves as gay or, as it was for the youth below, bisexual.

Four weeks ago when I met him through a Coalition meeting as a friend and then we decided to begin dating. We spent a whole day together with the movies and then back to my room. My roommate was gone and so he spent the night.

We were sort of friends and this whole issue of our sexual attraction was sort of at loose ends and we needed to resolve it. It was really mutually initiated. It was on the first real date, but we had been together for three weeks before as friends. I certainly wanted it, but I didn't really want to expect it. I was very happy. It sort of was the final confirmation but then, of course, I knew I was bi beforehand. It was a big step in my life. For the first time I felt that I was not entering the gay world but was in it. I knew I was bi but now it felt like I had made a major step. I still do have interests in females and we are still involved in this relationship.

Most gay/bisexual youths were satisfied that they had now crossed a critical barrier. Relatively few were upset that the sexual experience implied that they were now gay; most were convinced of this fact prior to breaking their gay virginity. Some, however, needed one final push.

There's this guy who's seven years older than me who lived on the street where my apartment is, and I always shadowed him. For some reason he felt like my mentor, like my chaperon, that he was going to lead me out of my state of wilderness. He had been away for a while during the second semester, and I was developing my own sexual identity. And I felt that he also sensed this when he got back.

We went for a walk and we were smoking cigarettes. He asked if I had a girl-friend and I said, "No," and then he asked if I had a boyfriend and I said, "No." Later, at his house, he started kissing me and suddenly everything clicked—this is homosexuality! He declared himself, that is, he had tagged himself. I pushed him away but I wanted to do it. I left. This was in his backyard, and then I just cried.

He apologized two days later and then he began crying and we did it in a very loving, emotional way. Now we're the best of friends after this put some distance between us. During the process I kept saying, "Is this what it is?" "Is this what it is?" "Do I like it?" "Do I like it?" And the answers were, "Yes! Yes! Yes! Yes!" It did confirm my sexual identity because I enjoyed it so much. I'd been wondering before this if this was just a phase, but this definitely confirmed that it was not just a phase.

The number of youths who initiated their same-sex sexual careers after high school was relatively small when compared to those who began during their adolescent or childhood years. In several ways these sexual experiences were quite unique. First, they were more often a negative experience for the young adult than for any other age group—although pleasurable as often as distressing. The first partner was likely to be an individual more than four years older, a stranger, and a date. Third, the context for meeting this individual was most often a gay bar or gay organization and not the family or friendship network. Young adults did not end their virginity to disprove their gayness or to affirm their heterosexuality. Rather, same-sex encounters served to confirm that which they already knew or to help them better integrate into a gay community.

Gay Virgins

It may seem unbelievable or unlikely to some that an adolescent could claim a gay or bisexual label *prior to* experiencing sex with another male. Youths who had not experienced sex with a male are here considered to be *gay virgins*. For them, the sex act was not a prerequisite for knowing their sexual orientation; in all cases, knowledge of sexual identity preceded the sex act. One youth, twenty-two years old during the interview, was still a virgin by anyone's definition, but he was very publicly out as a gay activist on his college campus, in his social world, and to his parents. "I'm proud. Now I'm a representative for the gays and lesbians on the campus student senate."

Few heterosexuals would doubt that virginity exists within the straight world or that a heterosexual orientation is determined or known prior to first sexual encounter. In fact, virginity is becoming increasingly visible with current emphases on "just say no" to all carnal desires campaigns. Studies of youths clearly document the existence of self-identified gay and bisexual males who have never had homosexual sex. Numbers usually range from 2 percent to 10 percent for gay male youths and slightly more for heterosexual male youths.[7]

Gay male virgins probably exist for the same reasons that straight male virgins endure: religious or moral concerns, disease and AIDS considerations, availability of sexual partners, an asexual or low sexual constitution, and unattractive personal characteristics. One gay youth stated that he did not want to lose his virginity to "just any guy who came along."

> I'm looking for someone very special, but it is really hard to meet such a guy. They all just want sex. I need to know the person; ideally we would be friends for a while. This I know is an elusive goal but I want to hold onto it.

Another youth attributed his lack of sexual experience to his shyness. He spent much of his time alone engaging in quiet pursuits such as stamp collecting, writing, and walking. "I never was much of a socializer, or drinker, or go-to-parties type." He never had a large circle of friends and his parents expressed some concern with his self-absorption. "I was never pressured to date but my family worried that I spent so much time alone. They wanted me to get out more with friends. I was sort of the 'best little boy in the world' type."

Other youths reported a dearth of sexual feelings and desires throughout their childhood, much of their adolescence, and now their young adulthood. Only lately, if at all, had they become aware of themselves as sexual beings. In many cases these youths had a late onset of pubertal and sexual development. The following youth never doubted that he was gay, because his fantasies had been of males; however, he did not self-identify until age twenty and did not disclose this to his best friend until three years later. He has never had sex with a male or female and has never masturbated.

> I was a late bloomer and so in junior high school I had no real sexual orgasms. In senior high I had an occasional wet dream but it was really not that frequent. This was the same both in college and now. I guess I've never felt the need for sex, although I would like to try it sometime.

These factors may be magnified or even distorted when personal and societal views of homosexuality are considered. Certainly, the rampant homophobic tirades and heterosexist assumptions that characterize the interpersonal world of many gay and bisexual youths raise the stakes for becoming sexual with other males. To engage in behavior that is so heavily condemned in their family or among their peers may be overwhelming for a youth.

> I knew I was attracted to boys in my class but I couldn't be gay because of all the horrible stuff that was associated with it. Me, a good kid, just could not be all of

that. To stick it up someone's ass, to prance around in dresses, to lisp and say, "Oh, Darling!" I just was asexual.

Although liberal or liberated parents can encourage their sons to accept some dimensions of their homosexuality by exposing them to knowledge about homosexuality or supporting gay rights, there is no guarantee that parents are sufficiently influential to facilitate the breakdown of the walls of virginity. Indeed, they may strongly discourage the behavior, similar to many religious institutions that love "the sinner" but hate "the sin."

> My family is not open to sexuality of any sort. They're Baptists. They can't even say the word. They fear it and I fear being cut off. It's a real hard dilemma for me because it's a close family. It's a very controlling family and they wouldn't understand. I would want to make sure they would accept me before I would tell them. They'd blame themselves and I'd feel guilty.

Gay virgins often suggested that engaging in secretive same-sex encounters would have made their adolescence more enjoyable and thus provoked a quicker resolution to their identity process. By avoiding such encounters perhaps they were attempting to shield their "deviancy," their personal horror, from others and ultimately, but unsuccessfully, from themselves. The reasons why one gay youth is a virgin and another is a homosexual veteran by high-school graduation cannot be understood solely by resorting to typical social-science demographic categories. However, for some adolescents the lack of access to willing male partners posed a formidable barrier—most pronounced for youths living in rural or conservative families and communities.

> I knew by probably age six my attractions to males because when I watched TV I was always attracted to the male actors. I never really knew anyone else like me, so I never had a chance. I grew up in Culver and there were no gay people there. In college there was no gay group, and I just studied really hard.

As a group, virgins had the latest onset of puberty and consequently the latest age of ejaculation. Once puberty finally arrived, they reacted in a less positive manner than did other youths, perhaps because it awakened desires they knew would be problematic. Also noteworthy, as opposed to the usual pattern of first orgasm by masturbation, more than other youths, virgins first ejaculated by wet dreams. During junior and senior high school, virgins were far less likely to masturbate, although considerable variability was evident. In fact, one individual remained celibate to others and *to himself* during his adolescence and young adulthood. He so enjoyed the homoeroticism of his wet-dream fantasies that his only sexual outlet was through nocturnal emissions: "The thought of handling myself is so unnatural and rather weird that I never masturbated."

Other virgins, however, made up for lost time during their prepubertal junior high school days by increasing masturbation from once or twice a month in junior high school to several times a week by the junior year in high school. One youth reported that he never came during early adolescence, but flourished during high school by increasing his level of masturbation to several times per day.

Despite the preceding accounts of group averages, not all virgins were alike. Some had few opportunities for sexual activity, and these gay virgins stand in stark contrast to those who experienced few barriers or the barriers were so permeable as to pose little opposition to acting on their same-sex impulses or desires. For them, it was not so much that sexual opportunities never arose but that they were not pursued when presented, for a variety of reasons that are embedded in each life history. As the stories of other youths testify, same-sex partners could be bountiful during childhood and adolescence. Openness to engage in sex may be more significant than the availability issue. Indeed, after listening to the virgin youths' life stories, far more important than availability or happenstance was an openness to engage in sex, which in turn was likely based on personal characteristics of individual youths, such as physical attractiveness, outgoing personality style, and levels of sexual energy and expression. Embedded in the youths' narratives are the dynamic reasons why virginity is elected by or imposed on these young men.

Reflections on First Gay Sex

Nearly half of the gay/bisexual youths who were interviewed initiated sexual encounters with another male by the time they completed junior high school. The others "waited" until their high-school or college years, or were still virgins at the time of the interview. The variability in the experience, timing, partner, setting, motivation, emotion, and consequence of first gay sex was immense. Also noteworthy are several clear developmental trends that are apparent when youths are compared based on the age at which they first had gay sex.

Youths who had their first encounter prior to pubertal onset were generally enthralled by their sexual encounter and were committed to continuing the interactions. These were experiences they sought for their own pleasurable purpose, although at some level of awareness several youths speculated that they "knew" that these playful activities were not merely whimsical and that they were more "into it" than their perceived heterosexual partners. Early sex did not make these youths gay, according to all but one of them, but merely made tangible that which would later became an abstract reality—their homosexuality or bisexuality.

Only *very rarely* was the first sex partner of children or early adolescents someone significantly older than them. Initiation of sexual contact occurred wherever children and early adolescents congregate, usually in one of their homes while their parents cooked dinner, mowed the yard, or watched television—or, perhaps, had sex themselves! Either partner was likely to initiate sex and their physical intimacies sometimes lasted years, through high-school graduation. Although sexual interactions were seldom interpreted as "homosexuality" during childhood, if they extended into early adolescence they acquired a greater significance—implying that the sex was somehow more than mere play or experimentation.

The circumstances that halted sex play varied, obstructed by the onset of puberty of either partner or terminated after one of the pair moved away or changed schools. Perhaps the effect of puberty was to intensify the sexual feelings present during childhood, fashioning an implication for a youth's sexuality that was too glaring or uncomfortable to ignore or to excuse as curious play or as merely a sexual adventure. The onset of puberty may have crystallized a troublesome and frightening possibility for a youth, bringing into penetrating focus the nature of his sexual desires, the likely consequences of that reality for his relations with family and peers, and his future life as a gay or bisexual man.

For other youths, the onset of puberty motivated an exploration of what they had felt but had not acted upon during childhood. For them, early adolescence signified the *possibilities of eroticism*. Relatively few of these youths, however, were inspired by their first gay sex to proclaim their sexual identity as gay or bisexual. What was most strikingly unique for those who began their sexual careers during early adolescence was the emergence of orgasms. Rather than increasing the rate of pleasure, however, orgasms appeared to swell the number of youths who felt guilty or ashamed about their sexual behavior and to augment the resiliency of psychological defenses intended to deny or suppress the meaning of the sexual activities. Children who engaged in sexual activity were fearful of getting caught and hence punished; early adolescents feared understanding the *meaning* of their activity. However, the majority loved the physical intimacies and sought repetition of such experiences. The primary developmental trend here is that the physical expression of homoeroticism became both more pleasurable and more distressing for the early adolescent beginner.

For the other half who began their same-sex activities during high school or later, several striking developmental transitions are apparent. First, sex partners are not so much one's heterosexual friends and family members, but strangers, dating partners, and gay friends. In fact, among those who began during young adulthood, a friend was the first partner in only 5 percent of the cases; a stranger, in nearly one-half of these encounters. Partners were also more likely to be significantly older than the interviewed gay/bisexual youth and to initiate the sexual aspect of their relationship. The settings where they met were much broader during the high-school years when chance encounters in public places became more normative, and then narrowed during college when gay bars and organizations became the primary context for meeting the first sex partner.

Unique among the four age groupings, high-school beginners were most likely to have only one encounter with their first partner. The possibility that a meaning other than pleasure lurked in the background was felt by some to be so threatening that it interrupted the sexual contact, and no future interactions occurred. For others, first encounters were viewed as gay in content but did not at first cause the individuals to label themselves "homosexual." For a select few, to be discussed in greater detail in Chapter Eight, the encounters entered the realm of romantic sexuality with clearer implications for sexual identity. Beginning sex during high school often brought with it distress because of the implied undesirability of the sexual activity, but it also had potential value as a source of learning about gay life and sexuality. In any case, relatively few of these youths reported that their first gay sex had "no effects" on their gay/bisexual identity.

Continuing the linear trend from childhood to young adulthood, those who began their sexual careers after high-school graduation reported the least amount of pleasure in their first sexual encounter. For them, the loss of virginity brought not so much pleasure as it did clarity and confirmation of their status as a gay or bisexual man. Few were upset by this, perhaps because it was a reality that they already knew; this confirmation brought relief, a testimony to their evolving sexual identity. They felt little guilt about their activity, expressed relatively few fears, and relied on older individuals, usually within the context of a date, to be their first partner.

Those who began having gay sex at an early age also began to have heterosexual sex at an early age, perhaps reflecting a strong libido or an increased ability to be in sexual situations. They were also more likely to begin dating and developing romantic relationships with other men at an earlier age. Having early sex may have allowed them the psychic space to feel free to let these relationships evolve. These issues are discussed further in Chapters Five and Eight.

In terms of other developmental milestones, youths who began their same-sex careers early also tended to have a slightly earlier onset of puberty, an earlier awareness of same-sex attractions, and an earlier positive identification of their sexual identity. They did not, however, name their sexual identity as gay or bisexual any earlier than did those who had their first sex at a later age; nor did they disclose their homosexuality to others at an earlier age. They were *not* more likely to be "out" in general, to be involved in gay politics and organizations, to be reared in small or large communities, or to have high or low levels of self-esteem.

By contrast, on nearly every developmental milestone assessed, youths who were so late in launching their sexual careers that they were gay virgins at the time of the interview were on average at least one year delayed. Virgins became aware of their attractions on average at age nine and labeled these feelings as "homosexual" more than five years later, not at twelve or thirteen as was true of other youths, but as they neared their fifteenth birthday. They self-identified as gay a year later than their peers and disclosed to others—including the first person, parents, and siblings—from six months to two years later than nonvirgins. As a group, they were the most closeted or least "out" of those interviewed. Surprisingly, however, they were as politically and socially involved as were nonvirgins. Their self-esteem level was nearly identical to the group average.

Most clearly, early gay sex was highly associated with early heterosexual sex— but many gay youths have never had, and never plan on having, heterosexual sex. It is to this developmental milestone that I now turn.

5.

First Heterosexual Sex

Observers of human behavior might be confused if they were to discover that some gay youths have sex with girls during childhood, adolescence, and young adulthood. It is perhaps less surprising that bisexual youths have sex with girls during their preadult years. As Table 1.3 indicates, few researchers have assessed the age of first heterosexual sex among gay and bisexual youths, and few educators, mental health professionals, and researchers have speculated as to the meaning or significance that sex with girls has for these youths. Perhaps they subscribe to the belief that sex with girls is an irrelevant factor in the development of sexual identity for nonheterosexual boys.

Previous studies with gay/bisexual youths suggest answers to three important questions—how many engage in sex with girls, at what age, and what do they do. Among sexual-minority youths in urban support groups, approximately 60 percent report that they have had sex with at least one girl during their childhood or adolescence. On average they recalled sex with girls as *following* quite closely on the heels of sex with boys, at age fourteen and fifteen years, respectively. Another study places first sex with a girl as occurring a year and a half *before* first gay sex, just prior to the boy's twelfth birthday. Among New York City gay/bisexual youths the nature of heterosexual sex acts was assessed. Penile-digital sex was the most prevalent, followed by penile-vaginal sex, vaginal-digital sex, and oral sex.[1]

Gilbert Herdt and Andy Boxer provide additional insight regarding how Chicago gay and bisexual youths perceived their heteroerotic experience. The boys sought sex with girls primarily to alleviate "pressure to conform to mainstream norms" (p. 195). Counter to the New York City sample, more had sex with males before sex with females than the reverse sequence. Apparently, the youths used sex with girls as a contrast for their sexual experiences with boys.

> Even youth who were ambivalent about their first homoerotic experiences found that comparing these experiences to heteroerotic ones helped them to admit or accept feelings otherwise difficult to comprehend (p. 193).

A prevalent theme in the Chicago youths' reports was that sex with girls was "'sex without feelings,' which they 'kept trying' but did not particularly find rewarding or fulfilling" (p. 193). Others found heterosexual sex to be unnatural and insufficiently passionate. In general, the boys were slightly more positive about their homoerotic than their heteroerotic experiences, rating the former as midway between "average/ok" and "good" and heteroerotic experiences as almost "average/ok."

Although these studies provide averages and some insight regarding the sex that gay/bisexual youths have with females, frequently overlooked is the wide diversity of experiences. For example, in the Chicago study the reaction ratings reflect average viewpoints. In reality, of course, some probably experienced their first sex with a girl as incredibly fantastic—most likely some bisexual youths did—or as devastatingly horrible—likely for those forced into a heterosexual experience because of personal, familial, or peer pressure. Also ignored in these studies are the significance of the age ranges of first heterosexual sex and whether these ages vary for bisexual versus gay youths, the meanings that sex with girls have for gay/bisexual youths, and other basic and perhaps important points of variability in the experience of sex with girls. Omitted as well are a sense of the variety of sexual experiences that gay/bisexual youths have with girls and a separation of the first sexual experience from all succeeding ones. These and other sources of diversity are a necessary consideration when appraising the sexual experiences that gay and bisexual youths have with girls/women.

First Heterosexual Sex

Fifty-two percent of the gay/bisexual youths had sex with a girl or woman prior to being interviewed. This chapter only considers this half of the sample; those without this experience were not queried regarding their reasons for not having sex with females, although several volunteered their reasons. Several generalizations characterized the narratives of youths recounting their first heterosexual sex. Nearly three-quarters first experienced sex with a girl during high school or college. Having an orgasm the first time was relatively rare (20 percent); nearly all partners were the same age or slightly older; and partners were either a date (50 percent) or a friend (50 percent). No youth first had heterosexual sex with a female stranger or with a woman more than five years older than him. However, one youth first had sex with a girl at age five; another, at age twenty-two. Some were exhilarated by the experience, while others were disgusted. Heterosexual sex could confirm a gay identity, a bisexual identity, or, temporarily, a heterosexual identity.

Seventy percent of the youths had their first heterosexual experience with a girl within a year of their own age. In one-quarter of all cases, female sex partners were at least two years older than the gay/bisexual youth. Compared to other first-time heterosexual encounters, gay/bisexual youths reported that sex with these "older females" was more likely to be a singular event, done as a favor to their partner, and either boring or disappointing. The exceptions to these patterns were bisexual youths who had sex with an older female; they enjoyed the sex and noted that it helped confirm their bisexuality.

> This was my sophomore year in high school and she was a freshman in college. This was sort of a long distance girl/boyfriend. At the same time I was also having sex with guys, not as boyfriends, but I never told her about them. We'd been dating for two or three months, sort of mutually initiated the first time. We continued to have sex whenever she was home over the six or nine months that we were together. We both always loved it. The thought crossed my mind that perhaps she herself was lesbian or bi, and I think she suspected that about me as well. And I must have been because I was having sex with both, but only loving one, her.

By contrast, only two youths first had sex with a female two or more years younger than them—a college senior dating a first-year college woman and a high-school junior dating an eighth-grade girl.

The gay/bisexual youth initiated the first sexual interaction in only one-quarter of all encounters. In these female-initiated events, sex was most often a one-time occurrence rather than an activity that continued for several weeks, months, or years. Less than one-third of heterosexually experienced youths reported that they engaged in intercourse during their first sexual experience. In the main, first sex acts consisted of the girl masturbating the boy, female to male oral sex, mutual masturbation, or heavy petting. Rarely did the girl/woman have an orgasm and the gay/bisexual youth climaxed only slightly more often.

First heterosexual sex was as likely to be perceived positively as negatively. Forty percent of the gay/bisexual youths described it as "strange," "awkward," "disappointing," or "disgusting." Nearly the same percentage noted that it was "pleasurable," "fun," or "fulfilling." The remaining 20 percent replied that the sex was "okay" or expressed ambivalent feelings about it. One eighth-grader decided to conclusively and inescapably verify his sexuality by arranging to have sex with his girlfriend. After a less than positive experience with her, he felt prepared to make his decision.

> It was sex but it did very little for me. We did do intercourse and neither of us came. I really can't remember if she did or not but I don't think so. It wasn't

absolutely horrible, but close, but she had no idea what to do with me. I kept losing my erection because she thought the base of the penis had some super sensitive spot on it. I don't know where she learned that but it did nothing for me! It certainly wasn't the same as with a guy the week before. So now I had done both and could make my choice. In fact, I remember thinking at the time with her, "I hope it gets better than this, or I'm going to be gay."

Although the next youth eventually came to the same conclusion, it was not because it was a negative experience. He very much enjoyed sex with his girlfriend during her high-school graduation party.

Nineteen years old and she was eighteen. We were dating very seriously, at least she thought so more than me. We did it at her house. Later at my house, my car, in the pool. I initiated all of it. Oral and vaginal sex. Great fun. Very erotic. I felt very good about it. I wasn't emotionally attached, though.

The third general reaction, ambivalence, was given by a college senior who had waited many years for his first sex with a woman. Opportunities had come and gone and he felt that if it were to happen, college was the right time. His boyfriend agreed to "introduce" him to a friend's friend.

I was certainly willing, a little nervous, but ultimately it was more her with me rather than me with her. I just could not get into it. I had ambivalent feelings. Overall, it was a neutral experience. It was one of those silly little "got to do it to have lived" things. I could have done without it, although physically it was okay.

Given this less than glowing postmortem, youths were asked what motivated them to engage in heterosexual sex in the first place. The number one response was "as a favor to her." One youth simply noted, "She had been such a good friend, so why shouldn't I do something for her?" Another youth felt sorry for his girl-friend because she had never had sex and thus was feeling unattractive and unwanted. He obliged, as a favor for someone he cared deeply about. She cried immediately afterwards, causing him to regret his decision.

I was fourteen and she was either eighteen or nineteen. We had been friends for a long time and we began to sort of date. She wasn't all that attractive but she was really nice. I initiated it. She'd never really had a boyfriend and she knew I knew this, so she wanted to experiment sexually. And although I really was not real interested, I said that I would help her because, in fact, I had seen movies so I knew what to do. I never ejaculated with her or any other female. I really did it to please her; it was a pleasurable experience I guess. Except she started crying afterwards. She wanted the real thing I guess and I just couldn't give her what she wanted. I tried.

The second most common response was that heterosexual sex was an effort to satisfy a youth's own physical or psychological needs. One high-school student attended a high-income boarding school and felt that he was missing out on the fun that his male friends were having. It was a need for physical pleasure and to feel accepted.

> I felt undesirable until then and I felt inadequate. With Lisa someone was finding me attractive. I was fifteen and she was sixteen. We'd been dating for a month. I liked her but it was not love. I just wanted to satisfy myself. I was always horny back then. I initiated it. I did not climax but there was intercourse. I knew I was interested in female sex after that.

Twenty percent of the youths were merely curious about what sex with a girl would be like. These youths wanted the experience because it seemed to be one of those things one had to have.

> We were seventeen and we had been dating. She was my girlfriend for four days. A group of friends and I were at a free college thing at the University of Iowa and she liked me, I wanted to have the experience. I had heard so much about it but didn't want to do it with the girls at home, so this seemed like an opportune time. It was in my room and I had brought condoms for us. She said that she wanted it and I said "okay." I felt bad because I didn't feel anything for her. We did it a couple of more times in the next three weeks and then I didn't care at all.

About 10 percent of the youths had sex with a girl because they were drunk.

> It was at a professional convention. She was a high, influential, ranking academic professor, my advisor, and her husband was the same in the corporate world. She kept flirting with me so I got myself real drunk, and the husband was passive so I was able to make moves on this woman. I penetrated her and reached orgasm but only by masturbation. I do remember during the time having sex of visualizing the man I was dating. This only happened one time.

Given the male culture that surrounds all youths in their schools and neighborhoods, it was somewhat surprising that relatively few (10 percent) gay/bisexual youths said that their primary reason for engaging a girl in sex was to brag to male peers that they had "done" a girl. The following youth felt pressure to have sex with his date because of her beauty and the consequent expectations of his friends. Dating her enhanced his macho image and others' perception that he was "straight as an arrow."

> One girl I dated I really got into when I was sixteen. She really pursued me and all the other guys wanted her. So beautiful! We did everything but intercourse because I was afraid of my performance. I got prestige and didn't interpret it any

which way. It gave me something to do to tell the other guys, who were always bragging. It helped my straight image and I liked that.

The consequences of first heterosexual sex for a gay/bisexual youth's sexuality were somewhat diverse. The most common effect was that it proved to a youth that he could perform heterosexually if necessary. Thus, if others were to ask whether he had tried heterosexual sex, a gay youth could say with conviction, "I've tried heterosexuality, and it's not for me." Paradoxically, heterosexual sex did not make a gay youth feel less gay, but it did help him to justify to others that he *is* gay because, "after all, I've tried all sides." One youth noted that on good days when he felt politically and intellectually sharp, he would ask his straight friends, "Can you say you've done the same?" It empowered him to rebut the charges against him that he was gay only because he had not had heterosexual experiences. This, of course, was a mystery to his heterosexual male friends, who had difficulty imagining how another male could not want to continue having sex with a girl after having the initial experience.

Another youth simply wanted to feel more complete. His sexual experience with a woman was unexpected and unplanned but it served an important function.

> Well this was two months ago. It was with this same female friend, a straight woman. Her best friend was the one that I told you before that I first told. We'd had a discussion, this was late at night, for about five hours about sex. We told each other what turned each other on. I would have been happy actually just to have gone back home to go to sleep or to have the sex; it really didn't matter. She said that she didn't want to have sex and we both said that we were not sexually attracted to each other, but we did and it was sort of mutually initiated.
>
> I started in the sense of massaging her but she was fully clothed, first her back, thighs, chest, and I know that I got really aroused. She then offered to massage my back and while she was doing this I fell asleep and while I was asleep she took off all my clothes and she gave me a blow job and I ejaculated and then I left and she never did come. She's two years older than me.
>
> I felt like I really wanted to have a heterosexual encounter because I'd only had half of the story, so to speak, so this experience helped me to feel more complete. It didn't change my label.

This same sexual experience could, however, be confusing if a youth unexpectedly enjoyed it.

> The next night I was feeling pretty good about myself knowing I could woo and seduce a girl, but then when I was thinking these things I was in town sitting outside a gay bar and watching guys go in and wanting each and every one of them. The

sexual experience actually confused me. I felt at some level I was gay but on the other hand this heterosexual experience felt good physically.

Sex with a girl or woman could either confirm a gay or bisexual identity, as it did for slightly less than 20 percent of the youths, or have no effect on sexual identity. An equal number of youths noted that the experience had no impact because they already knew their status as gay or bisexual. After a particularly grueling sexual encounter with a woman he was dating, one youth knew for sure what he was.

Intercourse with oral sex on me. I didn't like having sex with her. A real drag; she was on the rag. Then it occurred to me, I wasn't attracted to women! Large impact on my sexuality, emotionally and physically, maybe because I felt I had to prove something. I hoped it would develop into something more than it did. This event, it was a precursor to me coming out. This event made me sure that I was gay.

When he realized that he could only climax with his girlfriend if he was fantasizing about men, another youth knew the meaning: "Not because she wasn't a nice person, but it did take forever! So much easier and natural with guys. It actually confirmed my gay identity."

Heterosexual sex could also reflect the heterosexual side of a youth's bisexuality. In meaning it confirmed a bisexual identity, one that was apparent prior to the sexual encounter.

I felt that I had to do it at least once and so this seemed to be the time. I can't remember if I enjoyed it or not. I had the feelings of being attracted to girls before this, so this had no effect on my identity. That is, it didn't make me feel more heterosexual because I knew I had both attractions to girls and to boys.

Some youths believed that their heterosexual experience had no measurable effect on their *sexual* identity. One such youth used sex as confirmation of his overall conception of himself as a rebel and an outsider.

I enjoyed being unpredictable. The gay guys couldn't figure out what in the hell I was doing, and my straight friends couldn't figure out why I was fucking fags. I loved that "in your face" approach to life. I loved being impetuous.

Although many of the gay/bisexual youths reported a positive experience during their first sexual encounter with a girl, only 10 percent noted that heterosexual sex was so positive that it affirmed their desire to be heterosexual. One reported, "I don't know much about her feelings, but I liked it and I do remember it fueled my desire to be straight, which lasted for two or three years." During the course of a four-year relationship with his girlfriend, sex was sporadic but significant.

I had sex with her off and on and we had intercourse about two years after we first began dating. She really didn't want this very often because of her fear of pregnancy. It was fun and all but my lack of strong motive should have screamed out to me that I was not straight but gay, but it did not. There was lots of contact after we broke up because I sought her emotional support. The effect perhaps was that it helped me to believe while we were dating that I was straight, a ticket to normalcy, if that was what I really wanted.

An equally small number reported that they wanted to try sex with girls as a general learning experience. Although these youths probably learned something about themselves, the cost could be quite high, as the following youth discovered.

If she had stronger male characteristics it would have carried through. It allowed me to initiate things sexually, to find out what sex was all about. It has no present significance on my life. It was something I went through in terms of experience. There was something wrong with it. It hurt afterwards. She began to withdraw. I did, too, in terms of our contact. I blamed the end of our relationship on our sexual activity.

Although the 48 percent of youths without heterosexual sex were not asked why they had not had the experience, several volunteered their reasons. Most simply never had a desire to have sex with a woman: "Never did, never will." One youth noted that he made sure, "I was never even close. I'm just sort of disgusted with the whole idea."

Other youths had opportunities for sex with girls but squandered them because, they believed, they lacked the motivation or their curiosity was not sufficient to overcome their physical or psychological barriers. "I tried once to kiss a friend and to have a sexual experience but I just really wasn't into it and it just was so stupid to try it." Another had his hand placed on a friend's breast by that friend; another calmly sat eating his lunch while a work colleague pulled up her dress to show him that she was not wearing underwear. She then sat on his lap, "gyrating to some tune in her head." A third was told that anytime he was ready she "wanted it." Several other youths have outstanding offers to "father babies."

One youth noted that his pattern of dating ensured, in an acceptable way to others and perhaps to himself, that he would not be forced into a situation in which he would be expected to have heterosexual sex.

I went to the senior prom with the girl who was the most conservative, the most Catholic in my class. I asked her out, and we went to a museum and then to dinner and the movie "Home Alone." A very nice time was had by all, and then I knew I was supposed to take her to my house and there begin hand roaming—but not more. Her mother would not allow it! Which I knew of course. I've always been attracted to conservative females who would never give in to me. The only thing stopping me was the girl. This way, I did not feel guilty.

One very thoughtful youth compared the psychological needs of his curiosity, the political benefits of having sex with a girl, and the emotional consequences for the girl. In the final analysis, the last outweighed the other two.

No, I've not had any heterosexual sex. If it came up maybe I would try it, as an excuse maybe to straight men because they're always saying that gay men don't know what female sex is like. Many straight men seemed surprised that gays have sex with females, even though we do prefer males. To be fair to myself I would like to try it, but it wouldn't be fair to her; and if I can't give emotionally to her, then it would just be using her.

Nearly one-third of the gay/bisexual youths who have had sex with a girl did so before they had sex with a boy (15 percent of the nonvirgins in the total sample). These sexual situations were nearly always initiated by the female partner and were perceived by the youths to be positive experiences, especially by the relatively large number of bisexual youths who had sex with a girl before having sex with a boy. Bisexual youths were four times more likely than gay youths to have sex with a girl before a boy.

The narratives in this chapter describe the heterosexual experiences of the gay/bisexual youths who have had sex with a female. The girls and women they had sex with, the sex act itself, emotions regarding the sexual encounter, and the consequences of the act are described according to the four age groups used in Chapter Four.

First Heterosexual Sex during Childhood

Relatively few, one in ten, of the gay/bisexual youths had their first sex with a girl during childhood. All such experiences were with same-age girls, who were also neighborhood friends. The "she" rather than the "he" always initiated sex, which consisted primarily of fondling, oral sex, and petting; none of the youths had an orgasm. The boys participated primarily out of curiosity.

We were both ten years, at summer camp. She wanted to know the truth or if it was just a rumor regarding how well hung I am. We sneaked out to the woods. Curiosity, like show and tell. I think it was the counselors who had spread the rumor. She started it but I was into it. I was curious and popularity at camp was based on doing it.

> This girl and me were playing the proverbial doctor/patient game the summer before first grade and there was lots of exploring each other's bodies. She was the doctor. Just curiosity. Felt natural to do it.

Most of these boys reported that they enjoyed the sex play but that it felt a "little weird." None reported that it affected their sexual identity. It meant nothing to either partner; it was simply play.

Heterosexual sex play during childhood was nearly indistinguishable from gay sex play in several important dimensions. The partner was usually a same-age neighborhood friend and the purpose was to have fun through physical stimulation. Orgasms were rare. Regardless of sex of partner, sexual activities had little meaning for the youth's identity or feelings about himself.

In several other important ways, however, sex play with girls differed from that with boys. First and foremost, sex play with girls was far less frequent, about five times less frequent than with boys. This was true despite the fact that most of the gay/bisexual youths reported a preponderance of female friends during childhood. If the girl wanted sex she had to initiate it; if a boy wanted sex with our gay/bisexual youths, then he could count on initiating the interaction only half of the time. Third, sex play with girls tended to be a rather discrete, time- or situation-bound event. No boy reported that he was more into the sex play than was his female partner; the opposite was a fairly common observation when the first partner was a boy. No gay/bisexual youth reported that he fell in love with his first girl partner; several described emotional love attachments with their first boy partner. Finally, no youth reported being fearful that he would be caught or punished for having sex with a girl prior to pubertal onset. This fear was a primary concern among boys who had sex with boys. Thus, in many respects, as children the gay and bisexual youths appeared more interested in sex play with boys than with girls.

First Heterosexual Sex during Early Adolescence

Twice as many youths began their heterosexual careers shortly after rather than before pubertal onset. The girls were usually same-age friends or dating partners and the sexual encounter was equally likely to be initiated by either one. Orgasm for either partner was relatively rare and the sexual activity seldom extended beyond the initial event.

> I was thirteen and Jen was fourteen. I guess we were dating but really not in a relationship. It consisted once of her getting her hand in my pants while we were doing homework. She really initiated it but I did not resist. I wanted more but really not with her.

The early adolescent's motivation for seeking sex with a girl included a favor for a friend, curiosity, and self-satisfaction. Examples of each of these are given below.

There was this girl who was in love with me. She would get me aroused with her hands. I was fourteen and she was sixteen. She was a church friend; she initiated it. I never really touched her but only her breast. It was a bad idea the way it happened. I was gay so why did I do it? She wanted the sex but was afraid of getting pregnant because she had no birth control. Came close to having intercourse, but I just couldn't do it. I did all I could for her. Maybe she thought this would get me to love her.

It was the summer after eighth grade. I went to the shore with my family. Above my family lived this girl and we became friends. We were digging in the sand together after dinner one night, just sort of hanging out. It was more of a curiosity thing. We decided we wanted to do it, and we would fool around kissing and fondling each other. She was a year older. She really initiated it, asking me because I was such a polite person. We didn't do it the first time, that is, neither one of us came. I'm not sure if she did but I know I did the second time.

We did this whenever we were alone. We were not in love and there really has been no contact since. It really had no impact on my sexual identity. It was fun and it just felt like at this age you should be having fun and screwing girls.

The youths' responses to the sexual activity ranged from pleasure to disgust. The first narrative is from a youth who had been privy to the considerable escapades of his older brothers and their stories about the pleasures of "fucking cunt." With great anticipation he craved what puberty could also do for him—"to ejaculate like my big brothers."

This is the summer after my first year in junior high with Carol, who was a year older. I went to the shore with two other couples, including one of my brothers, with great expectations! We'd been drinking beer and we were walking the beach. We laid out on the sand and I took her halter off. No resistance. I went further and initiated more, and we had sex on the beach. I was well prepared and I was good. I climaxed twice through intercourse and it certainly did feel fine. The others were watching, laughing, and clapping after the first time, which was why I fucked her a second time.

The following twelve-year-old had his first sexual experience with a high-school sophomore. He had just begun growing pubic hair and had not yet had his first orgasm. It was a "strange" but "okay" experience.

We were somewhat close. I was just over at her house, just fooling around. Her parents were downstairs and thought we were studying. She was my math tutor. Experimented with each other. I began to play with her breast somehow. She was unclothed, so I thought that's what I should do. She then put me on top of her and I entered her from the front and moved about. Strange feelings. Didn't know what was going on or what I was doing. It was okay. We never did it again.

A third youth was thoroughly turned off by his first heterosexual experience. A thirteen-year-old doing the obligatory dating at summer camp thought he should try sex with a girl before he settled on a gay identity.

I think I initiated it. I really didn't like it. I ended up fingering her because she wanted it. This was outdoors. I didn't come. I couldn't have even if I had wanted to after that. I don't really think that she did. I just didn't like it, the bad odor, and it just felt wet and dirty. I never really wanted to do it again, and I would never want to do it with my mouth—give me a bucket!—so anyway I guess this is going to third base—and never wanting to get home!

The effect of first heterosexual activity on a youth's sexual identity was diverse, spanning confirming heterosexuality, confirming bisexuality, and confirming homosexuality. When sex affirmed heterosexuality then the youth "felt myself normal because I was not looking for any gay identity"; when bisexuality, then the youth was "experimenting" or "doing what came naturally." The following youth knew he was gay before he had sex with a female friend.

At the time it wasn't all that bad; at least I had an orgasm. I'm not sure if she did. I was angry with her for forcing it on me and at myself for not being able to say "no." This was sort of the last time I saw her. She realized then the truth about me being gay. It made me realize how strongly that I was gay. I resigned myself that I would want to have sex from here on out only with males.

Thus, neither first gay nor first straight sex had a strong or telling impact on most youths' future sexuality.

Perhaps more so than during childhood, the two types of sexual experiences diverged on several major dimensions. As opposed to first sex with boys during early adolescence, strangers and older individuals were never the first heterosexual partner, and orgasms were more common in sex with boys than they were with girls. Gay encounters were likely to continue beyond the first time; heterosexual ones, to be singular events. Youths commonly reported that their first gay sex was pleasurable and fun; first heterosexual activities were equally likely to be negative or neutral as to be positive. Perhaps as a result of this less positive experience with heterosexual behavior, sex with a girl was more likely than sex with a boy to confirm a youth's homoeroticism. Sex was supposed to be fun, and when it was not, it must mean something. Finally, although many early adolescents felt guilty or ashamed after their first gay sex, none reported these feelings after first sex with a girl. Sex that was socially desirable and thus did not evoke shame or guilt was not necessarily, however, construed as a positive encounter. Guilt, shame, social denigration, and pleasure coalesced with the experiences of gay sex.

First Heterosexual Sex during Middle Adolescence

Nearly half of the youths who had sex with a female at least once during their lifetime began their heterosexual career during their high-school days. The most common context in which these first encounters occurred was not friendship but dating. First partners were never strangers, and one-fifth were more than two years older than the youth. The following pairing was not an atypical first heterosexual experience for a gay high-school youth.

> We were both sixteen and dating for about six months. Both of us were totally inexperienced, so it was sort of a discovery kind of thing. I can remember first we did a kiss and then I touched her breast. I knew that we were supposed to do it by this point in our relationship. I can't really remember the very first time because it was such a slow evolution. I liked masturbating her. Nothing that she did really got me off. I really just didn't feel like I wanted to come, although I did at times. I never had any intercourse. I think we were just young and scared. This lasted for a year and a half and it just sort of mutually died when we agreed we wanted to see other people.

Unlike youths who began sex with girls at an earlier age, orgasms were more common, and sexual activity was more likely to continue after the initial event. These may well reflect the change in sexual context from friendship to dating. However, girls still initiated the vast number of first sexual encounters.

> We had been dating for some time and for my seventeenth birthday she initiated intercourse as a gift. I don't remember much but I was drunk, making out. Before this she had wanted more than the heavy petting that we did to orgasm several times. But I wasn't in love with her.

As this narrative illustrates, being drunk was not an unfamiliar state of consciousness for some high-school initiates.

Gay/bisexual youths were most likely to engage in heterosexual sex not because of curiosity or to satisfy physical desires, but as a "favor" to their date or to claim "bragging rights" with male friends. The following two sixteen-year-olds had been dating for several months and the girl was pressuring the boy to "consummate" their relationship. Realizing the significance of this act for her, the gay youth obliged.

It was a terrible time keeping an erection, so it wasn't a good experience. It kept flopping over and she was getting very frustrated. She was not very supportive. I was attempting to be straight. She initiated it although I tried to put her off because, "I loved her too much." I really got off making her feel good.

When one youth bragged to peers about his sexual exploits with girls, he deceived them regarding the real object of his sexual lust. The desire was for one of those very same peers.

Mike and I went double dating. He and his girl were sort of making out in the front and we were in the back seat. She gave me oral sex. I felt really unfulfilled, that there was something missing. I was excited, though, because it was the first time, and I bragged to Mike about it in order to establish my heterosexuality. He and I had not yet had our sexual encounter. We kept our girlfriends for a while, basically as a front. I've had her touching my genitals. I eventually had intercourse with her, more out of revenge against Mike who cheated on me by having sex with a female. This experience was satisfying physically but not emotionally. I was sixteen and she was thirteen.

At times it was difficult for a gay/bisexual youth to sort through his feelings. He may have felt very attracted to his girlfriend, but was this more of an emotional than a physical attraction? Their history together as a pair was important to him and he often did not want to relinquish their relationship. Such was the case for the following youth.

I guess I was emotionally involved. She initiated by kissing me. She did all of it at first. I would say it was a lot of intellectual dating, about 90 percent of the time. It occurred at my home. I realized I physically didn't want her. It was not until college that this question about love being both emotional and physical came up, that I was not in love with her. I guess at the time there was no idea of what to make of it. Heavy petting and no intercourse. Somewhat arousing, but it wasn't what I wanted. It didn't fit but I didn't want to lose her either. We'd known each other since grade school.

The reaction of youths to heterosexual sex was slightly more negative than positive or ambivalent. One youth, who was not particularly fond of heterosexual activity, found sex with his girlfriend "really turned me off because of her smell. It was very foreign, nauseating, repulsive, revolting, even offensive to me. I felt trapped. It lasted three months, from the summer to Halloween."

A fifteen-year-old had been dating for several months when the opportunity for sex presented itself. Although it was an "okay" experience, it compared quite unfavorably with earlier sex with a boy.

There was sort of sexual tension between us and I found out that she wanted it. We went down to a glen which was deserted, sort of on the rocks by water. It was by manual stimulation with her initiating it. I guess I enjoyed it but it seemed very strange, like she had done it to me but I wasn't quite sure what I was supposed to do to her. It didn't feel like it did with John, more uncomfortable because I was unfamiliar with her body.

Thoroughly enjoying sex, both emotionally and physically, with a girl was considerably more common among bisexual than gay youths. In the instance below, the relationship was a physical and not an emotional one.

This is when there was the three of us in the hot tub. They were going out with each other at the time. Mac was definitely bisexual. Me too. I'm a seventeen year old and they are like a year or two older than me.

It was a party, a hot-tub party, and Pam had on just a t-shirt with no bottom. They asked me if I wanted to come in and I thought they meant did I want to "come." Mac said that we should all take off our clothes and so we did. Pam had huge, drooping boobs. Mac was twice my size with the curve to the right, and very hairy. He was already erect, pointing the way. We began grabbing each other, sort of a group grope and hug. At one time I had Mac's cock in one hand and Pam's boobs in my mouth.

I was a prude at the time and perhaps there was more going on sexually than I was aware of. I was as excited as hell. So my first blow job was by Pam and this is my first real conscious ejaculation. I came very quickly all over the hot tub but I'm not sure why, but I can just remember seeing her rinsing out her mouth. After this I began masturbating.

I was just sort of behind the times developmentally but I would soon catch up. I didn't associate orgasm with sex acts, at least until I had this hot-tub experience with Mac and Pam. Nothing like this had ever happened to me before and I regretted waiting so long. Certainly there was lots of meaning for me sexually at this time that this happened, not so much that I was attracted to Mac, which I already knew, but that Pam turned me on.

This youth reflects the primary effect of the maiden heterosexual experience—demonstrating that a youth has the capacity to perform heterosexually. One youth reported that he "was relieved as hell that I could perform with a woman." Sex with a girl seldom confirmed homosexuality or, perhaps more surprisingly, seldom fueled a desire to be heterosexual. Both were characteristic because by their high-school years most youths already knew or strongly suspected their homoerotic nature. One youth found it somewhat awkward to have females touch him, but he always wondered what it would be like to do it with a female, "although many of the women, I feared, would want to change me."

Nearly half of all first heterosexual and one-third of first gay experiences occurred during the high-school years. Although dating was an important context for sex with both girls, and boys during middle adolescence, it was a far more frequent context for sex with girls, in large part, one would assume, because of social sanctions against same-sex dating. Thus, many of those desiring sex with boys had to rely on strangers, especially the older, more experienced kind. Perhaps as a result, many of these were one-time encounters. Girls willing to have sex with their gay/bisexual dates were considerably more accessible, present in the everyday world of the middle adolescent, and wanting, even demanding, multiple sexual encounters. Despite the inhibition against having a gay lover, romantic relationships, the topic of Chapter Eight, developed about equally with girls and boys. With girls, however, the relationships were public, visible to all. With boys, clandestine romantic relationships were more normative.

First sexual activity during the high-school years, regardless of whether the partner was a girl or a boy, was as likely to be positive as negative. Gone is the frivolity of sex play with friends and neighborhood buddies of former years. Sex is now more fraught with meaning and significance, especially for a youth's sexual identity. Sex with girls, which was frequently less enjoyable for these youths than sex with boys, was often interpreted as unpleasant because it disconfirmed heterosexuality. This realization did not necessarily, however, directly lead to a gay identity. Sex with boys might be perceived as negative because it implied that the youth could be gay. In either case, sex complicated life. By contrast, bisexual youths were often uplifted by their sexual experience with girls. If they had once thought that they might be gay because of previous same-sex fantasies or sex with boys, they now had counterevidence and could once again be heterosexual. Other bisexual youths were thrilled that they enjoyed sex regardless of who it was with, indicating to them a more natural, gender-neutral state of sexuality.

First Heterosexual Sex during Young Adulthood

The second most popular time to begin having heterosexual sex was during young adulthood—as happened with nearly one in three of those who had heterosexual sex. In several respects, the pattern returns to the early adolescent years: The woman was as likely to be older as the same age and to be a friend as a date. No subsequent follow-up to the initial event was the usual consequence. However, the sex act was more likely to be initiated by the woman than the youth, to involve vaginal intercourse, and to result in an orgasm for the gay/bisexual youth. Somewhat typical is the following narrative, which incorporates several of the major characteristics noted above.

> I was eighteen years old and beginning college; she was twenty. It was a woman in the dorm and actually she was attracted to me. The romantic process for her

began and now she was interested in sex. The relationship was by mutual consent, and we began as friends and then she tried to escalate it. The event occurred in the dorm and the sex was vaginal intercourse with a climax. This was our only time. From my vantage point we were just friends and always were friends.

No longer did gay/bisexual youths report that their primary reason for engaging in heterosexual sex was as a favor for their partner—as was true during adolescence. Now it was a favor for themselves—they sought satisfaction of their own physical, psychological, and social needs. All three needs were met for the following bisexual fraternity brother.

We were separated for a year and then we began dating again for about two to three months. She initiated the sex. I wanted it and was always horny when I was with her, but I had fears that if I initiated it I would be accused of rape, and I was really afraid of that. It just seemed like the right thing to do at the time. It was like a coming of age for me. I needed it and it calmed my fraternity brothers' concerns. It was both vaginal and oral. We both came. We then dated another three months after that and there was more sex. Maybe once a week or every other week.

Consistent with a linear developmental trend from childhood, first sex with a girl was now perceived as more negative than positive. It was rare that the reaction was ambivalent or neutral. The following youth first believed that sex with his friend would simply be "interesting" but later discovered that negative repercussions were more evident.

It was mutually understood that we were attracted to each other and it was mutually initiated, though maybe it was more of her. She invited me to her apartment, and we had our sexual experience. I was sort of amused by it, sort of a humorous situation. I fell asleep about four times because I really wasn't all that interested. I was hoping that she would stay asleep as well but she'd wake up and then would try to have sex with me. I just never felt like perhaps that I did it right. I never did come. Later I came to resent her forcing it on me.

Handicaps other than the sex act itself could interfere with a youth's pleasurable experience. Despite presex anxiety, the following pair overcame the hurdles they had created.

We had been dating for three months and we were in love. She initiated it. Previously we had petted and then we carefully planned the "Sex Event." The worse part was that it seemed so planned. I was so nervous so we put it off. Several days later it worked. It was no big deal; it felt fine once I could relax. We did it once a week, always on Friday night after services, for several months. Not the greatest sex I've ever had, but good and just sort of comfortable. I felt myself normal at the time so I was not looking for any confirmation. It ended when I moved away to go to Rabbinical school.

The major consequence of the initial sexual experience with a woman was to confirm a young adult's homosexuality. He seldom entered the encounter with this motivation, but it was an outcome, often fraught with sorrow or melancholy.

I started dating this woman and she was everything I could want in a woman, and it just did not click. This saddened me. We went to bed and I just could not do it. We kissed and held hands in public after that. She guessed it I think. It really helped my self-esteem to come out. If I could not love her, then I couldn't love anyone.

Another youth had multiple sexual experiences with a co-worker. He wanted to give heterosexuality a fair chance but he could not ignore his lack of emotional reaction.

I was nineteen years old and the woman was twenty-three. We worked together as matron and tutor in the boarding school. I also socialized through this means, meaning she was my companion during these social events. As I think about it, 65 percent of the time she initiated the event. It occurred at her place and I penetrated her. I can remember being uninvolved and detached and this disappointed me; this was all before I came out. As I look back on it, it helped me affirm on some level that I was gay and it assisted me with coming out.

The second most common aftermath of first heterosexual sex was for it to have "no effect" because the youth already knew that he was gay or bisexual. The following two narratives illustrate two different routes that youths took to believing that the sex had relatively little impact on their sexuality. In the first, a youth was seduced into sex under the influence of alcohol; in the second, an experiment was pursued that the youth had always wanted to conduct.

We had been drinking and we sometimes made out; but this time she just went further, and I did not protest sufficiently. This is outside by the fraternity on campus. Neither of us came. It didn't bother me but I did question what it all meant. Was this because I was drunk or was there some meaning to it? But it didn't have any effect on my sexual identity. We never did it again after this time.

Sex actually was a letdown; I didn't enjoy it. It also had to do with the person that I did it with. As I look back on it, the woman liked me as a friend and I was interested in exploring things at that time; so I went ahead and she was my subject. Now as I look back on it, it kind of proved things. Having sex would not change things. I was happy at the time that I wasn't a virgin anymore. It allowed me to say that I had tried heterosexual activity. Yes, I had done it!

Another youth was also very happy to have finally "gone all the way" with a woman. Rather than confirm his homosexuality it at least temporarily erased doubts that he might be gay. It did not, however, thus mean that he was heterosexual.

> I never really had sex before—or at least no orgasm—with women I dated. She was a sophomore and we would make out and we would progressively get further and further. I was actually happy about the relationship at first because it tended to prove that I wasn't gay. I was also interested in her and I was really walking on air after the screw because this meant I wasn't gay.

Finally, the following perspective was relatively common among youths who, despite some misgivings, decided to have sex with a woman. The female partner knew or strongly suspected that she might be having sex with a gay man, yet she requested somewhat covertly that the two have sex. The gay youth speculated that his partner's motivation was for physical pleasure or to convert him to heterosexuality. He came to regret his participation because of the damage it did to the relationship and because he felt that it was dishonest to "lead her on." He confessed, "I knew I couldn't be friends with her without telling her I had a more gay focus and gay feelings. We were never the same after that."

Unlike the large number of strangers and older individuals in the sexual histories of male-male sex, if the sex partner in heterosexual sex was not a date then she was a friend, usually a best friend. As such, the age difference was less dramatic—usually only several years older rather than a decade or more. The young adult perceived that his partner initiated the interaction, which was usually a singular event in their dating history. Regardless of sex of partner, having the first sexual experience during the young adult years was more negative, upsetting, and uncomfortable than it was at any other age. Most individuals by this time knew or strongly suspected their homoerotic attractions. Sex with a woman or a man simply confirmed a gay/bisexual identity or had no effect. Sex with a woman served an additional purpose, to satisfy a curiosity, perhaps before he committed himself totally to men.

Reflections on First Heterosexual Sex

Earlier research has presented a relatively superficial perspective regarding the importance of gay/bisexual youths having sex with girls or women. Lost in this neglect is the diversity of experiences and meanings that sex with women has for a youth's developmental history. This diversity is readily apparent in the narratives reported in this chapter. Sex with one girl is not the same as having sex with another, at one age rather than another, or for one youth rather than another. These differences may have a powerful impact on the sexual life trajectories of a gay/bisexual youth.

One-half of the gay and all but one of the bisexual youths had sex with a girl/woman during their childhood, adolescence, or young adulthood. Their sex partners were known to them, either as a friend or girlfriend, and with two exceptions, all were the same age (within two years) or older than their partner. Girls or women initiated three-quarters of such encounters. The sex was as likely to be a one-time event as an ongoing activity, seldom resulted in an orgasm for either pair member, and more frequently included oral sex, mutual masturbation, girl-on-boy masturbation, and fondling than vaginal intercourse.

The most pronounced developmental trend was that with increasing age of onset, first heterosexual sex was described in negative rather than positive terms—from fun in childhood to disappointment in young adulthood. This decrease in pleasure surprisingly parallels an increase in vaginal intercourse and orgasms from childhood through the post-high-school years. Perhaps the decline in the delightful hedonism of childhood most directly reflects the greater significance that sex with girls/women has for older adolescents' sexuality. That is, orgasms may have brought to mind not so much bliss as a frightening realization—the images remained centered on male objects and paraphernalia. Although sex with girls may have given a brief but illusory sense of straightness during the early years of adolescence and proof that one could "do it" with girls, by high-school graduation it failed to contradict the youth's growing sense that despite the best intentions of his female partner and his own hopes of being just like everyone else, he would always be inevitably gay.

More specifically, for each age group the initial sexual encounter with girls was construed as something different. For children, sex with girl playmates was fun and satisfied their curiosity as to what girls looked like. Orgasms were nearly nonexistent, as was intercourse. Rather, these children fondled, explored, and, occasionally, put their mouths on each other's genitalia. Perhaps the only noteworthy countenance of these experiences for the future sexual identity of the boys was the issue of motivation—the girl almost always initiated these "weird" aspects of play.

Early adolescents usually had a single encounter with their first female partner, frequently their girlfriend, as a means to fulfill the obligations of their dating relationship. For many, the sex was without intercourse, orgasm, or specific meaning. For others, it was a fun experience that was worth the effort. As one youth succinctly put it, "Why not do it?" When examined closely, many of these sexual encounters appear somewhat unusual. For example, sex was very sporadic, occurring only once or a couple of times. Given the highly charged sexual interests of many early adolescent boys, the infrequency is striking. Examples of sex with girls outside of a dating relationship were seldom reported. Most noteworthy was the attitude of the youths toward sex. It was "something to do" or "an obligation." One youth believed it "wasn't so bad"; another managed to perform heterosexually by having homosexual fantasies during heterosexual sex.

During the high-school years, sex with same-age girls was more likely to be repeated experiences. Heavy petting, sometimes to orgasm, was more common than intercourse. The sex was apparently not the best part of the relationship; rather, the gay or bisexual youth liked the idea of dating and liked his girlfriend but he did not like the pressure she applied to have sex.

While some middle adolescent boys took advantage of circumstances available to them and enjoyed their sexual opportunities, others "used" heterosexual dating to blind themselves and others as to their true nature. By so doing they attempted to disconfirm to themselves the growing encroachment of their homoerotic attractions while escaping derogatory name-calling ("fag") and gay innuendos. To be seen as a boyfriend of a girl lessened the gay image by proving to others that they were not gay, even though they were pretty sure that they were. The pressure to conform to the male norm was experienced by some as burdensome, especially if they were late in fulfilling the obligations of straight sex. Heterosexual sex was a small but necessary price to pay for acceptance from other guys. However, their motivation was less to be perceived as straight than as *not gay*. Despite the peer prestige that came with heterosexual behavior, something seemed "missing." They now had the experience they needed to prove to others and to themselves that they could "do it" with a girl. But this was not enough, perhaps because sex with girls also made them even more acutely aware of their attractions to other boys.

Those without heterosexual sex by high-school graduation often broke their virginity during their first or second year of college. Intercourse and orgasm were now more common but sex was still usually a one-time event initiated by the female partner. For some young adults, sex with women was a necessary experience to convince them that guys were better for them, or at least that they were of greater erotic interest. If the heterosexual relationship began to have a future in the eyes of their female partner, then gay, but not bisexual, youths usually opted out. One youth described sex with boys as "qualitatively different" than sex with girls, heterosexual experiences were not horrible or disgusting events for most youths. They did not prove heterosexuality but rather confirmed homosexuality or bisexuality. Although some young adults may have held out hope that they could be at least "partially straight," if the heterosexual experiment served any identity purpose then it was to reinforce the homoerotic aspects of their identity.

Bisexual youths differed from their gay peers primarily in that they were less likely to use their first heterosexual sex as a cover for their homoerotic attractions. Rather, sex with girls often occurred in the context of an emotional romantic relationship and was a pleasurable experience. Other youths who claimed a bisexual identity experienced some ambivalence about this "arrangement" of their sexuality. Without explicitly making the distinction, they often implied that their emotional attachments were to girls while their lustful feelings were directed toward boys. The heterosexual emotional attachment side felt safe and secure; the homosexual lust, dangerous and exciting.

Although comparable detailed data are not available on the first heterosexual sexual activities of *heterosexual* male youths, the experiences of the gay/bisexual youths reported in this chapter likely diverged significantly from those of their heterosexual peers. The mean age of first sex with a girl for White males is purported to be 17.5, considerably older than it was for the current sample of gay/bisexual youths.[3] However, breaking virginity statistics usually reflect "age of first intercourse"—a later event than the first heterosexual sex described by the youths in this book. Less than 30 percent reported vaginal intercourse as their first encounter with a girl/woman; over half described it as heavy petting. Thus, it is highly likely that the gay/bisexual youths had a significantly *later onset* of heterosexual activities than did their heterosexual male peers.

A gay/bisexual youth nearly always had his first heterosexual sex with a girl or woman who was his own age or older. It was rarely with a stranger but with a friend or date. Although comparable relevant statistics with heterosexual boys are not available, it would be surprising if so few had their first sex with a girl or woman younger than them. More strangers, fewer best friends, and more dates are also likely to emerge as a first partner for heterosexual male youths when compared with the gay/bisexual youths interviewed for this study.

Perhaps the most striking difference between gay and heterosexual male youths resides in motivation. Although a low degree of electrification of affective response may also characterize heterosexual males' first experience—perhaps because too much is made of the maiden event—it is doubtful that they would be so circumspect in their accounts of first sex with a girl/woman, as likely to make sex only a one-time event when their female partner was willing to extend the arrangements, or as prone to let their female partner initiate the sexual encounter as were the gay youths. In general, gay youths engaged in heterosexual sex not so much from an internal drive to satisfy lusts and desires (though maybe curiosity) as for external reasons, such as a favor to their partner or to appear heterosexual to friends and family. This portrait of motivations would likely be reversed for heterosexual male youths in their pursuit of first sex with a girl/woman.[4]

Most telling regarding motivations and driving forces was the sparseness of most gay youths' accounts and how void they were of heteroerotic feelings and details. Descriptions of female genitalia and secondary sex characteristics were nearly absent from their narratives and, at times, the youths appeared almost embarrassed that they had had such encounters. When probed for greater detail, little was forthcoming, almost as if they had forgotten this "insignificant event." But it was significant, even if for nothing more than eliminating options, and these heterosexual accounts stand in marked contrast to the youths' narratives of first sex with a boy, which are rich in homoerotic detail.

My best guess, then, is that gay, and perhaps bisexual, youths are not only less likely than a comparable sample of heterosexual males to have sex with girls/women or to have an early onset of the first encounter, but also more likely to have sex with an older girl or woman who initiates sex, helps her partner with the mechanics of sex in situations in which his motivation is low, and is supportive and understanding. Perhaps the most noteworthy difference, aside from the motivational one, is that for many gay/bisexual youths first sex with a girl/woman had meaning for their sexual identity. I doubt that many heterosexual male youths have said after their first sex with a girl/woman, "Wow! I'm heterosexual!" or "Good! I'm not gay." Heterosexual men assume, without the data that sex provides, their heterosexual identity, much as White people assume they have no race.

What is most clear from nearly all interviewed gay/bisexual youths is that their attractions to males did not disappear during this time of heterosexual involvement. In fact, many continued their sexual activities with males even as they professed their external heterosexuality by dating and having sex with girls/women. Sex with men and identification of self as gay or bisexual did not wait until explorations with girls and women had ended.

6.

Labeling Self as Gay or Bisexual

Labeling one's sexuality is generally a process unknown to heterosexual youths, who appear to naturally flow into the abyss of "normal sexuality"—that is, heterosexuality. For sexual-minority youths, however, the means by which they come to recognize that their sexuality has been named by their culture as an "other" is a vivid, memorable process that can never be forgotten. It alters interpretations of the past, current conceptions of the self, and future life trajectories.

Although the internal process of naming a sexuality is seldom an isolated event but is embedded within a progressive series of milestones for gay and bisexual youths, the critical developmental "crises" of self-labeling and first disclosing this information to others frequently occur in today's cohort of youths during the adolescent and young adult years. Both have been subsumed by the popular term "coming out"; however, labeling of self is distinct, both conceptually and temporally, from the disclosure process, which is discussed in Chapter Seven. The first often begins from earliest memories of feeling different and an awareness that one's attractions to males are sexual and homoerotic and resolves in an act of self-disclosure; the second is a process that begins with one's first disclosure of same-sex attractions and identity to another and ultimately concludes at one's deathbed, for one is constantly coming out to new others. The two are neither identical nor separate but "exist in a dialectic relationship: coming out to others constantly redefines one's notion of self, and the development of a self-identity drives the process of disclosure" (p. 76).[1]

The application of a sexual-identity label to oneself provides not only an explanation for formerly vague and misunderstood feelings but also affords a context in which future thoughts and emotions can be understood. Most youths ultimately navigate these terrains with difficulty but with success, becoming healthy, well-functioning adults. However, for a significant number of youths the self-recognition process is not an easy journey. Published reports lament the fact that all too many do not survive, ending their lives distraught because of their willingness to listen to the lies of family, friends, religion, and culture. The issue of gay youth suicide is addressed in Chapter Nine. Others are left with permanent scars that may be physical, such as HIV infection; emotional, such as depression; cognitive, such as self-depreciation; or social, such as being rejected by friends and family.[2] In its most benign form, internalizing particular negative cultural values and beliefs regarding homosexuality lead some youths to postpone their self-labeling process several years or decades.

Indeed, nonheterosexual labels are still beyond the reach of many youths. In a comprehensive study of sexual orientation among nearly thirty-five thousand Minnesota youths, about 1 percent of junior and senior high-school students defined themselves as gay, lesbian, or bisexual.[3] More youths were willing to report that they had same-sex attractions (5 percent), fantasies (3 percent), and behavior (1 percent). Furthermore, relatively few of those who reported same-sex attractions or fantasies or who engaged in same-sex behavior labeled themselves as anything other than heterosexual. These numbers correspond with the reports of adult men in which far more "confessed" during face-to-face interviews with a research stranger to having experienced desire for sex with a person of the same sex (8 percent) than having had sex with another man (5 percent) or having identified self as gay or bisexual (3 percent).[4]

Despite these numbers, an *increasing* number of gay/bisexual youths are self-defining their sexual identity at *increasingly* younger ages, largely because of the recent visibility of homosexuality in the macro culture (such as in the media), the reality of a very vocal and extensive gay and lesbian culture, and the presence of homosexuality in their immediate social world. For example, one student in my sexual minorities class reported that her high school had seven "out" teachers.[5] Thus, defenses are shattered because now homoerotically inclined adolescents have available to them a construct of homosexuality and gay role models (bisexual models are still scarce) that increase the likelihood of recognizing and labeling their same-sex attractions. Facilitative factors that ease the transition from an assumed but frequently unexamined heterosexual identity to a gay/bisexual identity have seldom been adequately explored and are thus largely unknown.[6]

Youths also now have available a number of support, advocacy, and recreational groups that can facilitate the transition from feelings of nonheterosexuality to a tentative identification as gay or bisexual. For example, the National Advocacy Coalition on Youth and Sexual Orientation, whose mission is to end discrimination against lesbian, gay, bisexual, and transgendered youths and to secure their physical and emotional well-being, lists nearly eighty participating organizations located in all regions of the United States. This public focus on sexual-minority youth further weakens the defenses of adolescents who try to deny or ignore their sexuality.

All too often, however, attempts are made to homogenize the developmental processes by which youths come to an understanding about their sexual identity. What is new and is perhaps the key development for many youths is the visibility and hence possibility of multiple ways of being gay, many of which break traditional images and stereotypes of how one must act, think, and feel if one is gay. Across individuals, sufficient variability is now apparent to warrant an expanded discussion of the broad outlines that are the essential developmental features of many gays and bisexuals during their childhood and adolescence.

Self-Identifying as Gay or Bisexual

The internal process of identifying as gay or bisexual is a very personal, private affair. As opposed to other developmental milestones, such as first gay or heterosexual sex or disclosure to another, in which an identifiable event marks the occasion, many youths consider the identity process to be an abstraction that is difficult to specify as an exact moment in time. Many notable exceptions, however, are apparent in the narratives cited in this section. For example, some youths recalled a very specific instant in which they said clearly and discreetly, "I'm gay/bisexual."

Youths identified their sexuality as early as third or fourth grade or as late as graduate school. The largest number self-identified during their high-school years or while in college—about 40 percent each. A much smaller number, approximately 20 percent, labeled themselves during childhood and early adolescence.

Nearly one in four recognized their homoerotic attractions and sexual identity simultaneously. One youth described this process as, "I really didn't make the distinction. The attractions just happened, and I didn't question them." The absence of a boundary between the two was much more likely to characterize early adolescence than any other time. Another quarter labeled their identity within one to three years after recognizing that they had gay attractions. A third quarter connected their attractions and identity within four to five years; the final quarter, from six to eleven years.

Excluding bisexual youths, nearly 25 percent of gay youths reported that they went through a "bisexual stage" on their way to labeling themselves gay. What prevented these "bisexual" youths from immediately embracing a gay identity was the same as that which prevented many other youths who also delayed naming themselves from moving beyond their heterosexual identity—they felt that their attractions to males would go away. When this temporary aberration did not abate, youths became confused, frightened, and anxious. Many had been taught, especially by their religious or cultural group, that being gay is wrong and they should make all efforts possible to change. Others had more secular fears—that they would be stigmatized by family members, peers, and the culture at large, or verbally and physically harassed.

This should not, however, be construed as a monolithic portrait of these gay/bisexual youths. Although much smaller in number than the previously described group, other youths were relieved that they had finally come to terms with their feelings. Being gay/bisexual was not a handicap or a disability but an extension of living a new life filled with exhilarating prospects for homoeroticism and romantic relationships with those compelling, passionate objects known as men.

When asked what led to their decision to identify as gay or bisexual, the most frequent response was, "I just knew." That is, something just "clicked" in their head, and everything made sense. It could be a sudden event or a gradual process. The second most common response was expressed by those who knew their identity based on the strength of homoerotic feelings that just would not go away. Masturbatory fantasies remained centered on males and sex with girls was just not changing anything.

Friends, both gay and liberal heterosexuals, were the third most frequent contributors to a youth's decision to "come out" to himself. To these individuals, a youth was able to verbalize, "I'm gay/bisexual," and in the process say the same to himself for the first time. The following youth secured the greatest gift a pregay could receive from a friend—someone who would become an even better friend in the process.

> I got very excited and nervous when we talked about gay people and I didn't know why. My friend was very confident and sure of himself and I was not. I'm asking him questions about gays and he was very positive. I remember I got upset with something he said. Somehow he knew that I was gay, which was something I didn't even know then. He tried to calm me down as I muttered, "I'm a faggot! I'm a queer!" He was very supportive. He said he figured it out a long time ago and that he was my friend regardless. He liked me as me. I said that I feared for what my life would be like and what my parents would be like because I was gay. He said he'd be there for me and we became great friends.
>
> So I was crying and very relieved. Part of me should have been developed much earlier but it never was. I missed out on normal development because I didn't even know myself. I was afraid what my parents would think, what my life would be like, no family, alone for the rest of my life. So I feared for the worst. But I had my friend.

Contrary to what many may presuppose, relatively few youths depended on their first sexual experience with a male to label themselves as gay or bisexual. This was evident in Chapter Four. More commonly, youths self-identified as gay after they fell in love with a man or after they accepted their undeniable emotional feelings for a friend. These strong emotional attractions provided the necessary fodder for what their feelings for another man meant, including exiting their "bisexual stage" of development.

> I was just sort of hanging out my senior year of high school at a cafe. I met this guy who turned out to be a male prostitute, and I told him that I had a female friend and he said that he was bisexual. I said that I was too. We drew closer and closer and I said that I loved him; then I told him that I was gay which was telling myself in my mind that I was gay, but I didn't really tell anyone else except him at this point.

Some, but not many, youths made the transition from straight to gay with the emotional support of a therapist, gay peer counselor, or gay hotline. After falling in love with a friend and not understanding what was happening to him, one youth told his therapist about his feelings. She gave him the encouragement he needed to realize that he was gay. Not all, however, received support from their mental-health provider.

> During my junior year of high school the feelings began to come back and I seriously thought that I must be gay, although I was not yet ready to call myself gay. During the summer before my senior year I knew I had to do something about it, so I told my psychiatrist, and he gave me that old spiel about how do I really know that I am since I had no experience sexually. He encouraged me to get a girlfriend and have sex. But I just knew that this is what I was but I didn't get very much good feedback from the psychiatrist. He just sat there a lot.

What eventually helped a relatively small number of youths make sense of their blocked feelings was living in an enlightened community or being exposed to gay images in the mass media. Several youths had an openly lesbian or gay relative, and that helped; others attributed their self-recognition to reading a gay-positive book or article or seeing a gay-positive movie or television show.

> At thirteen I felt I was my own person, and I can't recall any major concerns with my sexual identification. A year later I was gay. Before this I didn't have a name for it. Just sort of happened and then I had to deal with it. Which I did, probably because Ithaca is such an enlightened place that I knew what it meant to be gay.

The nature and influence of these factors and the reactions that youths had in making the transition in self-perception from someone with same-sex attractions to a gay or bisexual identity are presented in this chapter. The narratives are organized based on the age at which the transition occurred.

Childhood and Early Adolescence

Twenty percent of the youths first recognized their gay or bisexual status during late childhood or early adolescence. Compared with other youths, reaching this developmental milestone uncommonly early had particular perils. Although this precarious theme dominates the narratives in this section, several youths were extremely happy to have this aspect of their lives resolved at such an early age.

Over one-half who knew their sexual identity at a relatively early age named their sexual identity within a year of labeling their attractions as "homosexual." For the following two youths, no gap separated labeling feelings and self. Disclosing this information to others, however, was an altogether different matter.

> I never went through a period when my feelings and attractions and my identification were separate. I knew that I was gay but certainly what I was not going to do was come out or advertise it. I spent a lot of my childhood denying what I was but certainly by the age of fourteen I couldn't deny it. But I didn't tell anyone.

> I never did have the real split. I realize that the behavior and feelings and attractions were all labeled gay and that I then was as well. In sixth grade I was really wondering. I still denied it to others but there was a certainty by seventh grade that I knew I was gay.

Similar to these two, most of the other boys who identified themselves as not heterosexual at this age knew instinctively that it would be a mistake to disclose their sexual identity to anyone else. To cope, they played a game—they pretended. One said he knew, "even then that if anyone were to ask me I would have to pretend to be straight." Another reported, "I really wanted my feelings and myself to be heterosexual but I just knew that they really never were. I said to others that I was straight even though I knew within myself that that was not true." Nearly all youths kept their secret close to them and pretended to their families and social world that they were not gay or bisexual. (See further discussion of disclosure to others in Chapter Seven.)

One motive to hide one's homoerotic identity was provided by religion. God did not come to one youth's rescue, although he beseeched Him to come to his aid through fervent prayers.

> Around eleven years old, I began to label my attractions and myself as gay. I said to myself even then that I was gay, but I wasn't going to tell anyone because I knew that I would have to change. My aunt and uncle are born-again Christians and I went on a massive prayer crusade to sort of get rid of these feelings. I felt that I just had to find the right girl.

Others who struggled believed that their feelings for other boys were only temporary and would disappear with time. Other youths must surely have the same problem, they reasoned.

> At one point I thought maybe that it was just a stage that I was going through. If it was a stage, then it was probably no problem. In junior high I knew I had gay feelings but I was really only out about this to myself. I remember using sort of a Kinsey idea that everyone has had homosexual experiences, although I certainly knew that it was more fun for me.

Although not a common practice, some early adolescents sought refuge in the arms of bisexuality. To understand his feelings, the following youth took the "middle ground," labeling his "temporary" attractions to males as bisexual. Being bisexual was not perceived as so bad or as so permanent as being gay.

> At first I thought that maybe I was bisexual. I had the feelings but that I would probably grow out of it and get married. This is probably when I was in middle school. I would never have said to myself at that point that I was gay. But I really wasn't sure; I think I was just trying to take the middle ground. It was very much of a gradual process, not just one moment. By sixth grade I pretty well knew for sure that I certainly was attracted to guys. But I certainly could never have shared that with anyone.

After the hope of temporality vanished, these early adolescents expressed a number of fears that delayed naming their identity. Among these included one who said: "I was crushed because of what I had hoped to be, I wasn't going to be. I was not straight, not normal."

Given the struggle these youths had in naming their identity and placing themselves in a socially despised class of individuals, an interesting question emerges: What convinced a young adolescent that he was gay or bisexual? The overwhelming response was simply, "I just knew. Something clicked inside." Several had difficulty identifying a moment in time. The following youth expressed these themes.

> I can remember knowing that I had homosexual feelings but I really felt that these would wear off, that I could make the decision as an adult not to be gay. By eighth grade I knew in the back of my mind that I was attracted to males but I never really said it to others or to myself. I hoped that I would change, so I really never directly thought about it. It was about that time that I think I began to realize or at least that I began to remember that I had forgotten all about those feelings, then I began to put two and two together and began to realize what I was.

Other young adolescents named particular assets that they believed helped them make the transition from gay attractions to gay identity. The following three had the assistance of a family member.

My parents split very early on and my father moved to New York City so I spent a lot of time there with him and by the age of twelve I was going to gay bars with my older brother. So I was certainly familiar with the gay lifestyle.

Why so early? I'm not really sure. But certainly by the beginning of high school I knew. I certainly knew what it meant and I certainly knew I was attracted to boys. Maybe in part this was helpful because I had a gay cousin who sort of helped prepare me.

My parents always provided me with sexually explicit education so I knew what homosexuality was. So by thirteen I could consciously say to myself that I was gay.

Although relatively few in number, other youths relied on their sexual feelings to guide them in identifying their gay/bisexual identity. When comparing their attractions to boys versus girls, they came to the inevitable conclusion that they must be gay or bisexual.

I was going out with this girl but we like never did anything. We would hang out and then we broke up and it sort of hit me like a lightning bolt that I really was into girls only in terms of spiritual and emotional intimacy. But with males they were the object of my sexual fantasies. I knew that my sexual fantasies were of males and this told me that I was gay. It was very liberating to finally figure this out; it was a real positive experience.

One early adolescent came to realize his gayness because of his emotional attachments to other males. A new friend in school became something more than a "regular guy friend" to him, and as eighth grade closed he knew that his "love" had significance for who he was as a person. "I knew I wanted to be with him. It's sort of like the T-shirt that says, 'I'm not gay, but my boyfriend is.' That's sort of the way that I felt at that time." Another youth moved from hell to heaven during the course of early adolescence.

In junior high school I was confused as hell. I was in a Catholic school, an all-male school and I was going through confirmation class and at one point in the confirmation class it was very clear that homosexuality was bad and that everyone was going to hell. I just felt very confused because I had the feelings. I recognized that my feelings were homosexual but I decided that I could purge the feelings from me.

The second semester of the eighth grade I developed a serious crush on my [male] English teacher. At the time I said that I was bisexual because I had a girlfriend. At this point everything just clicked; it all made sense. I had to basically leave the church, and then labeling myself gay felt exciting yet scary. I knew that I would have to be closeted during my high-school career because I knew that if I was not I would get beat up on because gay bashing was a popular sport in my high school. But inside I felt blessed, a state of nirvana after the years of hell.

The 20 percent of youths who identified themselves as gay or bisexual during childhood or early adolescence were also considerably advanced of their gay peers regarding when they reported awareness of same-sex attractions, labeling those attractions as homoerotic, disclosing their sexual identity to others, and evolving a positive gay/bisexual identity. They were not, however, more or less likely to have gay sex, heterosexual sex, or same-sex romantic relationships or to do so at an earlier age. Although these youths appeared to be advanced in their cognitive awareness of their sexuality, they did not thus act on it in their sexual behavior or romantic relationships.

In summary, youths who made an important and nearly instantaneous connection at pubertal onset knew that their attractions to males implied something about their sexual identity. Others, however, waited a year or more, hoping that their homoeroticism was merely a temporary aberration, perhaps reflecting a bisexual phase. Some youths had a gay role model within their family; still others labeled themselves as the result of having stronger gay than heterosexual feelings or after having an emotional attachment to another male. For most, however, something just "clicked" in their minds and they knew they were gay or bisexual. The teachings of social institutions, such as their religious or ethnic community, frightened them from disclosing that which they knew was true about their sexuality. Despite these handicaps, as will be apparent in Chapter Seven, these youths were on their way to an early and long gay career.

The High-School Years

Nearly 40 percent of the youths came to the conclusion during their high-school years that they were gay or bisexual. For these youths, an average of three and one half years transpired after labeling their attractions as homoerotic before they labeled themselves as gay or bisexual. The range of time between these two, however, is more informative. The interval was either nonexistent, for 20 percent, or was extended to between three and five years for over half of the youths. Several delayed the identity process more than six years. One youth knew immediately during his senior year of high school when suddenly "a light switched on." Another "wasted" six years of his life.

> I spent a lot of time reading in the library about homosexuality. This was in the sixth and seventh grade. I still didn't identify as gay even after that because I was not like those that I read about. Then early in high school I was very, very devoted to my academic work and I just put all this on the back burner. By my senior year I

started to have very strong emotional feelings towards male friends. This was six years after I should have known; six wasted years.

Twenty percent of youths who became aware of their sexual identity during their high-school years were delayed in labeling their sexual identity because, according to one, "I spent all this time hiding myself in this bisexual stage." This bisexual transition—distinct from true bisexuality—could take several years and perhaps a broken relationship with a girl before a boy could finally say to himself that he was not bisexual but gay.

> I sort of went through a bisexual stage, but then doesn't everybody? In middle school I would have said that I was straight with bi tendencies. In high school I would have said bisexual and by eleventh grade, definitely gay. I felt pretty bad, but it's not easy given the rural, Republican community I grew up in. It was definitely not gay positive. I did have a girlfriend and I felt like I was using her because when I entered into the relationship I should have known that I was gay.

Other youths perceived that they delayed the naming process because they feared what their lives would be like if they were to be gay/bisexual. As such, several reported that they were under the strong, irresistible, and oppressive influence of religious dogma. Once they had thrown off the confines of religion and other institutions that oppress gay people, they felt liberated to name their sexuality.

> At age sixteen I said to myself that I was gay. I was in the hospital away from Thomas [youth minister] and all of his religious beliefs that led to this suicide attempt in the first place so that I could indeed think about it. It was at this time, in fact, that I was struggling with all the religious issues Thomas kept reminding me of, that I would go to hell and stuff like that.

Many youths simply hoped that they would outgrow their attractions to other boys. They had heard or read that such a phase during adolescence was not uncommon and so they decided to put all such thoughts out of their minds. This sometimes worked for a year or two, but seldom lasted beyond three or four. Eventually, they could not deny their reality.

> The feelings were not passing as they were supposed to. They were staying and I was beginning to get scared. At first, the label was very negative. This was when I was fifteen years old. I tried to engage in behavior that would encourage heterosexuality, such as looking at girls, imagining their breasts, and trying to date them. I read my Bible six times that one year to find a way out of my predicament. My senior year I gave up outgrowing it.

Extensive soul-searching, journal writing, or taking long walks could also be helpful. The contribution of sex was powerful for a few. One youth could not deny to himself that "at fifteen I wasn't dating girls and I was having sex with guys." Because first gay sex was most likely to occur between the ages of thirteen and fifteen years, the consequence for some youths of having this experience was that they concluded that it must mean they were gay/bisexual. That is, having the attractions was one thing but to actually act on them made these youths strikingly aware of their sexual identity.

The persistence of homoerotic fantasies and feelings was sufficient information for some to conclude that they were gay or bisexual. When one sixteen year old's sexual fantasies consisted exclusively of male images, despite his attempts to alter them, he looked in the mirror one day and said to himself, at first tentatively and then louder, "Gay! Gay! Gay!" This was not, however, a happy revelation: "For the next year or two I was depressed on and off." However, another youth was much relieved once the mystery was solved. "I remember that I had been fantasizing about men and at some point I just finally said to myself, 'Why am I denying this?' I had such relief that this was finally settled!"

For several youths, more important than sexual fantasies was the development of a strong emotional attachment for another male. This was initially experienced as a crush or an infatuation that just would not go away.

> There's this guy in my class I developed a crush on and yet I was still seeing a woman. I knew what my feelings for him were and that was what I was supposed to feel for her. I think this is sort of the beginning of my realization. I had concluded before that I must be bi because I had an emotional bond to women and I never really had that with guys. Then I discovered that one can have both an emotional bond and a sexual attraction to a guy.

Friends often helped a gay/bisexual youth make the jump from pregay to gay. Some were themselves gay, while others were understanding girlfriends or accepting heterosexuals. The following youth did not initially recognize that he wanted to walk across the "continental divide into the unknown abyss of homosexuality."

> I went to an all-Catholic military school and in my senior year I was friends with this guy who was obviously gay. You could tell by his handshake and his mannerisms. We were friends and then at one point I was freaking out because he was fucking with my mind. I had just broken up with this girlfriend and I was crying and he said that I needed to face the fact that I was gay and over the phone he got me to admit that I was. I hung up on him and then he called me back and we talked more. He practically outed me, asking me rather than me telling him. Even though he tried to be supportive, it was not something that I wanted to accept at the time. I am grateful now, but I wasn't then. Our friendship suffered for several years but we are okay now.

It was apparent to everyone, especially his friends, that the following youth was gay. They were not sure how to help him except to be honest with him about themselves.

> I was close to a lot of people and in particular, five of my very best friends, including my girlfriend, brought the whole issue of homosexuality to the forefront. These five included two who were gay, my very closest friends including my very best friend and he's the one who told me all about the gay lifestyle, and it was through this that I came to see that it was certainly something that I was all about. They actually suspected that I might be gay but it was not that they were trying to make me gay but it was just that we had the kind of relationship in which they confided in me these kinds of things.

Books, educational materials, and the media were occasionally helpful for gay/bisexual youths in understanding the meaning of their homoerotic attractions. This was not always the case, as the following narrative illustrates.

> I was wondering about homosexuality so I went and did some research in medical books on what it meant to be gay. Most of the stories were about young boys in boarding schools and the approach was either that it was temporary and something that would go away or that it was permanent, a lifestyle. This did not help me come out.

More common was the experience of the following high-school senior who found what he needed to make the transition to a gay identity.

> I was reading sort of all this educational stuff about homosexuality and it portrayed it in a positive way and that is, that they have their own culture and their own heroes and models. So at this point then I was able to say to myself that I am gay myself.

In some cases, an accumulation of knowledge proved beneficial when a decision needed to be made regarding the meaning of strongly felt attractions.

> I wasn't sure what homosexual meant but by the age of fifteen I had enough information to know. I'd always assumed that my attractions were shared by everyone else. What was helpful for me was having sex education in junior high. I knew that males could be attracted to other males and that this was normal and so I didn't really worry much about it.

One youth went to a movie with several of his female friends who were enamored with several of the male movie stars appearing in the picture. The event had a far-reaching effect on him.

> I had fooled around and then I saw "Making Love," and I realized at that point that it was me and that I could relate to it. I remember lying awake all night and I said to

myself, what am I going to do? The next day I told the two close female friends that I had seen the movie with that I was gay. They had suspected it, and I guess maybe the entire town as well. I really never dated and I really made no attempt to date.

As was true for this youth, many felt a sense of great relief that they had solved their life mystery. Although they knew that their daily routine would now be more difficult, the persistence of low-level anxiety and alienation was now over. Once he had named himself, one sophomore found "the answer to all of my struggles. I knew that my life would be difficult but at least I had my answer. I could now stop trying to be straight."

The following narrative illustrates several factors that helped a high-school youth name his sexual identity. It took an accumulation of "too much evidence not to be gay" before he understood the implications for himself.

I began to explore the whole issue of my sexuality. Like I would call 900 numbers and see if that turned me on or I would buy magazines or go to porno movies. It took me awhile to say that I'm gay. In fact, it took me a year until my senior year. I think I just gave up, not being gay. I never had dreams of sex with females; they were all of males. My friends kept hinting by saying they liked gay people. I knew that it would be hard being gay but I knew that I also had to be out to myself.

The decisive event of self-liberation varied considerably across the high-school youths. For some it was gay or heterosexual sex while for others it was introspection, a friend, a support group, a book, a television show, or an infatuation. Feelings of emancipation followed, offering a name for their feelings and attractions. An equal number, however, delayed this liberation until their college years.

The College Years

Forty percent of the interviewed youths did not name their sexuality until they had graduated from high school. Most were in college at the time. Less than one-quarter of these youths simultaneously recognized their attractions and identity as gay or bisexual. The majority waited at least four years, including one-third who had a gap of seven or more years between realizing their attractions were homoerotic and understanding the implications of them for their identity. One youth "had an inkling" when he was twelve; ten years later he finally believed it sufficiently to accept his homoeroticism.

I remember feeling guilty when I read about how bad it was, as a Catholic, to have thoughts about sex. This bothered me and I felt real guilty because I knew it was negative. In my junior year I said to myself, "I might be gay," but then I just shut off all feelings. It was not until my junior year of college that I was able to say "gay" and to accept it, if only for a minute. A year later I finally said it to myself and I accepted it. This was a little bit less than a year ago.

Unlike those who named their sexual identity at earlier ages, relatively few of these youths believed that their gay feelings constituted a phase to be outgrown. Also, few reported that they felt frightened, believed that their homosexuality was wrong, or were confused about their feelings. Most simply could not explain why it took them so long. Typical was the youth who modestly stated, "I felt I really was not being honest with myself."

This dual sense of having strong erotic attractions for males that did not disappear, even when involved with a woman, and of feeling an increased need to be honest with oneself characterized many stories. A mirror again proved critical for one youth to reflect on his true self.

> Always before because I was interested in females, as least as friends, I could not consider myself gay, but by this time I had to honestly say to myself that it was not going to go away. In high school I knew I was attracted to guys but I was not yet ready to deal with it. One day I said to myself in the mirror, "You are gay!" over and over until I believed it.

Another had to graduate from college to finally understand that his sexual feelings did not disappear once he left his liberal college campus.

The external factor that was most responsible for promoting an end to the charade of heterosexuality was coming into contact with friends who were gay. The chances of this occurring were considerably enhanced once away from the high-school closet and enrolled in a college where gay instructors, courses, and organizations existed. Such contact induced one youth to reconsider his previous assumed understandings and to conclude that he too was gay.

> In the dorm I met this guy who came out and he was very comfortable with it. He encouraged me to give up my act on a camp out I went with him. We talked and actually fooled around. I really didn't like this because I had never fooled around with a gay guy, which was different than just fooling around with guys. But he kept saying to relax, to relax, and by the third night I had come to accept these feelings. We fooled around all week while I was up there and so by this point I knew that gay actually had some positive dimensions as well. He wasn't all the negative things that I had heard about.

The friend need not be gay to be effective in helping a young adult recognize his sexual identity. Several youths noted that a liberal heterosexual friend "pulled it out of me." Another youth said to a straight friend that he was bisexual. "That was my way of saying it to myself. I had to say it out loud to someone I knew would be supportive."

One relatively common instigating factor combined internal and external components—becoming infatuated with another male. These youths were suddenly and unexpectedly startled into self-awareness; denial of their sexuality became less possible or desirable.

> Well this happened two summers ago when I was dating a female, as I have all my life, yet I always knew I was attracted to males. Then it all came together. I had a crush on a fellow student who was a bisexual male. Like him, I called myself bisexual at that point. I knew what bisexual meant since the age of sixteen because I have friends who were bisexual, including dating a female who was bisexual.

Identifying as bisexual posed particular difficulties not encountered by those who reached the conclusion that they had exclusive attractions to males. One youth who had feelings for both sexes tried to gauge which were stronger because he felt that he had to figure out if he was gay or heterosexual: "I was trying to understand how I should grapple with this and to make a *final* decision." Another with dual attractions wanted definitively to land on the heterosexual side. It was not so simple.

> I wanted desperately to be straight and the label implied some level of commitment. I dated females and realized that I was attracted to females and so I thought of myself as straight. I sort of let all of this go for awhile and then in the early months of my sophomore year I realized that my feelings for guys must mean something, and it must mean that I'm bisexual. Or, maybe what I was, was just sexual.
>
> I've lived with it as if it were a part of me but not that it was real important. With males I'm finding I'm very attracted to them and want to be close to them but really not have sex, and that's still sort of what I'm looking for, even now. I don't want to go out and just have sex but I want to find emotional attractiveness with males like I have with females. Now I know that I prefer males, though I'm probably more bi than most gays.

Struggles among competing sexual identities frequently lasted for many years for those who did not identify as gay or bisexual until after high-school graduation. Denial continued until self-revelation would no longer allow it, when sexual feelings for men intruded into their daily lives. Occasionally, falling in love with another male was the instigating factor; other times it was having gay or liberal friends who either presented a positive image of being gay or who helped end the charade of heterosexuality. Youths who desperately wanted to be heterosexual and had the sexual and emotional feelings to give credence to their desires often struggled with their attractions to males before they labeled themselves bisexual.

Reflections on Self-Identifying as Gay or Bisexual

In his review of the various coming-out models that were proposed during the 1970s, McDonald notes that the process of revelation to self is complex and highly significant.

> A developmental process through which gay persons become aware of their affectional and sexual preferences and choose to integrate this knowledge into their personal and social lives, coming out involves adopting a nontraditional identity, restructuring one's self-concept, reorganizing one's personal sense of history, and altering one's relations with others and with society . . . all of which reflects a complex series of cognitive and affective transformations as well as changes in behavior. (p. 47)[7]

The youths' narratives remind us that identifying as gay/bisexual was often an extremely complex process. Seldom understood but keenly felt attractions to males early in life could eventuate as early as childhood or as late as young adulthood in self-identifying as gay or bisexual. This could be an instantaneous event or a very long, protracted affair; a relatively easy process, or a feature of oneself that is denied or actively suppressed for years, perhaps decades. If the former, feelings were often long-standing and had evolved during childhood and adolescence as a natural aspect of the self. If the latter, youths tried to not think about their sexuality as anything other than heterosexual and a tone of fear dominated their stories. In some cases a youth was not aware that homosexuality was an option until eventually the evidence, consisting of recurrent same-sex fantasies or, less frequently, same-sex encounters, convinced him that he must be gay or bisexual. To combat overwhelming homoerotic feelings without taking on the mantle of the real thing—gayness—other youths claimed a temporary or transitory bisexual identity, remained "heterosexual," or decided not to decide.

Although many forces impact a youth's process of coming out to self, it is abundantly clear from the youths' stories that external agents neither created nor destroyed their desires, at least for long. Many youths related how macro-level forces such as family values and institutional heterosexism handicapped their understanding of what their same-sex attractions meant. To overcome these forces, layer upon layer of internalized homophobia—the incorporation of the hatred and fears that are readily apparent in our cultural biases and attitudes—had to be penetrated. The closer, more intimate aspects of their social world, such as best friends, as well as larger, more distant cultural customs, including gay positive media presentations of homosexuality and living in a liberal, often collegiate, community helped many of these youths overcome these barriers.

What had to be mastered internally was the stereotype many youths had of what it meant to be gay or bisexual and the kind of life they would have if they accepted "the gay lifestyle." The process was very individualized but most youths could point to some event, experience, or person that helped them make this leap to self-recognition. It was the rare but fortunate youth who had the guidance of an older gay or lesbian mentor who helped him see an alternate way of being gay that did not mean conforming to stereotypes. He need not be queer, transgendered, promiscuous, radical, or HIV positive; he need only be who he was before "becoming gay."

Yet, one factor, often ignored, that has increasingly assisted gay and bisexual teens to come to terms with their sexuality is the visibility of gay issues in our culture—a visibility that has sometimes been fostered by those very queer, radical activists whom these youths desired not to be. Counterbalancing this presentation of being a modern gay are other forces such as the gay-positive, famous heterosexuals who grace the covers of gay/lesbian national newsmagazines and the multiple images of homosexuality tendered in the media of renowned athletes, rock singers, artists, movie stars, and politicians who are declaring their gay, lesbian, or bisexual identities. This diversity has given young pregays the opportunity to better understand their experiences, regardless of their physical appearance, private thoughts, and public behavior, and not to think or feel poorly of themselves because of the experiences.

Although these external factors are critical, they may not be the most important catalyst for a youth to reach the decision to self-identify as gay or bisexual. Many of the narratives recounted intense self-reflections, an inner voice, that pushed youths to place honesty with self above the negative conceptions they had of being gay. Something clicked, and all became clarified. One fifteen-year-old never wrote one word in his daily journal about what was most on his mind. Then he began to write about "it" and his identification followed. "I kept it out of my journal but finally had to admit it if this journal was going to be an accurate reflection of my life." Another kept repeating to himself, "I'm gay," practicing, even trying on the concept, until it began to feel comfortable and right.

Thus, a single coming-out-to-self pattern did not emerge among the interviewed youths. The range was from one of ease and tranquillity to one of torture and disgust. At some point during their childhood, adolescence, or young adulthood, many youths felt threatened by their sexual fantasies, which did not, as planned, go away but in fact increased over time, especially after pubertal onset. The "homosexual" label was initially viewed as unacceptable by most, but not all, until high school or college, even though nearly all had strong suspicions before this point. Their willingness to label themselves as something other than heterosexual ranged from "absolutely" to "most likely" to "might be," and their comfort level from "feeling great" to "feeling ambivalent" to "feeling awful."

Some youths become more or less resigned to the inevitable, although they remained wary of the potential consequences of being gay for their future careers, pessimistic of the possibilities for finding a romantic relationship with a man, and racked with guilt for possibly destroying interpersonal relations with friends and family. The very clarity of their sexual identity frightened them immensely, and thus they developed elaborate defenses to protect themselves against that which they knew to be true, long-standing, and petrifying. They wanted to reject it but the evidence simply would not disappear, even with girlfriends, sex with girls, and a heterosexual persona in the eyes of peers. Once away from family and the hometown community, self-recognition of sexual identity for some was swift—most of those who identified as gay or bisexual in college did so during their first two years.

Others felt relieved that mysteries had been solved, sexual and romantic feelings could be freely expressed, and a basic sense of self could be experienced and expressed. One interviewee said, "I wanted to shout it to everybody. I really talked for the first time with my friends." Another said, "The fact that men found me attractive did wonders for my self-image in ways no female ever had." Of course, these timelines and the accompanying developmental milestones apply only to the interviewed youths. Many others, perhaps far exceeding in number those who disclosed prior to young adulthood, may never reach the point in their developmental trajectory at which they identify as gay or bisexual, or do so only in adulthood or old age.

Bisexual youths often experienced unique difficulties sorting through the complexities of their attractions. One reflected about his future, "Maybe I'll marry and deal with guys on the side." One began a gay relationship during his senior year of high school but was still disturbed by his continuing heterosexuality: "My 'Perfect Life Guard' wanted me, but I had Sally for so long, so why continue with him which would make my life so hard?" Some were not comfortable with the resolution of heterosexuality but it seemed the best compromise given the multitude of sexual feelings, confusions, and expectations from family and friends. One youth noted, "I was too scared to do anything or go to anyone. Was it really true? A phase? How could I possibly accept these gay feelings?" Another youth had sex with sixteen males and two females by the age of twenty-two and felt equally bisexual, which did not make sense to him. His homoerotic attractions came late, at age sixteen, when he was in the process of breaking up with his girlfriend since seventh grade. His working-class Catholic heritage still loomed powerful for him. Youths with emotional, romantic relationships with girls often tried to find opportunities to experiment with their male erotic feelings without disclosing their homoeroticism to their girlfriends. How many will be able to maintain this balance in adulthood is unknown.

Indeed, some youths reflected a theme of sexual fluidity in their longitudinal assessment of their sexuality. They may have understood themselves as bisexual but perhaps did not feel totally comfortable with the label or the absence of certainty. Whether these males are fluid in their sexual identity or momentarily uncertain is difficult to discern. The following youth represents a third alternative—confused and fluid; he wanted the best of both worlds.

> Well last summer I decided to tell my friends that I "might" be gay and that I "might" want to go to gay clubs. Sort of a couple of years before that I knew I wasn't straight and I was dealing with this issue in therapy a lot. I'm still today questioning myself as a gay person. Sometimes I want to say that I'm bisexual and then at times I wonder well maybe I'm straight, and this is when I contemplate marrying and having kids and having the pictures and all, but would this ever be meaningful for me? I'd have to have my own mister mistress.

Cultivating an acceptance of this self-identity and then disclosing this information to others are separable processes.[8] The youths themselves made this distinction. Openly declaring their sexuality was seldom a high-school event. Many too much feared that they would be battered and insufficiently supported to make the declaration to their hometown community. Given the complexity of the coming-out-to-self process, it is not surprising that sharing this information with others was often delayed until youths left home. The process of disclosing this new self-identification to others is the focus of Chapter Seven.

7.

Disclosure to Others

A developmental milestone that nearly all gay and bisexual youths vividly recall is the first time they disclosed their sexuality to another. Youths usually remember the exact circumstances, setting, date, time of day, feelings, and the reactions of the other person.[1] Initial disclosures occur throughout the process of self-labeling, but most usually ensue within a year or two after a gay or bisexual self-identification is at least tentatively adopted.

First disclosure is the opening salvo of a process of telling others about one's same-sex attractions. It may take a lifetime to fully resolve. Final disclosure, such that a gay/bisexual youth is "out" to everyone who cares to know, may never be achieved because people who do not know are always entering one's life. Most youths define themselves as "totally out" when they no longer care who knows about their sexual orientation. From first to final disclosure is often a formidable and protracted process because many elect to conceal or to selectively share their forbidden sexuality with others. Indeed, some choose to compartmentalize their lives by developing two distinct groups of people in their lives: those who know and those who do not.[2]

Disclosing a sexual identity to others poses a number of developmental hurdles. A sexual-minority youth often feels most vulnerable and out of control when he "comes out" or has his sexuality discovered by others.[3] He may more strongly fear immediate negative reprisals than anticipate the long-term positive, healthy consequences of sharing with others his true nature. Same-sex attractions may be kept secretive because a youth fears the unknown; wishes not to hurt or disappoint loved ones; or wants to avoid being rejected, verbally harassed, or physically abused by parents and peers.

It is a risky venture, and children, adolescents, and young adults may have legitimate concerns about their physical and emotional safety if their sexual orientation were to be known by those they love, as well as by those they do not know. At the same time, disclosure may result in a greater sense of personal freedom and of being oneself, of not living a lie, and of experiencing genuine acceptance from those who know the deepest, darkest secrets of one's life.

Conflicts between the possible benefits and drawbacks of disclosure are especially pronounced for youths who are still living at home or are attending college in their hometown community. Because many decide to disclose under these conditions, their lives contrast sharply with earlier generations of gay individuals, many of whom remained closeted until they moved out of the household and established independence. Clearly, adolescents who disclose their sexual identity to friends and parents while living at home must cope with the reactions and dispositions of those most important to them more frequently, more immediately, and for longer periods of time than those who wait until after they leave home.

Disapproving responses to the news place the newly out youth at greater risk for the *negative* outcomes associated with stigmatization, such as decreased self-esteem, running away from home, substance abuse, and suicide attempts.[4] As a result, most youths reveal their sexual orientation first to close friends who are most likely to understand and offer support.[5] However, other youths may vow never to disclose because they do not believe they fit gay stereotypes or because they have sufficient interest in heterosexual behaviors to "choose" that direction for their lives. These youths may thus never disclose to anyone their same-sex attractions, or do so only under very special circumstances or very late in life.

At the same time, adolescents who disclose to others are generally assumed to experience a diverse array of *positive* mental-health outcomes that are associated with openness, including identity synthesis and integration, healthy psychological adjustment, decreased feelings of loneliness and guilt, and positive self-esteem. Disclosure is thus assumed to reduce the stress that accrues to adolescents who actively hide or suppress their sexual orientation.[6]

Following the developmental focus of the book, narratives are discussed according to when youths first disclosed to another person. The two major divisions are between those who disclosed while living at home and those who waited until they graduated from high school. Because the youths chose prudently and selectively, nearly all reactions were at least positive, if not extremely supportive.

Disclosure to Others

All but two youths had disclosed to at least one other person the nature of their sexual attractions. The most popular time of initial disclosure was during freshman year of college, although the range is more instructive. One youth disclosed to his parents as he entered junior high school, and one did not disclose to anyone until just before his interview at age twenty-five years.

One-half of all first disclosures were to a female friend. She was someone the youth trusted with this potentially explosive information. Her response was inevitably and unequivocally supportive. In the following two examples, one taken from a youth who disclosed during high school and one during college, the initial disclosure was to the right person.

> This is a female friend of mine in music camp when we were both seventeen years old. Closer to her than any other person. Late one night I let out a big sigh and said, "I think I need to tell you something. I think I'm gay." Difficult, wrenching. I was trembling. At first she was just believing and then she said that she wasn't surprised, that she had wondered if I was but was afraid to ask. In the end she was honored that I could tell her. Telling her made us closer. I shared with her my diary to make it more real to her and myself.

> Freshman year and she was eighteen or nineteen. A very important person to me. We were in choir together, not dating but very good friends. Not sure why I told her. She had said one of her friends was gay and awhile after this I told her. I said I had a big thing to tell her and it was very difficult. She asked if I was gay. I didn't answer and then said I was. I found the support I needed and that was fine. I knew she'd be supportive. Very free-spirited, liberal, and accepting.

Not uncommonly, a youth was motivated to tell his best female friend because he sensed that she had become romantically or sexually interested in him and he wanted "to set the record straight." He did not want his friend to suffer by pursuing false hopes or to make his life more difficult. To do otherwise would place a burden on the friendship, potentially risking a very good thing.

> I was fourteen and she was fifteen, my best friend. She was becoming sexually attracted to me so I had to tell her to get away for her own good and to tell her I was gay. It solved the problem and she became my best friend.

> It was a woman friend, seeing the possibility I could be attracted to men. We lived together in a large apartment with fourteen people. She had an open mind, caring. It resolved the sexual tension around us as friends or potential lovers because obviously I was attracted to men. That serenity brought us together after I told her.

Other youths pursued the relationship as a romantic one, either because they truly felt love and affection for the women or because they needed the heterosexual cover for themselves. It was within the context of an ongoing dating relationship that some youths decided to disclose for the first time that they were sexually attracted not to their date but to men. One youth was in a long-term relationship with a woman, but their coupling was less than ideal. They both knew that the issue was his sexuality and she finally "guessed" the answer during a late-night telephone conversation.

> I was very, very depressed and she guessed that my problem was that I liked guys. Crying, I said, "Yes." It was a relief to her at first because we were so close that it helped her to understand my problems, like why I wasn't into sex with her and why I hadn't asked her to marry me. But then she wanted to salvage the relationship by saying that sex wasn't that important. She was, overall, supportive, but in other ways perhaps she really wasn't. She did ask me if it would still feel comfortable asking me what I find attractive about different males. But I was always afraid she held out hope for more.

Although no statistics are available, a significant number of the girls and women that the youths found attractive, at least from an interpersonal perspective, appeared themselves to be lesbian or bisexual. On such occasions, the youth was inevitably surprised to learn that his secret was also a secret of hers. They "came out" together to each other.

> Judith and I were nineteen years old and apartment mates. I found I wanted to get close to her; there was an attraction. It was in a coffee shop when I said the words and she shouted, "Me, too!" and she started to laugh hysterically. I regarded her as a close friend, but I never knew this about her.

The most popular person after best female friend to disclose to was best male friend. One-third of the youths first disclosed their sexual orientation to a male friend who was known or assumed to be heterosexual. The male friend was sometimes either a sexual partner or a gay friend or both. Similar to the girls and women, in nearly all cases these boys and men, even the heterosexual ones, reacted with support and, usually, acceptance. One youth found his close straight friend to be very supportive but hurt because the friend felt, "I should've told him before that."

Telling a gay friend that one is also gay was perceived to be a safe disclosure. Motivations for disclosing to such individuals were diverse. Some sought the inevitable support; who better to understand than a fellow traveler? Others desired sexual relations with the individual, and by disclosing their own sexual status they hoped that "something would happen." Still others disclosed after engaging in sexual relations with the gay friend, the act of sex providing the necessary impetus for a youth to finally say to himself and to another that which he had been feeling but had not yet felt comfortable telling anyone. The next three narratives illustrate this diversity in experience and motivation.

This friend and I came out to each other at the same time. He really helped me. He was seeing a friend of mine who was also gay. He came out to me after I said I was bi. He said he was gay. Later I admitted I was totally gay.

I fooled around with this guy and we would call ourselves bisexual because at that point I hadn't made the separation between the spiritual and the physical. But I really told someone I was gay at the age of fourteen when I met this seventeen-year-old guy in high school who I really had a crush on and we later had sex.

It was the guy that I first had sex with, on our second date, the guy that I met at that party. He wasn't like really surprised because we had had sex, but I needed to say it to someone and he was as good as anyone, even better than most.

The other 20 percent first disclosed to a family member, usually a parent or a sibling rather than an extended family member, or an adult who was usually in a supportive role—such as a therapist or residential worker. Perhaps because youths carefully selected adults or family members who they trusted would be receptive to the information, in most cases the response of the individual was indeed a positive one. The first three individuals the following youth told were family members; his father had to wait an additional year.

Was my younger brother. Not sure why but I needed to tell him. He was great about it. Said he suspected. Then I told my next youngest brother and then my mother. I knew she knew and that was confirmed when I asked her if she knew. I told my father several months ago. They were all okay about it.

One youth discovered during his first day of class as a college freshman that his professor wore a mysterious pink triangle on his coat. To make conversation after class he asked what it symbolized. When he discovered its significance he knew intuitively the first person to whom he would disclose, in writing.

I was in an English seminar at Amherst College, and I didn't know that my professor was gay until this point. I could not get this out of my mind and I came eagerly to class every day. I hung around him after class. I still didn't know why. He recommended a book to me for my final paper, My Son Eric. I concluded the paper by saying for the first time that I was gay, and he was of course very great, very positive about it. He gave me a list of books that he thought might be helpful for me to read.

As noted earlier, two youths had not discussed with anyone at the time of the interview the nature of their sexuality. They asserted that they always assumed that everyone knew as much information as they needed to know and thus they felt no need to "come out"—it was never deemed necessary or obligatory.

> In the dance company or soon thereafter, it seemed like everyone always knew. Maybe I had no problems because there were a lot of male gays and lesbians there, and no one really cared what you were. Or everybody assumed that everybody was gay or something weird, sexually or otherwise.

> There were lots of others talking about my outrageous behavior towards both men and women. It just seemed like the others seemed to know about me. I was never really in a confessional booth. So I never really used the words. Everyone just always knew, if they wanted to know. If not, well, fuck them.

These were the rare youths, so out to themselves and others that they could not remember the moment when they said to another, "I'm gay/bisexual." Most youths were extremely circumspect in whom they told, perhaps in order to elicit a very positive, supportive response.

Disclosure during Adolescence

When a youth made the decision to first disclose his sexual orientation during his junior or senior high-school years, he usually looked no further than his best female friend. These were seldom girls that he was dating, and very few of them "came out" to him at the same time—these classifications were more characteristic of youths who first disclosed while in college. With best female friends a youth was fairly certain of a positive reception and in many cases she had suspected this about him all along. One sixteen-year-old finally mustered the courage to tell his best friend the truth about himself, only to discover that she already knew.

> She was also a friend of my first love, the first guy I had sex with. This guy was a complete jerk to me and so I had to explain all what had happened to her and therefore that I was gay. She already knew. Someone else had told her. My reaction was relief. I didn't mind that someone had told her—but who else knew?

Although her response and those of many others were positive, this was not always the case. It was not that the best friend responded negatively, but that she was less than ideally supportive. For example, one youth found his best friend "distanced herself from the conversation and really intellectualized my sexuality." Another youth discovered that his best friend's initial response of "no big deal" was later belied by her growing discomfort with his sexuality. He regretted telling her: "If I had known, well, maybe I would have waited, but we just were talking about deep issues and it came up." Sometimes, as in the case below, a youth decided to disclose to a best friend even though he doubted that she would react in an ideal fashion.

I guess the theme of honesty is strong with me. It's also a sense of communication with others even when they don't want to know. The first person who I came out to that I wanted to know that I was gay freaked out. She was supportive but also disgusted and she did have some homophobic reaction. I wasn't offended by her ignorance. She was trying to instruct me to see how I think my life would be being gay.

Some youths used the opportunity to disclose to another to cross the bridge to self-recognition that they were afraid to take alone. Thus, by disclosing, they self-consciously placed themselves in a wanted but fearful position. They could never renege on their declaration; once out of the closet the door locked behind them.

I needed to talk to someone. She was a good friend, and I also knew at the point of telling her there'd be no point of return. She didn't understand initially, so I had to explain it in detail. She thought I was lying! I was excited but scared at the same time. She didn't make it easy on me!

The need to talk, to share this intimate aspect of oneself, had few age boundaries. One of the youngest to first disclose was a thirteen-year-old who told his best female friend during a school lunch of chili, celery sticks, chocolate milk, and chocolate cake. The choice was a good one because she responded in a very understanding and supportive way, even for an eighth-grader: "She was fascinated by it and said it was cool."

Although the girl who was first told was seldom a dating partner, in several instances a youth was motivated to disclose to prevent a romantic relationship from forming. He sensed that the direction of the friendship was not a mutually shared understanding.

She wanted to know why I really wasn't interested in her sexually, and I felt that at that point I really had no choice except to tell her. She was shocked but she asked a lot of questions and she really tried to understand. She didn't really know very much about the issue. She's still actually my very best friend.

Bisexual youths occasionally faced a formidable dilemma: whether to risk the relationship they had with a girlfriend by disclosing that attractions to boys were also present. In the following case, a bisexual youth was deeply in love with his girlfriend and thus felt the need to be honest with her.

I first disclosed my bisexuality to my girlfriend who I was in love with at the time. She was thirteen or fourteen years old and I was fourteen or fifteen. She dealt pretty good; she had already lived in Europe and for her it was no big deal. She grew up in a precocious background. It did become a central issue for us for awhile and we did get over that. For me it was hard because I was in love with her. There were expectations that I had and others had of me, marrying her.

Other bisexual adolescents discovered that they were dating or were friends with bisexual females. The truth came out for one couple with the help of alcohol, when the nature of their sexuality, long suspected by each about the other, was finally articulated.

> I first told the girl I was dating, who's been a best friend since tenth grade. We were drunk and she said she was bisexual. I told her that I too was bisexual. She thought it was funny and her reaction was, in fact, very positive. We laughed and laughed. It was hysterical. We dated for another year before each of us fell for this new guy in school. She got to him first, but I got to him last!

Disclosing to a girlfriend was seldom an easy task, especially if a youth felt a strong emotional attraction for his girlfriend. The hopes of both were often shattered under such circumstances and the strain on the relationship often proved ultimately detrimental. The following relationship did not survive the news.

> I loved her too much to lie. Her reaction was shock but, I thought, very positive. She had a friend come out to her as lesbian, so that helped. Draining, emotionally hard to say the words. I tiptoed around it. I did make a mistake in saying I felt good after coming out. She thought I meant I was glad we weren't a pair. We did not remain friends the next year.

One in three youths turned not to a female but to a male peer for the first disclosure. He was either a heterosexual friend or someone with whom the youth was having sex. In the former, the motivation to share was similar to that of disclosing to a female friend. For example, in the following narrative two best friends were having their own "love problems." Little did Bob, the heterosexual one, know that his best friend was having problems with "Chris"—a male.

> I had broken up with Chris, my second boyfriend. This is the middle of my senior year in high school. I was tired of Bob telling me all about his girlfriends and his troubles. I told him that I had broken up with someone, but it was not a girl. He was very cool. He really didn't seem to care one way or the other. But then I knew he would be okay with it. He just sort of intellectualized it.

In general, the reactions of male friends were positive, although not quite as supportive as female friends. At an Eastern boarding school one youth had the difficult task of deciding which of his friends to tell first. He feared most the reactions of his best friend—so he told one of his other friends.

> Well, it was a straight male in my hallway at the boarding school. I wanted to tell all three of my friends, and I knew he would be the accepting one. I told him first and his reaction was rather bland. Then I told the other two the next day, one of whom was my best friend but he was very homophobic and later on we weren't friends because he just couldn't be friends with a gay person.

Another prep-school youth decided the safest person to tell was not one of his peers but his floor's resident advisor. Although he knew that the advisor "had to be good about it," he later admitted to himself that he had a slight crush on him and had wondered if the man also had gay feelings. By disclosing to him he was hoping that the advisor would reciprocate, but he was disappointed.

> He was employed by the school and acted very professionally, cool, and he referred me to someone else to talk to. He never followed up or brought up the subject again. I think he avoided me. I wondered whether in fact he was gay himself.

In his desires, this youth was not singularly unique. Other gay/bisexual adolescents first disclosed to a male friend with the thought that he might not be "totally straight" or because they had developed a crush on him and were hoping that his friendship and kindness might indicate a similar sexuality. Although the gay youths were generally disappointed, most of the heterosexual male friends responded with kindness and support, but seldom with offers of sex or romance.

> Well a couple days after I accepted my gay feelings I told a friend, my best male friend at the time, that I had fantasies about other men. He was very accepting and he said he too had occasionally had fantasies, even though it was about 90 percent women and 10 percent men. I was very indirect initially but as we talked over the next couple of days I finally told him that I'm gay, and he said that was fine with him but he was straight.

> When I was sixteen I told my best friend Mike, also sixteen. He was very supportive and not particularly surprised. I think I dropped a lot of hints. I broke down and cried and cried and he was great. I know that I had a crush on him and was in love with him, and I think I wanted him to tell me that he was gay. I'm not absolutely 100 percent sure that he is straight, even though he has a girlfriend right now, but he certainly is a rare individual, being very open-minded.

As expected, given the diversity of life events experienced by the youths interviewed for this book, exceptions emerged. A best friendship turned into both a first disclosure and a first sexual relationship for the following youth. Although it did not last, no regrets were expressed.

> We came out to each other. It had been building so it was a big relief. Once I let it go I knew I'd never get it back. Was almost scared but a relief in the end. We had several sexual encounters but he seemed less than really interested. I thought this was very amusing but very suggestive. Later I didn't take him seriously, that he had gay feelings. Maybe he just wanted sex because he wasn't getting it from girls.

Another divergent scenario occurred when the first disclosure was to a male stranger. This person could become a friend, a sexual partner, or both. In the first example, a youth was surprised when his first disclosure was to a stranger who became a friend but never a sexual partner.

> I responded to his personal ad for sex (I was "young, blond, masculine, discreet, and fond of the outdoors") and so I guess he was the first person I told—when I was seventeen over the telephone. Turned out he was in my school! A senior. Even though he tried to be supportive, it was not something that I could accept at the time. But he persisted and finally I agreed, though not to have sex with him which was what he wanted. We just became friends.

The second example started out with sex and then became a mutually supportive friendship in which sexual relations merged with a high level of emotional support.

> I noticed this guy was following me on the street and we looked at each other. I knew what was going on. I tried losing him but then we sat down and talked. He asked me if I am gay and I said I didn't know but I was struggling with the issue. After sex with him I struggled no more! He was a stranger maybe twenty-two, but he would later become a friend—my lifeboat out of adolescence and darkness.

Very few youths who first disclosed during adolescence went much beyond their age group to share the nature of their sexuality. Even when the person was a family member it was more likely to be a sibling than a parent. Compared with youths who disclosed once they had moved away from home, youths who disclosed before high-school graduation were twice as likely to first disclose to a family member. The critical factor here may be one of proximity; the family member was present and offered a safe haven for the youth. One youth found his lesbian sister to be an ideal first person. "She was obviously very supportive but not particularly encouraging of the sexual part of my life with AIDS and all, but she certainly was of my identity as gay."

Another middle-school youth had "strange sexual desires and feelings" that he could not identify. Desperate to understand what was happening to him, he asked his fraternal twin brother if he had similar feelings. "He was very supportive, and I wanted to see if he felt the same way that I did. He didn't." Although he was disappointed that the two did not share this aspect of his life, he knew he had his brother's support and acceptance.

Only rarely, as characterizes the case below, was a parent the first person told. The circumstance provoking the disclosure was also extraordinary. After a high-school counselor feared that a youth under her charge would make a suicide attempt, she sent a letter to the family expressing her concerns and hinting that the problem was one of "sexually not fitting in." Pressured to disclose this aspect of his sexuality to his parents, the youth had very low expectations that they would be supportive; he was not surprised.

My mother was the first person. Father later the same evening. According to them, everyone had the same feelings. It was just a phase. It was about ninth grade when it happened. Felt under pressure, expressed that I thought I was gay. Parents actually had received directing memo from my counselor that I was suicidal and that's why they had pressured me, pressured me into committing, saying, or making a statement that I was gay. It was about three years ago to this day that I finally told my parents. I told them to accept this, to accept me. They never have like I'd want them to.

The following youth first confided in an extended family member—the only interviewed youth who did so. Although most youths reported having close relationships with at least one nonnuclear adult family member, these individuals were almost never considered to be the first person to whom to disclose. Perhaps youths feared that the information would not be kept secret or that the generational difference would be too great to surmount. For one seventeen-year-old, however, a favorite aunt was the one person he could tell.

I came out to my aunt, my mother's sister. I had always had a close relationship with her. I saw her more as a friend. I felt more comfortable to tell her than any other family member because she was so liberal and accepted everybody. She was the only family member who didn't live on a farm and who had black friends. She was very positive about the thing too. At the time I wasn't sure of my sexuality but sought her out to tell her.

In general, youths who first disclosed during their adolescent years felt most comfortable telling a same-age peer, usually a girl but not uncommonly a boy. The motivation was to receive support, to relieve the stress of keeping "it" inside, and, occasionally, to get gay sex. The girl was almost always a best friend, periodically a dating partner, and only rarely a sexual minority herself. Few adults in the lives of gay/bisexual youths were sufficiently trusted to be told this central aspect of the self. Even if a family member became the first outlet for the news, the person was usually a same-age sibling rather than a parent. One youth explained why he did not first disclose to his parents: "I did not want to hurt them, affect their jobs or status in the community where everybody knows everybody else."

Disclosure during Young Adulthood

Nearly 60 percent of the youths first disclosed their sexual orientation to another individual after they graduated from high school. Many took the opportunities afforded in a university setting to, as one youth stated it, "set the record unstraight." He had considered coming out while in high school but changed his mind once he discovered the extensive gay studies programs, support groups, and organizations at the university of his choice.

> I noticed that everyone there was gay! They had a gay coalition group and I could even major in it! Someone even told me I could live in a gay dorm! This was going to be my way out of my closet. There was a community. Why get killed in high school with the morons there? Cornell would be my salvation![8]

Despite the change in venues, females remained the primary objects of first disclosure. Now, however, they were nearly as likely to be women that the youths were dating as they were to be best friends. Because they were nearly always supportive, choosing these women was a wise decision. Few were shocked or greatly surprised by learning about their friend's homoeroticism. One youth found that he "couldn't say the words because I was unsure. She asked me about it rather than me telling her. I was so relieved." One woman guessed a year before the youth was ready to disclose to her.

> She was very happy for me, very supportive. I had always wanted to get involved with men, and I was, but I could never say that I was gay. She asked me actually a year ago, in a really joking tone, and I said "What!?!" and then I talked about other things very quickly.

The support was usually so comprehensive and inclusive that some women were upset that the youth had not sufficiently trusted their friendship to disclose sooner.

Similar to youths who disclosed before high-school graduation, a young adult sometimes decided to disclose to prevent a romantic relationship from forming with a woman he wanted as a friend, not a lover. The following youth feared that the relationship with his friend was becoming something other than a friendship in her mind. He was initially afraid of losing the friendship if he were to clarify his intents.

> She was a close friend, in fact, one of my best friends. We were spending a lot of time together and she was obviously very interested in me; and I told her that I had something important to tell her but, in fact, she guessed it even as I was telling her. Her reaction was quite fine. She was one of those bleeding-heart liberals. She was my best friend but philosophically, of course, she had to accept it. I told her primarily because I didn't want to have a romantic relationship with her and because I was feeling very stressed and needed to tell someone and she was the best person.

Even when a youth was romantically involved with a woman and decided to disclose to her, the reaction of the woman was nearly always positive, and remained so over the years. One couple still has plans to have a baby together.

It was a woman that I knew for about eight years. We were unconditional lovers. We tried sex once and it just didn't work, but one day she will bear my children. I told her because it felt like it was important to tell her for myself. After that everything was set, that is after I told her. She reacted by saying, "Now I understand." It really didn't change anything in our relationship.

For those who did not first disclose to a same-age female peer, the next most popular person was a male friend. Over one-third of the post-high-school disclosing youths first told someone they perceived to be a heterosexual male friend. When he was a gay individual he was not likely to be a sex partner but a friend. A heterosexual freshman roommate was the recipient of the following first disclosure. In turn, he gave supportive advice that he felt would make life easier for his gay roommate.

He didn't have a problem at all with it, but he was concerned with me because of ROTC and whether I'd lose my scholarship. He said not to tell my RA who is a radical gay person because he might tell everyone else. My concern was with not letting everyone know. I told him sort of at random because at the time I didn't have any real good friends on campus. If I had been home I would have told a couple of my very good female friends.

Telling a male friend could be a difficult task if that friend had previously expressed disgust with gay people or gay sex or made gay jokes. One college freshman first told a male friend who had previously assumed that there "weren't any fags around him" and that gay sex was "disgusting and vile." Although such an individual would appear to be a less than ideal first person to whom one would disclose, the gay youth took the chance and shared his secret. His rationale was two-fold: first, that their friendship would overcome the friend's ignorance and second, that his friend was a closeted gay. He based this on his friend's hyper concern with gay issues and his knowledge of his friend's previous same-sex experiences.

Even though I had been sleeping with men I didn't ever say to anyone else that I was gay. In all my talk I kept myself very gender neutral when I told others of sex. He was a very honest person and he never did say that he is gay but he is disgusted by gay sex. I know he's had homosexual experiences, but I felt I could be honest with him. I felt if he had a problem with it, who cares. Some part of me was afraid that he would tell others but another part was hoping that he would. He distanced me but still spoke to me. He did tell others, which was good.

Occasionally a gay/bisexual young adult had hopes, much like his peers who were open during adolescence, that disclosure to a particular individual might lead to gay sex or a relationship. Sometimes it worked.

I just felt that he was leading me on and so we never told the other one that we were gay. I had enough of this and I made my move. First time was at my apartment. Great sex! His response was great. Felt good. Looking back, I realize I was attracted to him, had a really intense crush on. We said the words to each other that night, "I'm gay."

This situation was, however, an unusual one. More commonly, disclosure was to a gay friend with whom no sexual relations, either actual or desired, were intended. More needed were support, advice, and friendship with someone who had been through it and had survived.

He lived down the hall and told his roommate that he was gay. The roommate freaked out and later I talked with this guy and told him I was gay. We gave each other support. Man to man support. He wasn't surprised I came out to him. I knew he wouldn't react badly, since obviously he was gay. After that we went to a support group, my first.

Another way to disclose to similarly oriented men is through a gay men's support group. Given the group's stated mission, a gay youth could be fairly confident of gaining support during his initial stages of coming out. Although such groups were available on most campuses where the interviewed youths lived, they were seldom the first choice of initial disclosure. The public aspect frightened them. Rather, support groups were the place to go after the initial disclosure had occurred. An exception was a youth who told no one until his time came to "share something personal about your last week. A whole room of people, twelve of us, men only. I was very young and they were surprised and very happy for me."

For some youths a more confidential and supportive source for the first disclosure was a psychotherapist. Although many older individuals have horror stories about the reactions of psychiatrists and psychotherapists,[9] most of the interviewed youths reported very positive experiences with a therapist.

He had reason to believe I was unsure about whether or not I was gay because I kept telling him that I was interested in females. He wanted me to be sure. He told me that it would be easier to be straight, but he was definitely okay about it. I started telling other people.

Less likely to be supportive were "persons of the cloth." Reactions of ministers, rabbis, priests, and chaplains were mixed. One of the worst was the following. After thoughts of suicide, a gay youth disclosed to his youth minister what was bothering him. The "religious advice" he received led to a serious suicide attempt. "He said that I really wasn't gay, that God wouldn't accept it, that hell was populated by people like me—that's what he felt at least."

By contrast was a youth who disclosed to a campus chaplain. "I trusted her. She was very accepting. I broke down and cried the very first time I told her." It probably helped that this chaplain was a *lesbian*.

Relatively few youths who disclosed after they left home as young adults first shared their secret with a family member. However, those who did usually disclosed to a parent and not a sibling. The initiation appeared to come as much from the parent as from the youths. One mother called a month after her son went to college several hundred miles away and asked him "the question." He initially told her, "No." The following day he called her back and told her, "'Yes.' For me it was a big relief."

Another mother made the association between her son having a gay friend and the possibility that her son might be gay himself. She asked "the question" and although the answer she received was not the one she wanted, it was the one she expected.

> Last summer I had a job at home and the assistant manager for where I worked and I became very good friends. We talked about gay issues and both of us were very positive, but we never said to the other one that we might be gay ourselves.
>
> On the last day my mother picked me up and she watched the two of us as we said good-bye. We gave each other a long hug. He was very effeminate and she transferred the fact that he might be gay to me. It was sort of a test pattern when she asked, "Are you gay?" She didn't really expect me to say "yes," but I had decided beforehand that I was not going to lie. She felt confused and lost and didn't know what to say, but she was very supportive and she listened to me. She said that she loved me. It wasn't so much the idea that I was gay that bothered her, but that she feared for what my life would be like.

After a romantic relationship with another man developed, one youth realized that he could not keep this vital aspect of himself secret from his parents. He wanted their blessing on this, his first relationship.

> I told them together. I had been visiting them every two weeks, and I came to a point where in my relationship with Tim that I felt terrible about lying, so I just felt like I had to tell them. I broke down in tears and I felt like I was confessing. I wish I had been stronger. They responded by loving me no matter what because I was their son. They were silent about it after that. They really just didn't want to deal with it.

In summary, most youths who first disclosed to another person their sexual orientation did so after high school, usually after leaving their hometown community. The first recipient was usually a female friend or a woman they were dating. They were more likely than adolescents to disclose to a male friend, usually a heterosexual man they felt would be positive, or a gay friend they met at college. Family members were rarely the first to know, although when it occurred the mother was usually the one to be told—or the one to guess the secret.

Reflections on First Disclosures

The decision to disclose to one other person the nature of their sexuality, usually within a year or two after self-recognition, was felt by most youths to be a monumental event. Many recalled exact dates, times, places, reactions, and feelings. Most (60 percent) did not tell anyone about their same-sex attractions until they had left their families and hometown communities because they were fearful of the consequences. The motivation to tell someone else was usually internally generated, reflecting a need to disclose this aspect of their identity. Telling others, even best friends, about their sexual identity was a frequently postponed and much debated process for the youths. As a result, they first disclosed to the safest, most supportive individual they knew, thus gaining strength and assurance that their world would not collapse if they were to be gay.

Adolescence was not perceived by a majority of these youths to be the ideal time to declare their gay or bisexual identity. For some, they simply had not reached a point in their developmental timeline where they could have disclosed to anyone because they had not yet disclosed to themselves. Whether the major impetus to disclose was being away from home, friends, and families or the allure of leading a gay life in college, which was felt to be a much safer and accepting environment, is unclear. Many youths declared that the major deterrent to disclosure during their high-school years centered on their fear of peer and family rejection and ostracism. Yet, 40 percent of the youths initially disclosed selectively, usually to friends and only rarely to family members and adults, during their junior or senior high-school years. Their intent was not to be known as gay or bisexual to their family or community but to be open and honest with their closest friend or friends. Although the responses they received varied, the vast majority experienced support, acceptance, and encouragement.

College presented many of the youths with an opportunity to "try out a new identity." Many took advantage of their new life and disclosed to their new friends during their freshman or sophomore year. Some were female friends; others were girlfriends. Now, however, gay, lesbian, and bisexual friends more fully entered the picture, providing models and levels of support seldom before experienced. Despite this inviting environment, some youths did not disclose to anyone until after they graduated from college and entered graduate school or began their work careers.

Several youths, although not prepared to initiate a discussion of their new sexual consciousness with anyone, were willing to let others guess or bring up the topic. This passive manner of disclosure was strongly preferred by those who were most frightened by the consequences of disclosing their homoeroticism. One youth, unable to tell his mother directly, was willing to confirm her suspicions once she raised the possibility. He was surprised when she was supportive, promising to love him "no matter what." Others "indirectly" told their sex partners without saying the words; in their minds they had not yet disclosed to anyone because, as one youth reported, "All sorts of straight guys have gay sex when they want to." Another confirmed his female friend's suspicions when he was in the eighth grade, but later tried to retreat into the closet once he discovered how difficult it was to be gay in his junior-high school. He questioned whether the verbal harassment and loss of friends were worth the liberation and authenticity that he now felt.

Youths who had difficulty sharing this aspect of themselves sometimes maintained a dating relationship with a girl through their high-school years, primarily as a cover for their secret. They felt particularly vulnerable, perhaps because they had internalized the negative stigma of homophobia, had religious parents, lived in a small-town community, or feared peer rejection. One youth never told anyone because his family was very prominent in the community. "It would be selfish of me to be gay when so much depended on me being a good family member. Why embarrass them?" Only later, in college, was he able to come to self-disclosure without the fear of humiliating those he loved.

The reason that female friends and dating partners reacted so positively to the news is largely unknown. However, various possibilities are suggested in the narratives. Several youths reported that the girl/woman they told had previous exposure to gay people or had lived in a home or community environment that was supportive of alternative lifestyles. Occasionally, she had experienced similar feelings or did not consider it so surprising that a male could be sexually attracted to another male. Given the greater fluidity in female sexuality,[10] women may be in a better position to understand how their best male friend might be attracted to girls, boys, or both and that these attractions could change over time.

Male friends were less frequently the first person to whom a youth first disclosed. Contrary to cultural stereotypes, many of the heterosexual males who were the first recipient of the news that their good friend, roommate, or teammate was gay/bisexual responded with support and acceptance. The youth was sometimes motivated to risk this disclosure as an act of friendship or because he had developed a crush or infatuation with his friend and desired to test the future of their potential sexual or romantic relationship. There was always the hoped for possibility that the other male was gay or bisexual himself, and the motivation to disclose to him was to set up a sexual encounter. More commonly, however, the goal was to secure support and understanding that would help the gay youth through this difficult period in life.

Given that any developmental generalization is difficult to maintain without noting the various trajectories, some youths reported only fleeting or nonexistent moments of disclosure. Others felt that they did not have a choice of whether to "come out" to others—they were pushed, even shoved out by others. For example, friends may have assumed that a youth was gay if he was gender atypical in behavior. His associations (e.g., "faggy friends") and interests (e.g., drama club) could also be used as evidence. Even if he were to tell no one, others often suspected. One youth reported that peers, including one guy with whom he had sex, called him "queer"; this enraged him because he feared his cover would be blown. Then, after his older sister and mother began calling him "gay" and "faggot," he vowed never to disclose to anyone—a promise that was quickly broken once he left home and entered cosmetology school.

In most cases the interviewed youths were relieved to finally disclose their sexual orientation. It was an aspiration many feared yet were afraid would never happen. One youth reflected this paradox when he reported, "I could never have imagined telling anyone a year ago and then I wanted to tell just one other person, to say it out loud, but not too loudly, but now I want to shout it to everyone, even if they don't want to know!" Whether this disclosure led to finding one's true love or to feeling good about one's sexual identity is disclosed in Chapters Eight and Nine.

8.

First Gay Romance

S ex with other males under any circumstance may come to be associated exclusively with anonymous, guilt-ridden encounters, handicapping one's ability to develop healthy, intimate relationships that blend sexual and emotional components. Yet, two adolescents of the same sex with erotic, sexual attractions for each other may long to share not only sexual intimacy but also an emotional bond that includes tenderness and a commitment to each other's future. By developing such a relationship, adolescents learn how to relate to another and to experiment in associating intimacy needs with sexuality. These romantic relationships help youths further clarify who they are and what they desire.

The intimacy needs of gay/bisexual youths are common, even normative. It is natural to become involved in an intimate relationship that connects one, according to writer Maggie Scarf, with "archaic, dimly perceived and yet powerfully meaningful aspects of our inner selves" (p. 79).[1] It is likely that humans are prewired for establishing loving and strongly experienced emotional attachments. If so, adolescents, regardless of sexual orientation, should pine for an emotional closeness within the context of a trusting, intimate relationship. In this relationship adolescents can feel safe, secure, and nurtured.[2]

Mental health-care professionals have written about these needs and their potential benefits. For example, psychoanalyst Richard Isay argues that falling in love is often a critical factor in helping his gay clients feel comfortable being gay. Clinician Christine Browning regards love relationships as opportunities for adolescents to validate a new identity, to give and receive love, and to provide emotional support at a developmentally significant moment in life.[3] According to psychotherapist Charles Silverstein, when gay youths establish a romantic relationship with a same-sex partner they feel "chosen," which helps to resolve issues of sexual identity and to create a feeling of completeness. Indeed, those who are in a long-term love relationship generally have high levels of self-esteem and self-acceptance.[4]

Despite the inherent value of romantic relationships, many adolescents despair of being given the opportunity to establish anything other than clandestine sexual intimacies with another male. This is graphically illustrated in the writings of clinician Alan Malyon, who recounts difficulties gay adolescents face in their homes, schools, and communities.

> For example, their most charged sexual desires are usually seen as perverted, and their deepest feelings of psychological attachment are regarded as unacceptable. This social disapproval interferes with the preintimacy involvement that fosters the evolution of maturity and self-respect in the domain of object relations. (p. 326)[5]

Falling in love with someone of the same sex and sustaining an emotional investment with that person suggest to many Americans an irreversible deviancy. So, too, youths may come to believe that a gay relationship is an oxymoron.

Given these dire obstacles, it is hardly surprising that a gay/bisexual adolescent may be, according to some writers, the loneliest person in his high school. Educator James Sears notes the explicit message that is given to all junior and senior high-school students that contributes to this loneliness.

> For the homosexual-identified student, high school is often a lonely place where, from every vantage point, there are couples: couples holding hands as they enter school; couples dissolving into an endless wet kiss between school bells; couples exchanging rings with ephemeral vows of devotion and love. (pp. 326–327)[6]

Indeed, some gay youths may believe that they will never have the opportunity to experience adolescent love.

A youth may fantasize about being intimate with a same-sex partner but have little hope that it could in fact become a reality. In a collection of coming-out stories, one youth reported this feeling.

> While growing up, love was something I watched other people experience and enjoy. . . . The countless men I secretly loved and fantasized about were only in private, empty dreams in which love was never returned. I seemed to be the only person in the world with no need for love and companionship. . . . Throughout high school and college I had no way to meet people of the same sex and sexual orientation. These were more years of isolation and secrecy. I saw what other guys my age did, listened to what they said and how they felt. I was expected to be part of a world with which I had nothing in common. (pp. 109–110)[7]

It is never easy for youths of any sexual persuasion to directly confront the mores of peers whose values and attitudes are routinely supported by the dominant culture. Nearly all youths know implicitly the rules of socially appropriate behavior and the consequences of nonconformity. This single, most influential barrier to same-sex romance, the threat posed by peers, can have severe repercussions. The penalty for crossing the line of "normalcy" can result in emotional and physical pain. Little social advantage, such as peer popularity or acceptance, is to be gained by holding hands and kissing a same-sex peer in school hallways, shopping malls, or other public places. The result is that some gay youths feel inherently "fake" and thus retreat altogether from intimacy with others. Although they may meet the implicit and explicit demands of their culture to appear heterosexual, it is at a cost—their sense of authenticity.

The difficulties inherent in developing same-sex romance during adolescence are monumental. First is the fundamental complication of finding a suitable partner. The vast majority of bisexual and gay youths are closeted, not out to themselves, let alone to others. A second barrier is the familial and peer prohibition of same-sex dating. A third impediment is the lack of public recognition or celebration of those who are romantically involved with a member of the same sex. Thus, same-sex romances remain hidden and mysterious, and are either ridiculed, condemned, or ignored.

Faced with this poverty of intimacy, the alternative for some youths is to explore their erotic sexuality, not within the context of an intimate relationship, but within the confines of clandestine sexual encounters, void of affection and romance but replete with anonymity and guilt. A youth may have genital contact with another boy without ever kissing him because to do so would be too meaningful. Thus, getting to the proverbial first base may be more problematic than "hitting a home run."

Despite the handicaps and prohibitions, youths who establish same-sex love relationships during adolescence and young adulthood appear to prosper from them. A report on gay youth suicide notes the potential redeeming quality of these relationships.

> The first romantic involvements of lesbian and gay male youth are a source of great joy to them in affirming their sexual identity, providing them with support, and assuring them that they too can experience love. (p. 3–130)[8]

From a research perspective, until the last several years same-sex romantic relationships of youths were seldom recognized. Eric Dubé, who works with the Cornell research team on sexual-minority youths, reviewed the literature on same-sex romantic relationships, conducted his own study of intimacy development among 166 gay and bisexual men, and reported that 87 percent of the youngest cohort, recruited primarily from community centers, youth groups, and collegiate organizations, have had a romantic relationship with a man. Slightly over 40 percent were in a relationship; at the time of the interview these romances had lasted nearly ten months. The average age of beginning a gay relationship for this adolescent/young adult sample was 18.2 years, nearly identical to the current study and more than three years after beginning a heterosexual relationship.

Although only a few published studies of same-sex oriented teens focus primarily on their romantic relationships, suggestive data such as the above debunk the myth that youths neither want nor maintain steady, loving same-sex relationships. Tony D'Augelli at Penn State University reports that one-half of his sample of gay/bisexual youths were "partnered" and that their most troubling mental-health concern was termination of a close relationship, ranking just ahead of telling parents about their homosexuality.[9] In addition, two-thirds of gay/bisexual youths in another study reported that they had experienced a romantic relationship; nearly 60 percent of these relationships were with other boys or men. Youths who had a large percentage of romantic relationships with boys rather than girls had high self-esteem and were more likely to be publicly "out" to friends and family. Individuals who initiated same-sex romances during adolescence were likely to report that they have had long-term and multiple relationships.[10]

A spirited narrative of how one youth developed a same-sex romance is depicted in the seminal autobiography of Aaron Fricke, *Reflections of a Rock Lobster*.[11] Once Aaron fell in love with a classmate, Paul, he discovered no guidelines existed on how best to express his feelings.

> Heterosexuals learn early in life what behavior is expected of them. They get practice in their early teens having crushes, talking to their friends about their feelings, going on first dates and to chaperoned parties, and figuring out their feelings. Paul and I hadn't gotten all that practice; our relationship was formed without much of a model to base it on. It was the first time either of us had been in love like this and we spent much of our time just figuring out what that meant for us. (p. 46)

However, with Paul's help Aaron challenged the prejudice he had encountered during his childhood and adolescence, giving him the courage to realize that it was possible to love another man without apprehension or loss of self-respect. Life gained significance. Aaron learned to express both kindness and strength.

Eventually, after a court case that received national attention, Aaron won the right to take Paul to his senior prom as a date. The satisfaction gained from this judicial victory was relatively minor compared to the self-acceptance and pride in being gay that their relationship won for each of them. Their example may well have eased the transition to a same-sex romantic relationship that the vast majority of youths in the current sample have experienced. Given the current climate for gay/bisexual youths, perhaps more important than documenting the existence of romantic relationships or the barriers they face in establishing them is to advance the discussion to a more complex and detailed level—how the partners met, who they were, when the relationships were begun, how they were terminated, and what significance they had for the youths' future.[12]

Characteristics of First Gay Romances

Seven in ten of the youths reported that they have experienced a romantic relationship with another male. Although the average age of first same-sex romance was shortly after the eighteenth birthday, a significant number of youths had their first relationship during junior (5 percent) and senior (30 percent) high school. More common, however, was the experience of the following youth, who became involved in a same-sex romantic relationship during his freshman year of college.

> It started in the residence halls two weeks after I arrived. I met the man when he moved into the room I was supposed to have. We became lovers through this contact. After two months I realized that it wasn't the thing I wanted.
>
> I was very excited about the relationship; it felt good and I talked much about it with other people. It was very confirming for me, and I find this fortunate considering others I've encountered. Their first relationship isn't as good. It's been fulfilling sexually and emotionally for me.

The youngest age at which a relationship began was when a youth was twelve years old; the oldest, twenty-five. Both were affairs of six to nine months, began slowly, and were evaluated by the youth as a good relationship with no contact since termination.

> Twelve years of age and lasted nine months. He was twenty-two years old, a science teacher in my school. It developed over time and was great. We became friends and I invited him over once when my parents weren't home. I practically had to force sex on him because he was afraid about losing his job. Ended when I went away for the summer and he wasn't a teacher at my school no more.

> Well I was twenty-five and he was twenty-seven. He responded to a personal ad in the newsletter and we began to exchange letters. We met and I said to myself, "Is this really happening?" I made a commitment to be honest with myself, but I was very scared because I knew nothing at all about him. Yet, it was very exciting. I was not immediately attracted to him, but it sort of evolved, my attractions. We didn't have sex the first time, which was sort of a relief for me. There's just lots of games going on. Over time we both decided that this really wouldn't work out. Neither of us was out to our family and friends and both of us were really afraid. It lasted for about six months and we mutually decided to end it. There has been no contact afterwards.

The first romantic partner was seldom younger than the interviewed youth and only slightly more likely to be the same age. Nearly 70 percent of the youths reported that their first relationship was with a boy or man who was older than them. Most often he was within two years of the youth's age; however, 20 percent were seven or more years older. At the outer extreme, 10 percent were over ten years older than the youth. The largest age-discrepant romantic relationship was a thirty-year difference between the partners.

> I answered a personal ad. He wanted youth and I wanted age! I'm "slender, fun-loving, and cute"; he was "bearded, masculine, and worked out." He was forty-six and I was sixteen at the time. We were together for ten months until I finally came to Penn State. I never lived with him. I'd go there to Pittsburgh maybe once a week or once every two weeks. He was very conservative and didn't want to take me out publicly. He hates outward displays of affection and he didn't want people to think he was my father. He sends me holiday and birthday cards. I think of him as my uncle. It was good for the time.

Nearly two-thirds of the youths perceived that their partner initiated the relationship. Most wanted the romance but were hesitant, perhaps because of their younger age, to make the first move. The following youth responded to an invitation proposed by a customer.

> I met him at a party and he really came on to me. I was working at bartending at the time. It was not really a gay party but there were certainly other gays present. He kept buying drinks and hanging around me making conversation. Before leaving he put his name card in my pocket—in case I "ever needed anything"—and so I called and so we had a first date.

Less than 20 percent of the youths reported that the initiative was taken by them to begin the relationship. In the vast majority of these pairings the two youths were the same age or the interviewed youth was older. In the following example a youth overcame his usual shyness when lust established its priority.

> I met him at a gay function, a reception. I'm very shy at socials, and I walked in and I lusted at first sight and invited him to dinner. He came over and we were friends during the three months with no sex. We went to a dance and then we had sex. This was when we started dating. This is over two years and it lasted until I came to Cornell. I tried to get back with him over the summer but it just didn't work. We're still close friends; it was his decision to break it off when I went away.

The most likely place to meet one's future romantic partner was a gay bar, but this represented only 20 percent of the first relationships. Listed below in order are the ten most frequently reported places for meeting one's first same-sex romantic partner.

• *Gay bar*

We met at the bar and it was love at first sight. I just fell head over heels, but maybe I moved too quickly. It lasted four months. He worked in a factory and he'd had no college experience. I really don't have much respect for his kind. It was sort of sex the first night but not to orgasm but certainly by the next weekend. He was the first man that I had intercourse with both ways.

• *Gay organization*

Someone that I had met at a gay meeting. I decided that my big "out" move was to go to the meeting. We were friends for about a week and then we became lovers. It was really great; he was really like my mentor. At first, we just sort of played around and made out before we did a lot of the other kinds of things.

• *A neighbor, friend, or acquaintance*

I told myself that this was the first time I'm in love. I wanted really to date someone and have a good relationship. Max was an acquaintance, a friend of a friend, and we talked one night and I decided to know more. I told him that I thought I was falling in love, and he said he was too. We went together for nine months.

• *School or work*

It occurred during the summer when I met this man who worked at the same place, a restaurant, that I did. I had the nerve to ask him out for dinner (we were both waiters), and he accepted. It wasn't easy for me but I made the move.

• *Introduction by a friend*

Well I was nineteen, a freshman, and he twenty-one and it went on for three months. I went to Hartford to visit an old female friend and he was her boyfriend. She introduced us and I stayed with them. When she was gone one day he began making the moves on me. He was a hockey player at the university there. I was sort of infatuated with it; it was very, very exciting.

• *Party (most common, fraternity)*

Well, I would go to fraternity parties and it always seemed like there were guys there that were trying to pick me up. Well, at one point then I was in a relationship that lasted for over two years with Peter. We were friends for a couple of weeks before I began to pursue him.

• *Personal ad or computer party line*

I was really tired of being straight. Then I joined a party line that was gay and I met this guy through it. We talked, agreed to meet for lunch, and a week later we slept together, which he initiated. This went on for a month and a half.

• *Public restroom*

We met through the Uris bathroom. At first we did nothing there, at least. We were both very closeted. We arranged a first meeting for very quick sex and there was no problem because we didn't have to say that we were homosexual. Then we found out we liked each other and we began to see each other on occasion.

• *Public place (most common, mall)*

He was working in this mall store and I was shopping. We made eye contact, and it felt like I was sort of teasing him and he was me with this kind of eye contact. He was very cute and I was really trying to make some kind of connection. Well, we went up to each other and he gave me his phone number and said that he would call me and he did. I didn't know really who he was or even if he was gay. I just knew that I was attracted to him. He asked me out in the sense that we would get together as "friends." It was a week or two before we actually had our first sex. This whole relationship lasted four months.

• *Peer counseling and support groups*

I met him at a gay peer counseling session three weeks earlier. I was upset one time and he comforted me, and this was when we had sex for the first time. We dated for a couple of months.

After meeting and initiating a relationship that would become romantic, the most common trajectory was to have sex that day or the next date—certainly within a month of meeting each other. This pattern characterized about 70 percent of the youths, including the following.

I met him at Charlies and he asked me to dance. We didn't have sex the first night because both of us were with friends and we felt that it would feel as if we were just using each other as a piece of meat. Two days later we had sex, but I did not sleep with him for another week.

Less characteristic, true for 15 percent of the youths, was to begin a relationship after being friends for a year or longer. The transition from a friendship to a romantic relationship was initiated by sex.

I'd had a series of one-night stands and I felt that I was getting burnt and I wanted more than that—I wanted a relationship! I was getting fed up with the gay scene. It was a wedding party of a friend of mine and so everyone was dressed real nicely. I talked to one guy for a long time and even though he was very seductive I resisted. We talked about politics, fashion, movies, and good government. But I wasn't attracted to him physically, but he was very nice and smart. He drove me home and he came inside; we talked and then he left.

Everyone thought we were a pair, but we weren't. We each dated others, but finally it was so obvious that we should try after a year to make it happen. We had been very affectionate, hugging, etc. but never sexual. The physical didn't matter I said to myself. I said we ought to try it and he agreed. It was great sex, but only for a short time. Then it went away, but we stayed loyal to each other.

I was pissed though at the end of the summer when he was accepted on a scholarship and moved to Italy. With this event in my life I began to understand myself as a gay person. I haven't seen the man since then and it's been painful, but I feel the event was better for my ego than anything else. Being gay is more than one-night stands.

About 20 percent of the sample began their first relationship one to four months after first meeting their future boyfriend. The following youth defined the transition from a dating to a romantic relationship as the time when they first shared sex.

It was four months after we started dating that we had our first sex. It was my first love, so I wanted to be sure. It occurred after dinner and music and dancing and we went back home to his place and we then had sex beautiful sex. Very romantic, and I'll never forget it. Gentle, affectionate, an all-night affair. We had sexual contact several times over the summer before we broke up.

Nearly all first romantic relationships lasted less than one year. By three months one-half of all relationships had ended; by six months 75 percent had dissolved. Fifteen percent endured at least one year with several lasting three to four years.

The extreme short and long relationships were one week and four years. The one-week affair was thwarted by the graduation of the youth. "It was actually on our second date, but the same week, that we had our first sex; but we both realized there was very little time because I was graduating, so this first relationship only lasted a week." The longest relationship, despite the efforts of both partners, could not survive.

I went to a gay group on campus and I met him there. I realized I needed to do something about not having a relationship, so I invited him over and we started dating. We went through a very turbulent period at first of questioning. He stayed around during my last two years at Cornell, working on research projects, so as to be near me. We went off to grad school together, where we both questioned whether we wanted to be in a relationship. So as a result the relationship was rather up and down. Finally, we ended it.

Termination of the relationship was rarely difficult to ascertain. Regardless of who initiated the relationship, the interviewed youth was most likely to abort the relationship. The partner terminated the relationship 30 percent of the time; less often the conclusion of the romance came by mutual consent (20 percent), as was true for the following pair.

> I really wanted a permanent partner, a deeply committed relationship that was good. This relationship was good, but it turned eventually into nothing more than a friendship after a month and a half. He didn't want a commitment and I didn't want just sex. So we just stopped it. He was just trying to please me and me him and when we found this out we laughed and went on to other people. We're still friends actually.

The ending of a relationship was seldom this easy. Indeed, in one-quarter of the relationships it was extremely difficult. The worst breakup was the following:

> I broke it off. He really didn't handle it very well. He was very bitter and accused me of being with others. Said horrible things about me and my utensils to others—like I had a micropenis surrounded by two peanuts. Told everyone I had AIDS, crabs, lice, herpes, and was not to be trusted. I tried talking with him, thought of suing him for defamation of character, thought of killing him for awhile. It just didn't work out.

Perhaps similar to many other types of relationships, the ending of a romantic relationship was not always obvious. Several of the relationships just faded, with no clear demarcation of a transition to another state or an understanding that it was over.

> Kevin came over after we had been friends for maybe two weeks and began to give me a massage. Then that led into kissing and then sex, very intense actually. I could tell that he wanted sex and I wanted more of a committed relationship. This was our point of disagreement. We had a big argument and we mutually decided that the other ought to end it. We were both eighteen at the time, so I guess it lasted a total of three months, but it hasn't so clearly ended. We became friends afterwards and we've had sex a couple of times. Since that point we got back together again but it's clear that he doesn't want what I want. I don't know if we can ever work it out. We have sex once a week and we've dated others, but not seriously.

Reasons given by the youths for termination of their first relationship were quite diverse, although the top two causes accounted for almost half of the breakups. A physical separation in which one of the two partners moved was the most common. One might leave for college or graduate school or change jobs. Also common were reports that the two youths simply "grew apart" or "discovered our dissimilarities." Listed below in order are the ten most commonly given reasons for ending the first romantic relationship.

- *Physical separation*

The relationship I was in was very attentive sexually; it was very good. It lasted for eighteen months. I ended up moving to Florida for school and therefore the relationship trailed off as we grew apart. It was a safe feeling; this was mostly how the relationship was defined, very affectionate. I didn't want to be promiscuous. But I had to move.

- *Grew apart, too dissimilar*

It ended because he was constantly on the go, partying, going to bars, and so forth. At first we spent all of our time together in my apartment, but then more and more we began going out. I'm very work-oriented and it began to affect my work. We tried to work it out but neither of us really was willing to change. We had nothing to say to each other.

- *He was frightened because it meant he was gay*

He was very closeted and really didn't want to be discovered. He wanted to spend time with others and not me necessarily, especially in public because I'm too queer-like. Being around him made me feel dirty and not good. I wanted to be out and proud, and he didn't. We couldn't hold hands in public and I couldn't even tell others we were going out. He was very superficial.

- *He/I had major problem that disrupted the relationship*

The whole relationship lasted four months. I pretty much ended it because I knew that it was not a relationship that was meant to be. I was very immature, just coming out, and I was not sure of what I wanted in a relationship. It just didn't work out as a relationship.

- *I needed room to grow*

I met him in the summer and he had a girlfriend. He began flirting with me with an eye-contact game, and then he did approach me. We had sex for the first time the week after we met. Soon we began dating. He practically moved into my apartment for two months. He's a townie, annoying and not very bright. I just needed to grow, intellectually, emotionally, spiritually, and I couldn't with him.

- *Sex/attractions faded*

It was the best sex I ever had. He was hot, but as happens to all good sex, it began to fade and wear off after a couple of weeks. It was just sort of a sexual outlet and I needed it less and less. We had sex maybe three days per week, but I don't know that we were in love.

- *He/I grew too dependent*

My first sexual experience, and was agreed that we'd have anal and oral sex and then get to know each other later. I grew to be dependent on him. It ruined my life, especially my social life because I was with him. I ended it because I could not handle it. Took courage from me. Felt bad that I had become so dependent on him, upset. Also that he became attached to me and I to him. Others saw me hanging onto him. When I thought it would work out I thought I was in love, but I wasn't happy.

• *I was frightened because it meant I was gay*
He wrote me letters and said that he loved me, but I never took his phone calls or his letters. I still thought of myself as heterosexual at this time. I just thought of our romance as sort of being a foreign thing, you know, while I was away from home. I don't know how I moved from a friendship in this to a love. I do know, though, that it ended when he said that he loved me because I knew what this means and I wasn't that.

• *He wanted sex, I wanted a relationship*
I wanted that it be more than sex but neither of us at the time identified ourselves as gay. It frightened me every time we did have sex because I wanted more, and it eventually made him leave. He would never sleep over and he would immediately go shower after sex. I felt that it was all dirty to have sex and not be comfortable with the person.

• *He found someone else*
I went away for the summer and in the fall he didn't return my calls and I got very depressed over it. A friend told me he met someone else and so it ended. We've not talked since.

When asked to evaluate the relationship, the most common response was that it helped a youth identify as gay or to feel better about being gay. This aspect was sufficiently positive for some youths to overcome the immediate sorrow and distress that often accompanied the end of a loving relationship.

We met at the Pub, then at his place afterwards, and he asked me to stay that night. At the end of the relationship eight weeks later I got a sense that what was actually happening was my partner felt that I was becoming too possessive. I couldn't believe he was dumping me; I cried for a week. For me, in terms of how this event happened, it was really important for me to link sex with actually what was going on and have me come to understand my own sexual identity. Up to then I had defined myself strictly as a gay man, but it wasn't until this relationship happened that I understood myself as a gay person.

A nearly equal number of youths reported that a relationship was primarily an expression of being in love or infatuated with someone. As such, it had to be good, even if the ending was bad. The following youth wanted to be with his partner, nearly twice his age, for the rest of his life. This aspiring passion, however, was not mutually shared.

> I began talking by computer with this guy who is a post-doc in comparative literature at Cornell. He seemed very kind and he talked and was very considerate to me. We met in a park and it sort of evolved into a romantic relationship. I wanted to live with him and be with him forever. He knew me so well, like no one else has ever known me. It ended because he had to leave Cornell after only being together four months. He just wanted to be my friend and to help me. It was a very intense relationship.

Many youths reported that their relationship was a fantastic experience, one that they will never forget. Through the dynamics of being with someone sexually and romantically, they learned about themselves and how to be in a relationship. Stereotypes were refuted and new dimensions of self were explored.

> I learned so much about myself. At that time, the only gayness I knew was the movies. I had these images and they were everything, everything negative or distorted. I had feelings that relationships would be only sex, but it was an emotional commitment, showed what a relationship could be. I just knew that it was hard growing up with no one around me to talk to about the feelings that I had.

Only 15 percent of the youths reported that the first relationship was a negative experience. This is not to assert that 85 percent were solely positive—only that the positive outweighed the negative. Some relationships, however, left strewn bodies and feelings on the landscape.

> We worked together as lifeguards. On break one afternoon he took my heart and my virginity. It lasted about four months. He dumped me and tore out my heart. At the time he was having conflicts. He was denying his own sexuality and blaming me for everything wrong in his life. It took me four years though to get over it. I am not willing to get into another relationship; I never want to be hurt like that again.

By contrast to this horrid conclusion of a failed romance, about one-quarter of the youths reported that they became friends with their ex-partner shortly after the breakup. When one interviewed youth met the man of his dreams, his then current boyfriend agreed that this man was better for the youth than he was. The "sacrifice" has resulted in a lifelong friendship.

> It lasted perhaps two months and then I met my current boyfriend, Dave, and he just literally swept me off my feet. Steve [first boyfriend] agreed that I should really go out with him because he would be much better for me. Steve and I are still best friends and I have a lot of contact with him. He's still very important in my life and always will be.

An additional 10 percent of the youths reported that they transformed their friendship with their former boyfriend into a "fuck buddy" relationship characterized by occasional sex. Several of these youths have current lovers but do not consider it cheating when they have sex with their ex because of the special relationship they once shared.

> We're now fuck buddies and we see each other a couple of times a year. We have sexual contact whenever we get together, which really feels wonderful. It was great sex with him then, which wasn't why we broke up—we couldn't stand each other— and it is even better now that it doesn't mean anything. Feels like forbidden sex, so we don't tell our current flames. I would never want to renew the relationship.

The most usual resolution to future contact, however, is to have none. Nearly 60 percent of the youths reported that they currently have little or no contact with their first same-sex romantic partner. He exists in their memories, but not in their daily lives.

First Relationship during Adolescence

Just over one-third of the youths began their first relationship with another boy or man before graduating from high school. In most respects they shared many of the characteristics of first relationships that were begun after leaving home for college, graduate school, or work. The variations, however, are noteworthy and are discussed in this section.

Compared to all other romances, relationships launched during adolescence were slightly more likely to be with an individual ten or more years older than the youth—20 percent of all such adolescent relationships—and to have been initiated by the older partner.

> I was fifteen and he twenty-seven, the mailman, honest to God! On and off for two years. The first time was when I came to the door to get a special delivery package in my sheer designer underwear, from American Male. I was changing to go back to school. He sprouted a boner, I got hard, he grabbed mine, I grabbed his, and we were off and running. Every day I'd come home for lunch; my mother worked. It had to be quick so he'd not get docked for late deliveries. He had a real thing for redheads like me. He was very forward, connected with me, and told me how hot I was. Talked about our backgrounds. It ended when he suddenly got transferred and contact became difficult. We visited each other and had sex, but it was hard and we agreed mutually because of the distance that it was better that we be friends and not lovers.

Adolescents met their first partners in places quite different from those of older youths. Rather than someone encountered in gay bars and organizations, which were inaccessible for most minors, the first romantic partner was likely to have been a neighbor, friend, or someone met during daily life.

> My neighbor. I was thirteen and he was couple of years older. The sex occurred off and on, but it was infrequent because his mom wouldn't let him out much to visit me. I know she suspected. Lasted for fourteen months. I entered a new school and found different friends. He was too dependent and a real nerd. I found other boys to have sex with in my new school, and so I dropped him.

Other frequent places to connect with a first romantic partner were high school classes, part-time jobs, and introductions by friends. The following youth met his first love at his high-school prom. They were introduced by his date, his partner-to-be's lesbian friend.

> I went to the prom with a female friend, Mary. We went with some of her female friends and their dates, one of whom was Rob who was dating one of the girls. So we went to the prom and various clubs and nothing happened that night. I knew that my friend Sue was a lesbian, but I didn't know that her date, Rob, was gay. I asked her about him and she said, "Yes," but we still hadn't done anything. A couple of weeks later as the group went out, we hooked up that night. Sue, matchmaker that she is, had told him about me. It lasted over the summer. When I went to school it ended. I don't think he wanted it to end, but perhaps I was frightened of it. I think I hurt him. It was not true love but there was certainly some emotional aspects to it.

Perhaps as a result of meeting a first romantic partner in these kinds of places, the most striking and distinctive first relationships were those that originated with a friendship and, according to one youth, "migrated into a torrid relationship." This pattern was four times more likely to characterize relationships begun during adolescence than those of other youths. Meeting and immediately having sex was half as likely to occur among adolescent relationships than those begun once a youth left home.

> He was maybe a year younger and I met him when I was fifteen or a freshman in high school. We were both friends for a couple of years and both of us said that we were straight. We were inseparable and now looking back it seems a bit odd that we didn't start it sooner or someone else didn't figure it out and tell us what was going on. We got drunk one night and I kissed him and he didn't resist. We then did oral sex with each other; I threw up. I attributed it at the time to drunkenness. I wanted us to be brought closer together because we always felt that we were blood brothers, so we blew each other every weekend. We would always drink a beer to be "drunk." It lasted, eventually, for nine months. He told me that he loved me; this was four months after we began being lovers. Me too.

The vast majority of adolescents reported that they decided to terminate the relationship, as might be expected, because of an impending or actual physical separation. It was not so much that the youths grew apart or discovered their dissimilarity (because so many were friends before the relationship began, they knew each other very well), but that one of the youths enrolled in college or one of the families moved. In the following example, a youth went to Norway for a student-exchange program, effectively ending his first same-sex romance.

> I met him through friends at the lake. We obviously liked each other and we went to his place where we fooled around. We spent a lot of time together. We had similar interests in music, movies, and clothes. It ended, however, when I had to go overseas, so it lasted just the summer. We're still friends and we do correspond. When I came back, things just didn't pick up where they were. There were a couple of weeks in which we were extremely sexual before I had to leave.

Adolescents were more likely than older youths to terminate a romantic relationship because one of the partners grew anxious that the relationship implied that one of them was gay. In the following narrative, neither youth was prepared to grapple with the profundity of their relationship.

> He became more reluctant over time because he cannot accept who he is. I felt as if he cheated on me by having sex with his girlfriend. This all ended when I came to college, and this is probably best for both of us. I never really viewed our relationship as legitimate. I was very homophobic in the relationship, not publicly so, but very much in my mind, so I ended having sex with him. I wasn't gay; he was.

Another major impetus for the dissolution of the first relationship was an adolescent feeling that he needed room to grow and develop outside interests. The relationship, although gratifying in some regards, felt confining.

> It ended because I didn't feel that he was really on my level. We couldn't really share very much and I didn't feel that he really understood me because he was so self-centered. I knew I could never grow with him and that I'd have to leave. The sex and being with someone was not enough. It was really hard for him because he thought that everything was going well, as it was for him. Now, we are somewhat friends; he was just too immature and I needed to mature.

The primary evaluation of the first relationship, spontaneously reported by one-half of the youths who began their romantic careers during their adolescent years, was the belief that the relationship was an expression of love or infatuation for their partner. One youth, however, wondered if the infatuation was with his partner or with the concept of being romantically involved with another male.

> My best friends took me to a club for gay teens and at the club I met this guy. After

a brief introduction we danced all night, fast and slow, and then afterwards we went out to eat and we exchanged phone numbers. He then called me the next day. It felt great actually, getting involved with someone, and it lasted for two months, but it ended very poorly. I ended it because I distrusted him. I checked up on him and discovered that indeed he was seeing other people, and when I confronted him, that was the end of the relationship. I did fall in love with him but it was more of an infatuation. Maybe, indeed, I was just infatuated with the idea of being infatuated.

Somewhat surprising, very few youths reported that adolescent romances helped them define their sexual identity as gay or bisexual. In large part this was because if youths were advanced enough to establish a same-sex relationship during the throes of adolescence then they were also early developers regarding other milestones, including knowing their sexual-identity status. Relatively few youths reported that their first relationship during adolescence was a negative experience. However, similar to the accounts of others, very few of these youths continued to have contact with their first romantic partner after the breakup.

Age-Discrepant Relationships

One-third of the first romantic relationships were with individuals at least four years older than the interviewed youth. Comparing these with relationships in which the partners were close in age reveals several distinctive qualities. Age-discrepant relationships did not vary from those in which the two were of similar age in terms of the meeting place, the length of the relationship, or who was most likely to initiate the relationship. None of these age-discrepant relationships began as a friendship that evolved into a romantic relationship. Also, similar to all other relationships, these romances could have both positive and negative outcomes, as exemplified by the following two narratives.

I was eighteen years old. The man was twenty-seven. The first move occurred in a Florida show bar, a place where guys, amateurs, go up and perform a striptease. The man on the stage got right in front of me and stripped everything off, wiggled his dick in my face, and I knew I was in love. He made a move after the show to find me and I then pursued him. The relationship evolved over two years and just recently ended because I moved here. It couldn't have been better for what I needed at the time—hot sex, warm body, good location.

We were of different generations, and that hurt us. He hates gay people who are political activists. So whenever we went out we could never show any affection. It was like he was my father or something. We could never hold hands. He was the first person who ever fucked me. I learned to like it better. If I hadn't moved here I would have broken up with him. I don't think I would have ever been anything more than fuck buddies with him.

These relationships were more likely to be terminated by the younger partner. However, it was extremely rare that the age-discrepant relationships ended in a fight in which one of the two participants was distressed or angry.

> It lasted about a month. I was fourteen and he was twenty-six. This friend was a friend of this guy, and he introduced us. This guy invited me to a party the next night and I went. That night we slept together. I was thoroughly infatuated with him. It was my third experience and it never did get beyond the infatuation stage. I finally woke up and realized this wasn't what I wanted. He kept on visiting me and hanging around and sort of helping me with my physics. He left to go back to the West Coast when I told him it wouldn't work out.

Similar to other first relationships, the end of age-discrepant relationships was most often provoked by physical separation. Another common reason for the breakup involved differing perceptions of the relationship. Most frequently, the older partner wanted sex and the youth wanted a romantic, emotional affair. The following pair shared both reasons for the conclusion of their relationship.

> I was twenty-one years old and the person I had the relationship with was thirty years old. It lasted a couple of months because he went off to school. We met each other in a theater; he was doing volunteer work for the summer. He invited me to go out to have a drink and then he started making advances toward me. We ended up having oral sex during that period of time. I thought this other person was very immature as hell; sex was the only thing he ever thought about. He was married; actually it was a marriage of convenience. I remember him mentioning that they slept in separate bedrooms. In terms of how it ended, I just remember being pissed off at him. He started placing his hands in my crotch one too many times and taking advantage of me, and I didn't like this. I wanted more, more than sex. I tried, but bad choice.

Perhaps the most striking differences in these age-discrepant relationships was the manner in which the younger partner viewed the relationship. They seldom regarded it as merely an infatuation but as an opportunity for growth and development.

> I was eighteen years old and he was twenty-four and it lasted about six months. I was coming out at the time, and I actually called this man after he placed a flyer in my mailbox about this gay group. This flyer had gone into everybody else's mailbox also.
>   One thing led to another and we started having sex. The relationship ended

abruptly when I realized he was looking at me as more of a sex object and the relationship was more sexual and not an emotional relationship. I went off in a huff after that particular incident when I realized this and basically told him that I didn't want it anymore. Now I think it was a good experience, the first training ground in being in a relationship. It started to develop a thought in me of what I wanted in a relationship.

Another benefit of many age-discrepant relationships was that they helped a youth feel better about being gay. This was seldom anything but an extremely positive outcome.

I was eighteen and he, twenty-nine. Probably the best kisser in my whole life. Lasted for a month and a half. We gave each other these shit-looking grins. He was attracted to me and I was shocked that he was attracted to me. During Christmas break he moved. I wrote letters and phone calls. I chalked it up to a sexual encounter to get over it. Long distance sucks anyway. Looking back, we had dinner a lot and we discussed gay issues; he was well off financially. It contributed to my comfort being gay because he found me attractive.

Very few youths who coupled with a considerably older man viewed this first romantic relationship as a negative experience. Most concluded that the good outweighed the bad, even if they ultimately discovered that it was not what they wanted. They were slightly less likely than other youths to have continued contact with their partner after the breakup.

Reflections on Same-Sex Romances

Myths that perpetuate the belief that gay and bisexual youths are unwilling and unable to develop intimate, erotic same-sex relationships are belied by the youths interviewed for this book. The vast majority had at least one romantic relationship with another male; those who had none wanted one and expected to have one in the near future. Separating passion from affection, engaging in sex with strangers in impersonal and sometimes unsafe places, and enduring estrangement rather than reveling in intimacy were seldom preferred by the interviewed youths as lifelong patterns.

The ways in which the youths initiated their first same-sex relationship were seldom univariate. For example, some began at pubertal onset; others, a decade or more later. Despite social prohibitions and peer stigma, fully one in three was in a romantic relationship with another male during his adolescent years; others were so manipulated by negative messages that they waited until they were far from their hometown community before daring to love another man. Although most experienced difficulty initiating their first same-sex relationship, nearly nine in ten evaluated their first romance in glowing, extremely positive terms.

The youths were most attracted to, at least for their first relationship, males older than themselves. First partners were found not only in gay bars and social/political organizations but also in many "normative" heterosexually oriented spheres of daily life—grocery stores, Boy Scouts, fraternities, summer camp, and next door. Sex was usually immediate, first or second date, but some youths were acquainted with their partner for weeks or months before having sex. Several youths knew their first love years before the relationship was sexually cemented.

In most cases, a first romantic relationship did not last very long—perhaps the fate of most first relationships. By six months, 75 percent had dissipated, in part because the initial infatuation or sexual lust had lost its luster. Few relationships ended with a "big scene" but through a slow ebbing of contact, interests, and desire; occasionally the couple made a conscious decision that the relationship was not working out. Youths were more adept at terminating than initiating the first relationship, which most frequently ended because of the mobility inherent in this age group. Schooling and careers were in transition and not uncommonly these were more important than maintaining the romantic relationship. Perhaps because future romantic relationships could now be envisioned—ones that would better match a youth's personal needs and interests—a youth felt he had more options and thus could end a current relationship that was assessed as less than ideal.

Characteristics of the first same-sex relationships varied somewhat based on the age of the youth and the age discrepancy of the couple. Youths who were involved with another male *before* graduating from high school found their lovers among neighbors, friends, and acquaintances in school clubs, athletic teams, and classes. Most distinctive, the maiden relationship for these males was more likely to begin as a friendship and to last more than three months, but not to extend beyond the ninth or tenth month. These couplings were also more likely to include an adult who was more than ten years older than the adolescent. Contrary to stereotypes, however, the older partner was not a "lecherous old man" but someone in his twenties with whom the youth was infatuated and to whom the youth was grateful for being a positive influence on his development. Also, in contrast to stereotypes, relationships with widely discrepant age differences between the partners appeared quite similar to those in which the two were of the same age. They tended to be positive relationships which, on reflection, helped the adolescent more readily identify as gay, feel better being gay, and learn much about himself. Tensions within the pair were largely based on the youth feeling that he needed more growth than the relationship was able to offer him, that the older partner wanted sex and not romance, and that the two were too different in their personalities, interests, and goals.

Perhaps the most important benefit in reporting the interviewed youths' narratives of their first same-sex relationships is to counter the assumptions that such romances do not or should not occur during adolescence or that they are problematic or negative experiences. Instances in which a youth was mistreated were seldom reported in the narratives. Few, if any, felt that their first same-sex relationship was one that they did not want or, however subtly, did not arrange or manipulate into existence.

Many of these romances, however, were hidden from friends and family because the youths knew that they would be deemed deplorable and seldom recognized, supported, or celebrated. Although these conditions may have delayed their initiation into same-sex relationships, youths did not as a consequence deny their desire for or their participation in romantic trysts. Whatever the price, these gay/bisexual youths were not defeated. They had their first romance, loved it, grew from it, and moved to other, more developmentally appropriate and helpful romantic relationships.

Future generations of adolescents will no doubt find it easier to establish same-sex relationships because of the efforts of youths such as Aaron Fricke and those who gave their stories for this book, who, despite the odds, established love relationships with other males during their adolescence and young adulthood. Also helpful has been the dramatic increase in the visibility that adult same-sex relationships have received during the last few years. The mid-1990s debate about same-sex marriages, the domestic partnership ordinances in many cities and counties, victories for spousal equivalent rights in businesses, and court cases addressing adoption by lesbian couples have raised public awareness that same-sex romantic relationships exist. Public media figures such as talk-show hosts, newspaper columnists such as Abby and Ann Landers, National Public Radio newscasters, actors such as Ellen DeGeneres, musicians such as Melissa Ethridge, and public figures are spreading the message that gay people form and maintain same-sex relationships and that in many ways they look strikingly similar to heterosexual ones—beginning for the same reasons, serving the same interpersonal needs, and ending as many do for a multitude of reasons.

9.

Positive Identity

Conceptualizing the final stage of the sexual-identity process is rarely a moment of consensus among those who propose coming-out models. Sexologist and clinician Eli Coleman refers to his decisive stage as "integration," in which the public and private aspects of a gay identity are joined to form one harmonious self-image. Once completed, individuals become fully functional and behave in an open, warm, and caring manner. Healthy, committed romantic relationships become possible, and individuals are in an excellent position to attend to future developmental tasks. In essence, according to Coleman, the gay component of a personal identity becomes merely one among many defining characteristics.[1]

Vivienne Cass, a clinical psychologist, defines the developmental conclusion of the gay identity process as "identity synthesis." Anger directed at heterosexuals and pride about being "homosexual" decline in intensity and a more integrated, soothing self becomes possible.

> A homosexual identity is no longer seen as overwhelmingly the identity by which an individual can be characterized. Individuals come to see themselves as people having many sides to their character, only one part of which is related to homosexuality. (p. 152)[2]

By contrast to these two clinicians, sociologist Richard Troiden's last stage in his developmental model is "commitment." In this, an individual does not meld his sexuality into other aspects of his identity but commits himself to "adopting homosexuality as a way of life" (p. 110).[3] Hallmarks of the "committed homosexual" include same-sex love relationships, disclosure of gay identity to others, viewing homosexuality as a state of being rather than merely sexual behavior, and satisfaction with a gay identity ("would not change even if I could"). He may choose to blend in with heterosexuals by acting in a gender-appropriate fashion and by making special efforts to keep his homosexuality from looming too large in his life. Thus, similar to Cass's identity-synthesis stage, his goal is to achieve social respectability. An individual in Troiden's final identity stage may also decide to confront rather than evade the stigma of homosexuality and seek social/political changes.

This political activism is the basis for sociologist John Alan Lee's final, two-step "Going Public" stage.[4] Step one in this "resolving and announcing one's sexual orientation as 'homosexual'" process is being identified in the public media; step two is becoming a spokesperson for the gay movement. Only rarely does an individual reach this point; most stop well short of going public. Lee's model addresses degrees of outness but not internal representations or feelings about the adopted sexuality.

A consensus emerges among clinicians and psychologically oriented researchers regarding the need for a healthy gay man to accept his status as a gay person, even though this acknowledgement may not be viewed as the conclusive and decisive act of identity formation. When an individual shuns the judgments of society and evaluates the self as worthy, *as is*, then self-validation has been achieved. This can be attained only once an individual has disclosed to himself and others, especially those who matter most. Thus, self-validation implies that an individual has placed himself into the new cognitive category of gay or bisexual, accepted that self-recognition, and shared it with significant others in his environment.[5]

To some extent this is not Cass's final stage of identity development but an earlier one, "Identity Pride," although her reference point is more directed to feeling good about placing oneself in the category (gay pride) than it is about feeling pride in being gay, per se.[6] The conclusion of Troiden's stage three, "Coming Out," in which an individual redefines homosexuality as a positive characteristic, is also similar to self-validation. Nearly 90 percent of his sample of twenty- to forty-year-olds reached this juncture one year after self-definition as gay. Before this revelatory point, all but a few had concurred with society's view of homosexuality as a mental illness; now they perceived homosexuality as a natural variation on a heterosexual norm. How was the dramatic transition engineered? The men attributed their change in attitudes to being exposed to the gay world, establishing friendships with gay men who had interests and attitudes similar to theirs, coming into contact with gay men indistinguishable from heterosexuals (that is, not effeminate), and ridding themselves of negative stereotypes of gays. Cass notes that gay pride is enhanced once an individual immerses himself into the gay subculture, especially through gay literature and gay friends. Sociologist Barry Dank identifies learning from other gay men, accessing accurate information through educational material, rejecting of societal definitions of gays as deviant, and living in a tolerant society as factors that beget a positive identity.

Cataloging factors responsible for developing a positive sense of self as a gay person have some congruency among coming-out theorists. In order of frequency and perceived importance are the following five:

- exposure to gay communities and subcultures
- friendships with gay men
- pro-gay educational material and accurate information
- elimination of negative stereotypes, especially gay people as mentally disturbed and gender inappropriate
- a tolerant societal atmosphere

Coleman intimates another factor may be critical in evolving a positive sense of self as a gay person—"ongoing process of development" (p. 39). That is, an internal process in which individuals incorporate both changes in cognition (e.g., gay is not acting like a woman) and evaluation (e.g., gay is not bad) is responsible for moving an individual from self-recognition to self-acceptance as a gay person.

The Youths' Narratives

Each interviewed youth was asked if he "had a positive view of himself as a gay person." If so, further probes explored when and how he made this transition to a positive sense of self as a gay/bisexual person. Nearly 80 percent reported that they currently had a positive sense of themselves as a gay person. This positive sense emerged, on average, just after their nineteenth birthday, shortly after first disclosing to a family member, nearly a year after beginning a same-sex romantic relationship, and over two years after labeling themselves as gay or bisexual. Three-quarters of the youths evolved their positive perspective after graduating from high school.

The age range, however, was expansive. One youth reported that he felt positive about being gay at age ten; another felt at age twenty-five that he had finally achieved his goal of feeling good about being gay. The ten-year-old perceived being gay as a natural aspect of himself; thus, once he recognized his gay status he felt good about it. He believed that his positive self-attitude owed an assist to the fact that he was sheltered from negative images of gay men during his first ten years of life.

I knew at ten years old and I didn't question it. I knew and liked being gay. I've never been around gays who are flaming, or those who were effeminate, or any who had psychological problems. I guess I've had positive, straight-acting gay men through my entire life. I have a very positive, intellectualized sense of self.

Although the time lapse between recognizing a sexual identity and feeling good about it can be instantaneous, as it was for the above youth, for others the process is often prolonged. The twenty-five-year-old struggled through eight years of turmoil.

> I think the whole process of coming to terms with my gay identity began when I was seventeen and has progressed very slowly. I now have a more positive feel about the gay side of my identity. So generally, yes, at least compared to many and also the way I used to be. I'm now talking with other people who are far more accepting of this aspect of themselves who do not judge me negatively.

One in five youths had not yet achieved this point in the coming-out process. Their reasons were usually unique. One young adult was dubious that he had achieved the status of "gay and proud," although this was a goal that he was working toward with the assistance of a gay therapist.

> I have a ways to go yet. I still have some internalized homophobia. Being with people who I perceive to be homophobic and not being able to be honest with them, like at work. It started sort of my sophomore year in college when my friends came out. I hated and yet respected them. I recognized that I would have to come to that point as well.

Of primary interest in this chapter are the critical factors that assisted the youths' movement from a negative or ambivalent gay status to one of a positive gay identity. It is particularly noteworthy that sex was an extremely rare context for evolving a positive gay concept. An intensive one-time sexual experience proved to be highly significant in altering the life course of only several youths. The following is one of these exceptions.

> I think having my first sex with this incredible guy made me feel better about my identity. I could see that nothing was wrong with it; it felt great. I felt chosen. Of all people, he chose me to have sex with! If it felt great how could it be wrong!

Most youths noted multiple sources that helped them establish a positive gay identity. These are counted in the narratives presented below. The six factors that garnered at least 10 percent of the responses are reviewed here.

Self-Assessment

The most prominent reason given by youths for their successful evolution, spontaneously reported by nearly four in ten, was that through a critical self-analysis of their attractions and desires they had come to accept themselves as a gay/bisexual person. What was added to their previous knowledge was an extensive and sometimes brutally honest self-reflection: Given their status as a gay/bisexual person, they should feel good about who they are. One youth remarked that he just "got tired of feeling guilty. Tired of being the way it is. I'm sick of it. I'm understanding myself being gay positively."

Another youth took time after leaving home to be by himself, to "reflect hard about myself, to discover myself." One issue he had not yet resolved was his sexual identity.

> Now I have a positive gay identity. It sort of began last summer when I was living in Vermont by myself and I worked part time. I spent a lot of time in the woods by myself thinking. I went on a diet and I began to work out a lot more. This was after my freshman year of college.

Only one other youth noted that a positive sexual identity was related to salvaging aspects of a physical self. He felt much better about his life in general after joining a recovery group.

> I'm a recovering addict. I've been sober now for two years and I think for awhile I saw homosexuality as part of this horrible part of me that perhaps I was addicted to, but with my sobriety came my greater acceptance of my own homosexuality.

Other youths named a number of events or factors that they felt were important for their positive sense of self. Ultimately, however, these appeared to matter little until they went through the necessary self-analysis.

> After my relationship with my girlfriend began to disintegrate when I was twenty, I felt lousy over the guilt of its breakup. I never went through a period when I felt that gay was bad, and I was always able to find friends who basically felt the same way. So all of these pieces began to fall into place around when I was twenty, a relatively hellish year. It began to occur to me that perhaps it was a good thing because I was beginning to discover myself.

Few of these youths could recall times when they hated themselves, either for being gay or for reasons independent of their sexual orientation. Perhaps because of their reliance on self-analysis rather than the evaluation of others, they displayed a level of self-contentment that served as a protective factor against the ravages of public opinion and societal homophobia. One youth best exemplifies this comfort-with-self perspective.

> I don't think of myself as bad and so if I'm gay then I can't be bad. I have a positive identity and being gay is a part of that. I felt the stigma from society, but that's all external. I never hated myself for being gay. I never felt that it was my fault that I was gay. I protected myself from self-abuse. I simply looked inward. It probably started during my freshman year in high school when I became increasingly internally comfortable with the idea. I never felt any guilt and it was a gradual process, although I didn't fully understand it initially.

For many youths, however, self-analysis was insufficient. They needed the affirmation of friends, both heterosexual and gay. These two factors were the second and third most frequently noted assists in forming a positive conviction of oneself as gay.

Heterosexual Friends

One-third of the gay/bisexual youths reported that straight friends were the most important factor in the development of their positive sexual identity. The *acceptance* of heterosexuals appeared to be relatively independent of any *support* they might offer. That is, support proffered by straight friends usually followed acceptance and was of secondary, though certainly appreciated, significance. In most circumstances, but not all, the embracing friends were female. One youth amplified this dynamic in his response.

> My close friends, especially very important female friends, built my self-esteem. I've met a lot of people who are very positive about homosexuality, but this was too frightening for me to experience in high school. It was my girlfriends who accepted me.

Another youth recounted that his self-acceptance began when his best *male* friend encouraged him to come out in high school. Knowing that his school was not "a safe place, I sort of basically decided that I would wait until college." Yet, that vote of confidence began the process of self-affirmation, completed once he escaped his suburban school for a more accepting college environment.

Several other youths noted that moving out of their hometown community was invaluable because it allowed them to develop a new set of friends who were understanding and worldly.

> There's a special side of me that is unique. It's not bad or wrong or deviant. It started about my freshman year in college, about eighteen years old. I was coming out to my best friend and she was accepting it. I felt safer here, here at Cornell. I was out my senior year in high school but still feared rejection, as if I was the only one in high school.

High school was usually perceived to be a bad context for developing a positive sexual identity. One youth was an exception, largely because he was in a high-school drama club that provided him with a ready-made pool of liberal friends. With them he knew that he would be accepted for who he was, with no questions asked.

Gay Friends

Third on the list of influential factors was the presence of gay, lesbian, and bisexual friends. They provided the nascent gay/bisexual youth with not merely acceptance—which was perceived to be a foregone conclusion given the similarity of their sexuality—but support, role models, a sense of community, and guideposts for behavior and attitudes. If these friends could feel positive about themselves, then the youth could as well. Gay friends provided perspective and a sense that one is not the only person on the planet who is gay. Some youths discovered that their longtime friends were gay, and eventually this knowledge had an impact on their self-evaluation. Most memorable are cases in which friends simultaneously "came out" to each other.

> My friend helped me to accept it at first. I realized it wasn't bad. This friend and I came out to each other at the same time. He really helped me. He was seeing a friend of mine who was also gay. He came out to me after I said I was bi. He said he was gay. Later I admitted I was totally gay.

Through his buddies, one youth determined that "being gay was more than being sexual."

Routes to finding gay friends were, at times, most unusual, as was the following youth's path. Wanting to come out and feel good about himself, he decided to join a particular collegiate fraternity that had a reputation as a "fag frat." He rushed, pledged, moved into the house, and had drunken sex with his "brothers" during after hours. Soon he developed deeper and more personal relationships with his gay brothers and through their example and encouragement he eventually marched in a gay-pride parade.

> There was a point at which it seemed to be a heavy weight on me, but it does feel natural and really nothing feels that different. I guess I had a negative view of my self-image as gay in high school, perhaps because I never spoke to anyone about it and there was all this name-calling. It's like my attitude changed somewhat, in large part because I did nothing at all about being gay when I went to college.
>
> I fooled around with girls during my first two years in college. I knew that I was gay, but I really did nothing at all about it. Then I joined a fraternity and had lots of sex with the guys, always after beers and always nothing was said the next day. In one of our conversations this guy in the fraternity named four other brothers who were gay. Then this one guy that I was good friends with told me that he was bi-sexual. This was not a shock, and it certainly didn't rock my world, so I came out to him and he said that he had pegged me as one.
>
> Two weeks later I was marching in Gay Pride in New York City, but this wasn't a shock to me. There was nothing that really surprised me at this point. It was just time for me to be visible and so I was proud to be gay.

One youth was convinced by his gay friends that it was even better to be gay than to be straight! This was not a concept with which he was familiar. But the argument was a source of self-validation.

I was in a dorm at Rochester with five other guys and they were out before me. Two of them had been out a long time, actually as children. Their reasoning and comfortableness being gay and with themselves was very important for me. Somehow it made too much logical sense. It was better to be gay than straight.

The final narrative in this section recounts one youth's transition from homophobic high-school friends to homophobic college friends. It was not until he was thoroughly accepted and celebrated by gay friends in a support group that he felt comfortable with himself as a gay person.

I had these friends in high school that I was very close to, but they would always make these homophobic comments and so I never brought up the topic of homosexuality with them because I knew I would be going away to college. In my second semester of my freshman year, I discovered my best female friend who goes to Ithaca College had apartment mates who were not tolerant and had no exposure to homosexuality. They became my friends, but once again, they didn't know about me.

Then I began going to a gay support group but telling my friends that I was going to the library. Then by the end of the semester these friends and me began going to the Common Ground [a gay bar]. I grew to be comfortable with myself, and I saw the full spectrum of gay behavior. This really began to bring me out of the closet socially and gradually I became more comfortable with myself and out to these homophobic friends in the suite.

Closely related to having gay friends was the fourth most frequently given reason for developing a positive gay identification. Rather than friends, the critical factor was exposure to gay culture and communities that offered support, role models, and information.

Exposure to Gay Culture/Communities

One in five youths reported that gay communities helped them evolve a positive gay identity. Living in a locale—usually a large urban area such as New York, Chicago, or Boston—in which vital gay communities existed was a necessary prerequisite. The factors within these gay communities that were perceived as promoting a positive identification varied among the youths. A frequently cited reason, was abetting positive images through an increased exposure to diverse gay people.

Ridding oneself of stereotypes of gay men usually implied negating impressions that all gay men are effeminate or are drag queens. Many of the interviewed youths could not or would not identify with this sterotype, including the following youth.

I didn't know anyone who was gay for a long time. Well, there was this big drag queen who lived on our block, but I knew that I wasn't like her. I didn't have to be a drag queen to be gay. I am finding that one can be gay and not feminine but indeed can be masculine.

Another reflected that what was most helpful in joining the gay community on campus was the exposure "to positive role models, countering my stereotypes that all gay men are sick, weird, or sexually promiscuous."

During coming-out week at Albany I experienced all these different gay persons, and I realized that they were like together, had their shit together. They were not sick or bizarre and it made me realize that being gay was not going to be a problem. Now for the first time I had a option, where before I didn't.

Many other youths particularly appreciated the diversity evident within gay communities. One noted, "It was the reassurance that I needed. I've met a lot of different gay people. There's much diversity in meeting these new people, and they have made me feel more comfortable." The following young adult discovered that he could tolerate far more diversity than he originally thought possible.

When I came to Cornell I tried to suppress my homosexuality because queenie men really turned me off because of their long hair and mannerisms. I almost went to a gay meeting several times, but I just couldn't do it because for me gay meant like queens or being an interior decorator, and this just clearly was not what I wanted or what I wanted to be. This frightened me a great deal. So in many ways I went back into the closet.

Then I was going on a winter skiing trip and I heard that a lot of the guys who were going were gay and so I thought, here are normal jock-type guys who are gay; and this sort of started for me, this positive gay identity, at the first meeting that I went to. This was early on and I was very frightened and I was trying to pace myself because I was scared to death. I walked up to the room behind someone who seemed very typical looking. We both went into the room and this helped to be a motivator for me to go to this group because he was so good-looking rather than queenie.

My image of gay people began to change by being involved. This also took place when I went to the Gay Pride March in New York City in June. I went to a Men Supporting Men meeting and then a group at Ithaca College, then a coffee house. All of this within a week and a half when I was beginning to come out.

I know that gay people would like to be liked. My attitude has now changed. Mainstream should be much more accepting, more tolerant, at least should allow a diversity in expressing ourselves; even the drag queens have a place in the community.

Youths valued gay culture because of the acceptance and affirmation they received from the community. First, however, they had to find a community in which to be a part. The following youth had an unusual introduction—through the parents of his girlfriend.

> It has been a long process accepting my sexuality. Have had to readjust to the outside world. Intellectually, I thought of gay as being nonsuccessful. Those were the negative images. Positive identity formed when the woman I was dating introduced me to other gay people and I realized they were okay. I also discovered this woman's parents were lesbians. They made me more available for contacts with gay culture and I find that satisfying, beginning to find a gay community.

After a very difficult time in high school, one youth resolved to be heterosexual once in college. His fortitude, however, was broken by, of all people, a heterosexual woman.

> In high school I was harassed every day by others. I came to college in order to be straight. I was very antihomosexual and then a straight female argued for gay rights in front of me and we had an argument in the dorm. I think I was very homophobic and I went to her afterwards and she recommended becoming involved in the gay community on campus, and against my better judgment, I joined it. That led to my turnaround.

Once in a gay community, many youths discovered that in reality there was not just one but *many* gay communities and that they offered different perspectives of what it means to be gay. Coming into contact with the great diversity inherent within gay culture helped some youths counter negative stereotypes of what it means to be gay.

Other youths reported that they were only able to feel good about themselves once they had refuted their image of gay people as lonely, sex-starved creatures and had established a romantic relationship with another man. Being in love, feeling lovable, and loving another formed the nucleus of having an overall positive view of oneself.

Romantic Relationships

Slightly over 10 percent of the youths felt positively about being gay once they discovered that it involved more than having anonymous one-night stands or casual sex among friends. Within the context of a same-sex romantic relationship, the following youth learned he could love and be loved.

> I think this positiveness is a result of falling out of traps of promiscuity that I formerly thought was necessary in order to be gay. The negativism ended when I was better

able to understand sex within the context of a relationship. This started when I first met my first boyfriend because up until then I had doubts that gay males could have relationships and that all of them ended very early.

For one youth, dating someone for two years who had a positive view of himself as a gay person taught him that he could feel the same way. Another listed many factors but decided because of his desire for a traditional family that his romantic relationships were the key to his gay self-esteem.

I feel much more at ease. I used to want sort of the classic Catholic family with many children and wife and so forth, and in some ways I still do but now only with a husband. The most important part of my developing a positive gay identity has been my two relationships, especially my first one with Rex. It made me feel good and natural rather than weird.

I think I've done a lot of work lately on trying to feel more comfortable being gay, and they've helped. Right now it just seems second nature and I feel pretty comfortable being out to everyone. I don't go around shouting about it, but I don't really try to hide it. I feel most comfortable with girls letting them know that I'm gay; some of the guys, especially if they're jockish, I still have some fears in regard to my safety but I feel like it's none of their business. If they can't deal with it then it's their problem.

Through relationships youths found a way of fitting in, a way in which they could mimic or lead a conventional life—only with a husband rather than a wife. Others, perhaps because of the importance of education in their lives, found that through educational material they discovered what it means to be gay and proud.

Educational Material

About 10 percent of the youths reported that information derived from many different kinds of educational materials was instrumental in the development of their positive gay identity. Specific sources ranged from gay pornography to scientific, academic books. Of critical importance for one youth was being exposed to correct information that allowed him to self-educate. "Gay magazines and gay newspapers helped. Course work on human relations, multiculturalism, and education connected me to oppression beyond myself. I could see that it was good to be gay."

Not uncommonly, a youth conducted a gay-related project for a high school or college course. Through the process of working on it, he "worked" on being gay or, in the following case, being bisexual.

I did a gay-studies project for one of my classes, and this helped me to see that there are many different ways of being gay and that one can be attracted to women and men at the same time. I also began talking with my girlfriend about a year ago, who also turned out to be bisexual, and she gave me books and suggested people I should talk to.

Although few gay-related classes exist on college campuses that provide accurate and timely information about being gay, women's studies courses often offer solace and an alternative—and not just for women students.

It happened last semester when I took Sandy Bem's class and hearing her theory about bisexuality and that society pushes people to the extreme. I like to think of myself as androgynous and I simply am who I am. I'm attracted to people regardless of gender. Then I was just not being myself, but now I am.

These six factors accounted for the vast majority of influential factors in the development of a positive sexual identity. Crossing the barrier from knowing that one is gay to gay pride was most often the path not taken until high-school graduation. One-quarter of the youths proved to be an exception. These individuals reported that they had a positive sexual identity during their adolescent years.

Early Awareness

Why some adolescents and not others evolved an early positive self-identification was not easily decipherable. Two themes that run through their narratives were leaving the home environment and finding accepting gay friends, usually in a gay youth group. Whether being away from home instigated a search for a positive sexual identity or a youth left home motivated to find self-confirmation was uncertain. Below is an excerpt from a youth who, after leaving home, realized an unexpected benefit—one that he cherished and exploited.

I think the real key was moving out of the house my senior year when I was an exchange student in Norway. The family I stayed with was very open and encouraging. They made sex exploration very easy. Everything was okay with them; they did not question anything I did, so I did a lot.

Other youths, all living near urban areas, found the impetus for self-validation closer to home—gay friends their age in youth groups. One discovered the New York City Gay and Lesbian Community Center and its youth group.

Well, I think this was when I sort of started going to the gay youth group in New York City. This was at a community center and has helped me to get a positive ID because I was able to make friends my own age. I was able to read literature, even porn, and other stuff that had a very positive image. There were role models that I got through reading and meeting other people. So definitely it's because I believe and understand I was not the only one.

Another found through the Chicago-based youth group Horizons "what I needed for myself, that there were other gay people and that gay was not just a phase and that there were older role models."

Although coming out in high school proved to be very negative, even repulsive, for most youths, one adolescent was enrolled in a gay-positive school setting.

It was a private religious school but not really by denomination, sort of a Judeo-Christian school. The atmosphere was very positive for gay people. I was sort of a member of the druggie, theatrical crowd and there might have been a couple of gay people in the group. I knew the school would support me.

If not the entire high school, personnel within a school could be a source of support for gay adolescents. One youth found that he was "fortunate enough my senior year to talk to a counselor in school, and she helped turn me around." Another found a teacher who supported his efforts to be authentic.

In eleventh and twelfth grades I had a nongay teacher who was very open and positive. I came out to her later when I had a confrontation with people in the school, and she confronted them and I was pleased. She knew that I had written a paper about gay rights in high school.

Other youths also had the benefit of a particular individual who helped them overcome the adversities of being young and gay. This could be a lesbian sister or, perhaps just as exceptional, a best friend who led one into the gay world with confidence—and with the proper attire.

Eric was a year younger, very confident and sure, and he seemed to know what he was talking about. I'm asking him questions and we talked for a long time and I remember I got upset with something he said; he knew that I was gay. He tried to calm me down, and I said that I feared for what my life would be like, what my parents would be like, because I was gay. I had to be so secretive. I was afraid my parents would think what my life would be like, no family, alone for the rest of my life. So I feared for the worst.

He lent support and answered my questions. The next day he took me to a gay club in New York. He dressed me in real trendy clothes; he introduced me to gay culture. I met a lot of nice, friendly men. I started making connections, and the media and the masses were wrong about what gay people were like. I began to see gay as positive and it changed my negative image. This all happened at the end of my sixteenth year.

Finally, one youth depended solely on himself for self-validation. Shortly after

pubertal onset he began a course of self-education that resulted in a positive identification even before he disclosed to others.

> I actually had a positive gay identity before I came out. I made an effort in seventh
> and eighth grades to read all about men's emotions and feelings, sort of the Men's
> Movement stuff. I knew that I felt deeply and that I felt that I was unlike most men
> and that I had feelings. I liked reading stories too about gay men. I especially liked
> *Reflections of a Rock Lobster*. So when finally I came out in tenth grade, it was with
> a positive identification.

This was a lucky youth. Twenty percent of those volunteering to be interviewed
replied "no" to the question "Do you believe you currently have a positive gay
identity?"

Youths Struggling to Feel Positive

Many of the gay and bisexual youths who had not yet achieved a positive sexual
identity were reluctant to forfeit their heterosexual intentions or lifestyle. Some of
these youths experienced strong heterosexual interests, and others saw little hope
in satisfying their need for an emotionally stable romantic relationship with a
man. Three interviewed youths with a bisexual orientation reflect these dilemmas.
One felt a strong attraction for a heterosexual lifestyle but was ambivalent with
this selection because of strongly experienced homoerotic impulses.

> I know that I just can't do it. I just can't play that role. It would be unfair because I
> know I'm part gay but I'm also attracted to certain women—perhaps more so than
> it used to be—but I know that I'm not totally attracted to any one woman or to any
> one man. In some places I'm still very closeted, and perhaps that's in part because
> I don't know what's best.

The difficulty for the second youth involved overcoming religious prohibitions
against a "homosexual lifestyle" and finding a man who sufficiently swept him off
his feet. "I really would like to get married to a woman and have children because
it certainly is easier than trying to develop a relationship with a man."

The dilemma for a third youth was that he was not so much attracted to
"particular genitalia as I am to the person." Once he graduated from high school
and went to Williams College he did not know how he could properly label himself or how to affirm this perceived ambiguity of sexual interests. He thought that
he "must be bisexual," but his gay peers thought him merely trying to be "politically correct." This lack of support in his collegiate gay community and the
enigma he presented to his heterosexual friends eroded the development of his
sexual self-esteem.

The absence of social support was frequently experienced as detrimental to a positive identification. One youth feared what would happen to him if he disclosed his sexual orientation to others in his workplace. "I'm out to those I'm close to, but I'm fearful for my physical safety or the repercussions of being known as gay at work or certain social circles." In these situations, "I pretend not to be gay, such as I feel I won't keep my job unless I'm straight, but I don't feel good about it." When asked if he had a positive gay identity he replied, "I can't really until I quit pretending not to be gay. I just can't accept being gay until everyone else accepts me."

Several youths reported vacillating between a positive and a negative identity. "I've lapsed back at times, but now I'm feeling better. I'm gaining confidence. It comes in spurts in which I feel positive, but there's still the negative aspects." He felt most positive when dating an attractive man and most negative when alone or coerced into anonymous sexual activities. Another youth felt his gay esteem was based on his ability to disclose to others in his environment. "Up until now I've been very closeted. I still have some negative feelings about myself when I'm around nongay people, but I am advancing."

One youth's impasse was his relationship with his father. He believed that if he could just say to him, "I'm gay," he would feel "free to be myself, but another part of me doesn't want to sort of push the issue." He concluded that until he discloses to his father or reduces his need for his father's approval, this aspect of his life will remain unresolved.

The youngest gays sometimes, but certainly not always, had the furthest to go in terms of evolving a positive gay identity. One youth directed the blame on his homonegative high-school environment, where he felt "very much alone, perhaps in part because I am gay but also because I did not feel like I really connected to anyone. I just really do not feel good about myself."

Accounts such as the aforementioned have led many clinicians, mental-health providers, and youth-group leaders to fear for the psychological well-being of gay youths. One of the most fertile areas of recent research has addressed an extreme outcome of personal turmoil—suicide.

Suicide Risks

That gay adolescents are at high risk for suicide attempts was brought to public attention by clinician Paul Gibson in a report he prepared for the U.S. Department of Health and Human Services.[7] He concludes, some would contend based on questionable data, that gay and lesbian youths represent nearly one-third of all adolescent suicides; less controversial is his claim that gay youths are two to three times more likely than their heterosexual peers to report a suicide attempt.[8] Gibson asserts that one primary culprit "is a society that discriminates against and stigmatizes homosexuals while failing to recognize that a substantial number of its youth has a gay or lesbian orientation (pp. 3–110)."

It has long been recognized that *adult* gay men and lesbians are at considerable risk for suicide attempts.[9] The ratios are remarkably invariant across studies—between 25 and 40 percent of individuals with homoerotic attractions report that they have seriously considered or attempted suicide. Multiple reasons have been given, from gay people being inherently weak to a "rational" response to the oppression that gay people face. Although early studies seldom included youth, isolated studies dating to the early 1970s demonstrate that sexual-minority adolescents are at high risk for suicide attempts. Later investigations have observed similar suicide risks among gay youths.[10] These rates increase for special populations of sexual-minority youth, including those who face violent assaults, live on the street, seek assistance at service agencies, feel rejected by others, or have a double minority status because of their ethnicity.[11]

Clinician and researcher Gary Remafedi and colleagues report that suicidal thoughts and behaviors among gay/bisexual adolescents frequently follow sexual milestones, such as labeling self as gay/bisexual or disclosing that status to others. Many youths in his study who have not attempted suicide indicated that it would be a viable option in their future. Summarizing the psychosocial data that predict suicide attempts, Remafedi and colleagues conclude:

> Compared with nonattempters, attempters had more feminine gender roles and adopted a bisexual or homosexual identity at younger ages. Attempters were more likely than peers to report sexual abuse, drug abuse, and arrests for misconduct. (p. 869)[12]

Attempters were more likely to come from dysfunctional families, to act out in other antisocial behaviors (more than half had been arrested), and to feel hopeless, worthless, alienated, and lonely. Many received no treatment after their suicide attempt. Compared with nonsuicidal gay youths, attempters were significantly younger when they first became aware of their same-sex attractions, first labeled their feelings as homosexual, and first became involved in a same-sex romance. Attempters had more male sex partners and were more out about their sexuality. Although most were aware of their same-sex attractions prior to their first suicide attempt, few had identified themselves publicly as gay or felt positive about their sexual orientation. Attempts were most likely to occur during the time that a youth was simultaneously questioning his heterosexual identity and having sex with males. These social and intrapersonal stressors inherently characterize many youths as they come to terms with their emerging sexual identity, predisposing them to attempt suicide.

Another group of researchers document the family connections for those at risk for suicide. Attempters experienced more gay-related stressors, including losing friends who would not accept the attempters' sexual orientation, disclosing to parents, being discovered as gay by parents or other family members, and being ridiculed or victimized (chased, physically assaulted), especially by fathers and siblings. Attempters had lower self-esteem and more mental-health problems, including drug and alcohol abuse.[13]

Problems with these empirical investigations are legendary, beginning with the population of youths recruited for study. In most cases the assessed participants are clearly not representative of the gay-youth population, either because they seek the assistance of a youth-serving agency from which they are recruited for study or because they are at-risk adolescents from urban areas (e.g., homeless or street youths, hustlers, HIV-positive youths). Furthermore, information about the rate of suicide attempts does not inform us about the rate of successful suicides. That is, although gay youths may be more prone to *report* suicide attempts than their heterosexual peers, they are not necessarily *more likely* to attempt or to commit suicide. For example, gay youths may be more inclined than youths of nongay sexualities to use suicide attempts to "cry out" regarding the difficulties of their lives, to emphasize the oppression that they both expect and receive, or, perhaps, to live up to particular stereotypes about what it means to be and act gay. Postmortem studies that address the sexual orientation of completed adolescent suicides are rare, and interpretations of these studies are open to question, both on methodological and statistical grounds.[14]

In the present investigation, also comprised of nonrepresentative samples of gay/bisexual youths, relatively few of the collegiate youths spontaneously mentioned any suicide attempts in their past. Although no specific questions were asked about suicide, many opportunities to discuss the issue were presented, including questions regarding harassment, peer ridicule, family and peer relations, difficulties identifying self, and disclosure to others.

Six youths (7 percent of those interviewed) explicitly made reference to suicide, all during their high-school years. Two of these youths reported that they attempted suicide, two thought about it, and two were feared by others in their environment to be at risk for suicide. The following two considered suicide just prior to identifying as gay within the context of a family or religious environment that did not appreciate its gay members. The first youth attempted suicide after he labeled his attractions but not his identity as "homosexual."

> In freshman year in high school the urge was strong to identify as gay but I suppressed it, which led to an attempted suicide. Then I had to admit to it. I grew up in a strong homophobic family environment. I had to admit it or commit suicide. I didn't seek suicide out but remember discussing it with a friend.

The second youth, discussed briefly in Chapter Seven, was hospitalized at age sixteen after a suicide attempt brought on by his first disclosure. He had fallen in love with his youth minister, who reciprocated in part, but then gave stern warnings about the dangers of homosexuality: ". . . hell was populated by people like me. He said that I really wasn't gay, because that would mean he was gay too."

Two youths reported that they thought about suicide. One was distressed after he had sex with his best friend and the friend refused to speak to him for a month. "I was so angry and very suicidal that I would risk a friendship for the sex." The second, a gender-atypical youth, was adversely affected by the ridicule he received from boys in his class.

> I became introverted, guilty, thought being gay was wrong. Took awhile to come to terms with it; hated that time. They were supposed to be happy times, your adolescence. But I dropped out of social life, thought about suicide, skipped school, and ran away from home once that I can remember.

Two other youths reported that others were concerned that they might be at risk for suicide. One, discussed in Chapter Seven, was thought to be at risk by his high-school counselor, who sent a letter to the youth's parents expressing her concerns. This led the youth to disclose his sexual orientation to his parents; the parents in turn were not the least supportive. He did not, however, attempt suicide.

The second youth was dating a longtime girlfriend but was distressed because his fantasies were solely of males. He believed that his parents were very concerned about him, although they did not know what it was that was tormenting him.

> It really bugs my parents, though, that I was very depressed, and they thought I had suicidal tendencies. This was my sophomore year. I think it had a lot to do with my sexuality and dating a female and sort of the whole discrepancy between my behavior and my feelings.

Other youths recalled friends and relatives who *committed suicide* as the result, the youths believed, of issues related to being gay. One was the first sexual partner of an interviewed youth.

> We never really talked about it and by the time we were in junior high we basically went our own way. We found different kinds of friends. I know that he committed suicide when he was twenty-one, and I often wonder about him being gay.

Two youths had uncles who committed suicide because, they speculated, the men were gay. In one case a distant uncle was not able to survive family pressure to marry. The second case was clear to the youth.

> I suspect that my uncle was. He was an artist and very flamboyant. Shot himself in the head. Suicide. He was married to my aunt and they had no kids.

By contrast to these interviewed youths, 71 percent of suburban Detroit youths in a support group (Sample Three) reported seriously thinking about suicide.

Nearly 40 percent replied that they had attempted suicide. Of the six (12 percent) who reported attempting suicide in the past twelve months, four had multiple attempts and three required medical attention.

Unlike the Detroit youths and other empirical reports of gay adolescent suicide and suicide attempts, the interviewed youths appeared to be at low risk for suicide. Few spontaneously reported past suicide attempts or strong suicidal ideation. Does this suggest that these youths are not typical of other gay youths? Are they simply not telling the truth? Perhaps the content of the interviews did not solicit such memories or reports of suicidal tendencies. Or, previous studies of gay youths may be biased by the population sampled—youth in urban or collegiate support groups organized and operated by mental-health personnel. One other possibility merits mention. When assessed by research instruments designed to measure suicidal risk and behavior, gay/bisexual youths may be more inclined than other youths to reply in the affirmative, either because they believe they are expected to respond in a particular way or because they want to use the researcher in a triangular fashion to convey to a larger audience the distress they encounter as gay individuals.

Reflections on a Positive Identity

The vast majority of the interviewed youths reported that they had a positive sexual identity and that it developed primarily after they were away from home and in a gay-positive environment such as college. Once there, they found affirmation and support from both gay and straight friends, romantic relationships, gay communities, and a sense of the diversity that is inherent among gay people. Negative stereotypes about what gay people are or must be in order to be gay were countered, refuted, or accepted as part of the "rainbow of diversity." Perhaps most importantly, the new context afforded the necessary space for gay and bisexual youths to reflect on their lives, their attractions, and their sexuality. The result was a positive conclusion—a movement toward the mantra of gay pride.

Counter to many coming-out models, however, having a personal sense of gay pride did not necessarily lead to more or fewer sex partners, greater outness to others, or to greater political or social activism. It may very well be that gay activism is greatest not among those who have resolved their gay status in a positive manner but among those who are attempting to move in that direction. The stressors they face are evident in the occasional stridency of their voices. Political activists may be individuals who through their ventures bestow on themselves a need to rid themselves of a personal albatross that they must render asunder, as well as to provide a public service.

Youths who had an early onset of other developmental milestones, such as recognition of self as gay/bisexual, disclosure to others, and first gay and heterosexual sex, were the same individuals who also reported an early age of feeling good about their sexual identity. That is, youths on the "fast track" of feeling and being gay were most likely to be "young, gay, and proud" during adolescence, prior to young adulthood.

These findings, as well as the observed low rate of suicidal ideation and attempts during adolescence among the interviewed youths, are somewhat inconsistent with the argument that the best time for gay youths to self-identify and disclose to others is after the adolescent years.[15] Although the psychologically best time to identify as gay/bisexual and to disclose that information to others is an issue few have addressed and is probably highly individualistic, speculation based on the clinical judgments of those who have conducted therapy with gay youths suggests that becoming aware at a relatively early age of one's nonheterosexuality is not highly detrimental to mental health if that revelation is shared only, if at all, with a select few. The rationale of these clinicians is that gay youths in junior and senior high school do not have peers who will accept and support them, accurate and positive information about homosexuality and gay people, models who will counter negative stereotypes about what it means to be gay, and defenses to negate the verbal and physical harassment of peers and family members. In most circumstances, self-disclosure following high school is usually considered best, once the interpersonal and social world is positive and supportive. Adolescents thus avoid the negative repercussions of being known as gay in junior and senior high-school settings. By taking their time, disclosing their sexual identity to safe persons who will provide social and psychological support, they learn crisis competence and develop an internal sense of self-respect and ego integrity that prepares them to face the cruelty of a homophobic society. This conclusion, however, may need to be reevaluated as an increasing number of lesbian, gay, and bisexual youths attend support groups in schools and local communities and find heterosexual peers and adults who accept them.

Yet one unresolved critical question remains: Is the difference between the narratives of the interviewed youths and the clinical reports of psychotherapists based on sample or cohort differences? If the issue is one of samples assessed, then youths who come to the attention of clinicians or who frequent youth support groups would need to be significantly different from those who volunteer for collegiate research about growing up gay. If cohort accounts for the discrepancy in reports, then previous generations of youths experienced an interpersonal world significantly different from current populations of gay youths, from which the interviewed youths were drawn. In either case, many of the interviewed youths, though to different degrees and at different points of their lives, found the necessary straight and gay friends; accessed educational materials that presented accurate and positive gay images in libraries, on television programs, and in movies; and were exposed to media models and personal experiences that showcased the diversity apparent among gay men. Many also found peers and adults who stopped the needless harassment of gay people and parents whose reactions appeared not to be as negative as previous accounts document.[16] If these factors are experienced in sufficient quantity during the adolescent years, as is now increasingly apparent, then disclosing to self and others and feeling good being gay can all occur before the eighteenth birthday.

Also in contrast to coming-out models, the most important factor leading to positive self-validation was not exposure to the gay community or the development of friendships with gay men, which were each endorsed by 20 percent of the youths, but by self-analysis or reflection.

Why this reflection led to positive rather than negative self-regard is not clear, but may be related to the Chapter Two finding that most of the youths felt that their homoeroticism was a natural part of who they were. If it were natural then it had to be good. In addition, most felt good being gay *before* they were exposed to gay communities or developed friendships with other gays.

Second on their list of factors that led to positive gay esteem was not noted by any coming-out theorist, perhaps for political reasons: feeling accepted and supported by *heterosexual* friends. I believe this is political because some would like to believe that gay pride can only be achieved through the work of gay communities and their role models, friendships, educational materials, and support groups. These were indeed important for some youths, but relatively few spontaneously registered the significance of educational materials or courses, the negation of stereotypes about gay people, or the tolerant political and social climate in which they live. Although the youths seldom noted that living in a tolerant society aided them in feeling good about being gay, it was within this cosmopolitan context that all other listed things were possible. Current cohorts of gay/bisexual youths may be taking our increasingly tolerant society for granted.

This is less likely to be true for ethnic-minority adolescents with same-sex attractions who face a hostile White world, regardless of their sexuality, as well as a hostile ethnic community if they declare their sexuality. This negotiation is a formidable task—integrating a personal identity and a reference-group orientation within the context of two at times competing and antagonistic social worlds. This is the focus of Chapter Ten.

10.

Ethnic Youths

The pressure to conform to traditional definitions of what it means to be a boy or young man—including wooing, dating, and marrying a woman—can undermine a gay youth's psychological integrity. If in addition he is faced with the task of integrating an ethnic identification with a sexual orientation that are both deemed undesirable by the majority culture, then developing a healthy self-concept may be sabotaged.[1] Such youths often encounter racism in gay communities and homophobia in their cultural community. As a result, many must create dual identities, assume multiple roles, and endure inevitable emotional conflicts. For example, because such individuals can seldom hide their ethnicity, they may feel extreme urgency to maintain silence regarding their sexual orientation in order to avoid being dually oppressed. Progress toward establishing both a healthy ethnic-based self-concept and a positive gay identity is often construed to be an uneasy journey for ethnic-minority youths. They must resolve three developmental tasks not experienced by White gay youths:

- cultivate both a sexual and an ethnic identity
- resolve potential conflicts in allegiance to a cultural reference group and to a gay community
- negotiate stigmas encountered because of homophobia and racism

Although ethnic-minority youths share many of the same challenges as do majority youths in disclosing their sexuality to family members, unique problems emerge because of the centrality of the family in many ethnic cultures. Psychologist Edward Morales describes the constellation of the traditional ethnic family, which centers on integrating the extended family within a youth's support system.

The ethnic family support system resembles more of a tribe with multiple family groups rather than a nuclear family structure consisting solely of parents and children. For the ethnic person the family constitutes a symbol of their basic roots and the focal point of their ethnic identity. (p. 9)[2]

Disclosing to the extended family may be a very onerous experience, one never desired and perhaps never imagined. How can an adolescent or young man destroy the very foundation of his support during, as Morales reminds us, "the arduous times of experiencing discrimination, slander and inferior treatment" (p. 9)? To embarrass, to alienate the family by publicly disclosing the "sin of homosexuality" jeopardizes, according to Morales, a youth's ties to his close-knit family across and within multiple generations, his associations with other ethnic-group members, and progress toward a healthy sense of self.

Thus, even if a youth advances to the point of accepting his sexual status, the inhibitions against stating this publicly can block further self-development. To "go public" would, in his worst nightmare, so devastate his family that he would likely decide that it would be better to construct a wall of silence around himself. While shunning associations with his ethnic group might relieve apprehensions that his homosexuality will become known, the alternative, to renounce same-sex attractions, is seldom an attractive option for the ethnic/sexual-minority youth. He may, however, choose this option until he is away from home and surrounded by a "family of creation."

Ideally, an ethnic/sexual-minority adolescent should have opportunities to acquire information and emotional support from two distinct and rich sources. Gay communities can offer youths of color acceptance and support that cultural communities are frequently unable or unwilling to provide, including affirmation of a sexuality, a place in which to openly explore same-sex feelings and relationships, and information about activities and organizations that cater to sexual-minority individuals. Similarly, ethnic ties can reinforce a cultural identification, offer a deep sense of ethnic heritage and values, and provide a sense of self within the context of a family that shares a youth's struggles and oppressions.[3]

This ideal juncture is thought to be rarely realized. Ethnic-minority youths with same-sex attractions may desire to closely identify with both ethnic and gay communities but feel conflicted because the two place demands that are inherently contradictory. Each community presents adolescents with dissenting information about "appropriate" sexual or ethnic behavior and the importance of choosing one identity over the other. A gay Chinese American adolescent summarized this dilemma:

I am a double minority. Caucasian gays don't like gay Chinese, and the Chinese don't like the gays. It would be easier to be White. It would be easier to be straight. (p. 263)[4]

Although the formation of an integrated self-identification that embraces ethnic and sexual identities is a protracted process that has been presented as necessarily having negative ramifications on sexual-identity development and self-worth, from another perspective being gay and of color may prove beneficial. That is, it is possible that because of their ethnicity, youths of color with same-sex attractions may be *stronger and healthier* than their White gay brothers. Learning the necessary skills to integrate and manage an ethnic-minority status may facilitate the subsequent synthesis and regulation of a second dissonant group identity, a sexual-minority status. Having endured the complications from an early age of being "ethnically different," such youths may have developed coping skills that assist them with their "sexual difference." This perception is rarely, however, articulated in the literature on gay youths of color.

One important caveat must be noted at this point. Although the following discussion is organized around generic ethnic groupings, within each ethnic group exist many communities and considerable diversity. Not all nationalities within an ethnic group are identical. For example, psychologist Beverly Greene notes, "African Americans are a diverse group of people with cultural origins in the tribes of Western Africa, with some Indian and European racial admixture" (p. 245).[5] Latinos include youths who grew up in Puerto Rican, Mexican, or one of many Central or South American cultures. Chinese, Japanese, Filipino, Indian, Vietnamese, Laotian, Korean, and Thai youths are Asian Americans but have diverse experiences being Asian in the United States. Thus, Greene reminds us that gross descriptions of ethnic influences can never be applied with uniformity to all members within an ethnic group or across ethnic groups.

Mindful of this warning, the present review emphasizes the common experiences shared by the interviewed gay/bisexual youths from various ethnic communities. They comprised one-quarter of the total sample and are here separated into three groupings—African Americans, Latinos, and Asian Americans. They did not differ from White youths in their sexual-orientation self-ratings but were more likely to be from urban areas.

African American Youths

African American youths were developmentally advanced on several indicators of sexual identity. They reported an early onset of labeling their sexual attractions as gay, prior to their eleventh birthday, and of recognizing themselves as gay, at age fifteen, both of which were approximately two years before White youths.

African American gay/bisexual youths also reported a higher frequency of orgasms during junior high school (daily) and began having sex with both boys and girls, usually other Black youths in their friendship play group, at an earlier age, at age twelve and thirteen, respectively. They did not, however, thus have more sexual partners; in fact, they reported fewer male partners during their lifetime, between three and four, than any other ethnic group, including Whites.

African American youths disclosed their sexual orientation to family members—including their mother, father, and closest sibling—at a younger age than any other ethnic group, during their seventeenth year. Most African American youths reported, however, that they did not directly disclose their sexual orientation to family members in a face-to-face meeting. Rather, they chose indirect means (e.g., leaving hints around the house or being vague in their gender language) or assumed their parents already knew. In fact, one youth questioned whether the coming-out concept applied to youths in his community, especially if it necessarily implied saying the words directly. More typically, less destructive means were used to preserve the son/parent relationship.

> It's a tough concept to discuss or understand, the coming-out process. It does not really apply to the Black male gay experience. You just don't say those words. Parents don't ask, and you don't tell. You know they know, and they know you know they know, and that's it. They may not like it, but that's all that's necessary.

Trying to avoid a showdown with his mother, one African American youth deflected her indirect questions and found a nonconfrontational way to tell her about his gay life.

> When I was eighteen and in college we met in Syracuse to discuss why my grades were so low. I could not tell her why, although she asked me at the time about a gay friend of mine and I said no, though he was. I was not surprised by these questions because they were in line with how sex in general was talked about in my home.
>
> I came out to her in a letter and discussed it later while we were driving in a car where she could not avoid it. It was awkward. She admitted after coming out to her that she knew, but she blocked it out.

Occasionally, however, an African American youth defied this unstated prohibition against directly approaching the family. These circumstances were typically when no other means seemed suitable.

> I was fifteen when I had a crush on a man and we had broken up. I was very depressed for a long period of time over this. My mother asked why and so I took the opportunity to tell her. For her she felt it was a phase and was very shaken up by the news. At the same time I also told my father.

African American youths initiated romantic relationships with men at an early age, just after their sixteenth birthday. These men were not always age peers, as was the case for a West Indies–born youth who waited until college for his first same-sex romantic relationship. He fell in love with his comparative literature professor, whose sexual identity was less advanced than the youth's newly discovered sexuality.

> I was nineteen and he was thirty-two. We went out for about three years. He was a professor in college. Taking classes with him and I decided to go to the movies with him and one thing led to another. Graduate school forced the ending of it and it was graduate school for me.
>
> A very positive reaction to it but there was too much secrecy to it. It was hard also trying to distinguish what the pupil versus teacher role was. He was also a Black man. The problem was that he didn't self-identify as a gay man. He just thought it was two friends having sex. Actually, I remember looking upon myself more as a Black man; the gay identity was already in place.

African American gay/bisexual youths were similar to others in terms of disclosing their sexuality to nonfamily members and becoming involved in gay social and political activities. The vast majority speculated that they were born gay, although most dismissed the question as irrelevant, including the following two youths.

> I don't have a theory. I don't look for one. I don't seek for an explanation. I think there are gay people because we have a lot to teach the world.

> Well, from a scientific point of view it's got to be sort of genetic, which I don't really understand; but then there's no real need to. We are all God's children and we are all created equal. There was no choice in it for me; it's just something that happened. Perhaps God had a reason for me being gay.

Compared to other youths, African Americans reported few clinical indications of mental distress and had high levels of self-esteem. One youth, still in the midst of resolving his gay identity felt proud with his ethnic identity—being Black.

> I'm still in the process of developing a gay image. I don't necessarily have negative connotations with that. Same time working through my gay identity I've worked through my racial identity. Closest friends were aware I was gay and I was able to talk more with them because of it. Began to develop it myself, and that was validating to me and I was also validated by them. Friends were basically Black, both men and women.

Most African American youths had little to report when asked whether their ethnic culture influenced their sexual-identity development. Responses were usually comparable to White youths and reflected the impact of parents' attitudes and chance environmental circumstances. Although few identified specific aspects of being Black that affected their sexual identity, one exception was the influence of the Black church. For example, one youth raised by his pastor father and church organist mother identified with many of his African American gay/bisexual brothers in his desire to make his sexual encounters count.

> I think my Blackness has affected me as a result of being raised in a Black church from the beginning. That has influenced me the way that I am, the way that I handle relationships and my sexual morals and values. I am more conservative than most of my friends on sexual behavior and I just don't feel comfortable in just jumping in and out of bed.

On many of these dimensions, African American gay/bisexual youths did not differ markedly from Latino youths. One notable exception was the number of same-sex partners that Latino youths had during their lifetime, about twice that of African Americans.

Latino Youths

Latino youths with same-sex attractions reported becoming aware of their attractions to males just after their sixth birthday, earlier than any other ethnic group and two years before White gay/bisexual youths. One year later, at age seven, they knew the meaning of the word *homosexual.* Not surprisingly, Latino youths were also among the earliest to label their attractions and identity as gay or bisexual, during their twelfth and fifteenth years, respectively. They disclosed this information to a first person earlier than any other ethnic group.

Latino youths were out to their mother and closest sibling, to most of their friends, and to their social world—everyone, that is, except their father. One Mexican youth feared what his father would do to him physically if the father were to find out: "He would probably call me every name in the book and take out his belt, even though I'm almost twenty-one." Latino youths were more likely to socialize with other gays and bisexuals and to be politically active than White, African American, and Asian American youths.

Although the following youth was out to everyone who cared to know, he was frustrated because he had difficulty finding other Spanish-speaking gay youths on his college campus.

> I've had a good network of friends, both straight and gay, but I'm looking for more gays in Spanish culture. I'm trying to reach a level of understanding and educate those White gays I care about, but I get mixed reactions. They want me to be White and when I don't act it, when I stopped giving, the friendships deteriorate. I'm in a process now after a couple of these experiences which have strained my Latino identity.

Latino youths had the largest number of male sex partners (eight) and were late having sex with a female, just before their seventeenth year. The ethnicity of the first partner was usually another Latino male, as it was for the following youth.

> I was doing research at Dartmouth and I saw this gorgeous Latin guy in the dining hall and I knew immediately that he was gay. We made a lot of eye contact, he came over, and somehow he got my phone number. He called me and asked if I was gay and I said I was. And then he asked me out for a movie and for coffee. The second date was our first sex. It lasted for eight weeks.
>
> We agreed to end it at that point. So there was a lot of freedom, no sense that we would have to be together or that even we could be together. We were very open and honest with each other. It was sad to have it end, but we still have contact with each other. He was twenty-four and I was nineteen at the time. It was a very affirming experience. Because he was from Chile we had a lot to talk about in terms of our experiences.

According to the interviewed youths, a traditional virtue common in many Latino communities is that boys should appear defiantly heterosexual—embracing and enacting the social construct of "machismo." Thus, male homosexuality is equated with behavioral effeminacy and not homosexual behavior per se. One youth noted this within the context of his first sexual experience—with a "heterosexual" Puerto Rican.

> This occurred at age seventeen. People are very closeted in Puerto Rico. If you're not queer looking then you can hide your sexuality and people do not assume that you are homosexual. So what these men do, who are more masculine, or at least not queer looking, is they look for other males on the street, while they are married and have children and lead a heterosexual life. This was the case for the man that I first had sex with.

A Peruvian-born bisexual youth could not accept the meaning of his lusts after his first sexual experience. In his cultural depiction, people who engaged in anal intercourse were transvestites or male prostitutes. "That was my image of what a gay person was. That's what it was portrayed in Peru, that is, that homosexuals were those who wanted really to be women."

Many Latino youths named the Catholic Church rather than their ethnicity as the primary instigator and socializer of traditional values, rigid sex-role mandates, and internalized homophobia.

> I grew up in a Catholic family and a Catholic country, and gay males have always been presented in a negative image. This was the image I had while I grew up. Being gay was associated with being feminine. Same-sex attractions were unspeakable even though I grew up in a very liberal community. In my school there's a lot

of diversity and certainly the people there were not as homophobic. It's like being in an island of irrationality.

Once here at college I didn't feel like most of the other people did when they talked about their ethnic background affecting how they are gay. It just never seemed to be a big issue except for growing up in a very Catholic country.

Catholicism dictated to a Latino family a conservative outlook on sexuality and morality and imposed constraints on a youth with same-sex attractions. A youth from Puerto Rico and another from Bolivia discussed these issues at the conclusion of their interview.

Well, my culture has a lot to do with how I have been shaped during my life. It's a very Catholic and conservative country. But my family is even more conservative than the culture because we are second-generation Spanish. Those of my friends who have been on the island longer tend to be from more liberal families.

If I'm away from my culture then I can be more out and more gay. It's very difficult to be Puerto Rican and gay. I could not be as out as I am in the United States in Puerto Rico because being gay is not seen as positive. There's lots of prejudice. People who know me are okay with it. Those who know me first as a person and then find out I'm gay are okay with it. But those who know me first as a gay person have a lot of problems with it in Puerto Rico. There's still a lot of rejection which I can feel from the community there. I'm gay in this culture but I'm not gay in Puerto Rican culture. In Puerto Rico, all gays supposedly act like females.

Dual identity is tough. I feel strongly about my Bolivian heritage. I love the Andes, but I must totally hide my life when there and I have had to give up much of my Bolivian heritage. I'm strong now as a gay person; it's the center of me and I'd be bitter to have to give it up. Never, never tell anyone in Bolivia because I'd be disowned. Worse thing you can be there is a faggot. I've not felt discrimination in the gay community because of my heritage, but I've seen others face it, especially those with Latino dress, accent, and behavior.

The effects of these religious and cultural mandates were often difficult to overcome. One Puerto Rican youth, only seventeen at the time of the interview, was still uncertain how long he would or could be gay.

Around nine years of age I was able to say to myself that I am homosexual. I also knew that I would have to learn to hide my feelings. I felt badly about this. I knew that I would have to hide my homosexuality forever. I want to marry and lead a heterosexual life and that would mean I would spend my life hiding my true attractions. This is characteristic of many men in Latin culture.

Another Latino youth felt positive about his same-sex attractions and himself as a gay person only after he left his ethnic community and joined a White gay community. He knew this was not ideal but he felt he had no choice. "I had to get out of my Latino community and begin building my own foundation, reading books, and a more philosophical focus on myself. I could not have done it if I had stayed."

Despite these cultural hurdles, most Latino youths developed a positive gay/bisexual identity at the same age as White, African American, and Asian American youths. Their self-esteem level was higher than all other groups, save one—Asian American youths.

Asian American Youths

Compared to all other youths, Asian American gay/bisexual youths deviated most strikingly from other groups, reaching particular developmental milestones at a significantly later age. As children and adolescents, for instance, they were the last to become aware of their same-sex attractions, at age nine, one year after Whites and nearly three years after Latino youths.

One Chinese youth attributed his lack of awareness to a linguistic difference between Chinese and American culture.

> You know the Chinese do not have a word for *gay* and *homosexual* is a very clinical-sounding term and is very bad. One could never say that he is homosexual; the language just doesn't exist for it. There's no real identity in Chinese for the concept of gay.
>
> In high school I began to think in English for the first time. So, in some ways that is the reason why I never had the concept of gay until this point. Now for the first time I had the concept of gay in the English language. But no one ever asked me what I was.

Asian American youths were also the last to have sex with another male, midway through their sixteenth year. This was two and a half years after White and Latino youths and four and a half years after African American youths had their first gay sex. This striking difference can be attributed in part to the taboo status that sex has in many Asian families and communities. Sex is usually considered a highly sensitive, delicate subject, open at best to awkward and infrequent discussion.

In nearly all cases the first partner was a White male. This may reflect the invisibility or dearth of sex play among Asian youths, thus making it more difficult to find an Asian partner. Alternatively, the later age of first gay sex may open the possibility of fulfilling a personal preference for White partners in college. One Asian youth suggested: "Having sex with a White guy is like incorporating Whiteness and its power and prestige."

Without a tradition of talking about sexuality, it can be very difficult for an Asian American youth to discuss his sexual identity, beliefs, and practices with others, including his first sex partner. One youth waited until his freshman year of college for his first sexual experience, and then he suffered anti-Asian abuse from his White partner.

> Well, I was not exactly thrilled. There's this White guy in the dorm and he pressured me. I wasn't all that attracted to him; it happened twice. I sort of regret it and resent the fact that he was the first time I did it. He had been pursuing me for two weeks, telling me I wasn't going to get anyone else. He was a friend, but we had difficulties after the encounter.
>
> It really didn't help me being gay because he told me I would be unattractive to Americans because I'm Asian. This made me feel really terrible about myself and my future.

Due to shyness, one Japanese youth did not undress during his first sexual encounter, which was construed by his White partner as disinterest, low eroticism, and rejection. Two Filipino adolescents had an elaborate system by which they maintained a sexual relationship while still honoring their sexual "shyness" and their heterosexuality. Eventually, their sexual relationship became less ambiguous while the romantic relationship festered until the gay component became too explicit to maintain.

> It was my freshman year of high school and he was the same age, a casual friend in the same group as me. He had heterosexual pornography and asked six of us guys to come over one day. It was real cool and all of us liked it. And then he asked us to come over again and this continued about every week for a month or so. However, after a while, the group got smaller and I was the only guy eventually who came over.
>
> So he and I would watch the heterosexual porn and then afterwards we would jerk off. This went on for about three months. Then what we began to work out was that rather than jerking off afterwards, we would do it during the porn but we would take turns going behind the other and jerking off so we would not see each other. This way we had the facade of heterosexuality going.
>
> Our friendship began to grow and we began to spend more time together. He would come over to my house and at one point we were at my house talking of sex and he said that he needed to jerk off. And so he did, once again going behind me. I did as well after him. This continued for a little while. Then one time when we were in the midst of this, I was doing it and my cat walked by and meowed and he looked at the cat and he saw me doing it. He made a big joke about it, that he saw my penis. And so the next time we were doing this, I joked that since he saw mine that I ought to see his. This is quite striking for me because I am usually very

reserved. So then this began the process where in fact we would jerk off in front of each other. It would always be him first. We did this two or three times. It was clear that the sexual tension between us was there.

Then at one point he said that he wanted to taste my cum. I said okay and he took the lead. So he gave me a blow job and I came in his mouth and he swallowed. Then I gave him one, even though he gave me instructions on how to do it. The second time we did this we actually kissed for the first time. We then started going out and developed a relationship, which continued for about six months.

So, from the first time to this that we watched the first porn was about one year from beginning to end. At this point I think I was getting deeply in love with him and I thought about how great it would be if we were to get married. However, after six months we broke up because we had many arguments. And then he said that he was not interested in doing it anymore. We never used the word gay.

The breakup occurred my sophomore year, during Valentine's Day. I was very hurt. I was devastated. We had spent a month arguing and then finally we said this was not worth it. He then went out with a woman for two years. We never talked again until high-school graduation. He is very closeted, whatever he is. Maybe he's bisexual or gay or maybe he was just experimenting. He too is very Catholic.

Youths of Asian descent were also the last to have a heterosexual encounter, one year after first gay sex. This was from one (Latino) to four and a half (African American) years after other ethnic youths. Only a few had sex with a girl; as a group they averaged less than one female partner during their lifetime, fewer than all other youths.

In other respects, however, Asian American youths were on par with other youths. They had normal frequencies of orgasms during their junior and senior high-school years, had the same number of male sex partners (four), and had their first same-sex romantic relationship at the same age, except for African American youths, who were precocious on these accounts. These numbers indicate that Asian American youths were not less sexual than other youths, but that they began expressing their sexual self at a later age.

The unwillingness to share their sexuality is most strikingly apparent in the domain of being out to others. Asian American gay/bisexual youths had disclosed to relatively few other people or, in some cases, nearly to no one. They seldom socialized with other sexual minorities or joined political organizations or activities. An exception was the following Chinese youth, who experienced the best summer of his life, one in which his social and political awareness soared and became an integral aspect of his life. But to do this he needed to disclose to a best female friend, a process he feared would be so traumatic that he needed special arrangements to utter the necessary words. She, also Chinese, felt the same secrecy was necessary.

My senior year after high school was going to be very difficult for me, so I asked her to turn her back so I wouldn't have to face her. After she did this, I told her that I was going out with a guy and I said that I was gay. Then she told me to stay turned because she also had something to tell me, that she liked girls!

Then my other best female friend, whom I told the next day, said as well, "Guess what? I'm a lesbian!" So the three of us had a great summer that year exploring gay New York City, The Village, the Hetrick-Martin Institute, and so forth.

It was a great summer! It was like learning and being involved in the whole history of the queer movement during this one time period in the summer. I felt more proud that I was interconnected. I felt empowered and that I had been part of a common struggle.

Many Asian American youths deferred their self-disclosure or never divulged their sexuality to parents. Of all youths, Asian Americans were the least likely to disclose to their parents and when they did, to do so at a later age than White, Latino, and African American youths. One Chinese youth believed that he could never have such a discussion with his parents.

Hell, no! I'll never tell my parents unless they ask. But I won't lie to them—but she has to ask. My dad is a very traditional, conservative Chinese man.

Another youth's parents still live in India and are financially supporting his studies in the United States. Although they respect him and his decisions, before telling them about his "failure to fulfill their dreams," he intends to graduate and be on his own financially.

So I'll tell them within the next two or three years. How do I think they will react? Well my father is more open minded. I'm not sure what he knows about gay people though. I don't expect either him or my mother to give me much support, nor do I think that they will overreact because they know me well enough to know that I would not do anything corrupt or horrible. My mother perhaps will be more negative towards the idea of homosexuality because of the pressure to marry, to have a family, to have grandchildren, and to carry on the family name.

In terms of being out to their closest sibling, Asian American youths were commensurate with other youths, although they disclosed to a sibling two years later than other ethnic-minority youths. The closest sibling was almost always a sister and she was told before and perhaps in lieu of parents. Although siblings did not always understand or offer unconditional support, they were usually supportive. The following Asian American youth received what he wanted, acceptance from a sibling.

In terms of my sister who is at Georgetown, she was really angry that I didn't tell her before I told my friends. It was getting rough at high school and many rumors were around. This was my senior year. I did not actually tell her but she asked me if I had a girlfriend and when I hesitated she said, "A boyfriend?" She is intellectually very supportive.

A sister may be told so that she can become a confidante and an invaluable source of support, especially in advance of disclosing to parents. One youth strategized first disclosing to his sister: "She is educated and seems to be very good about issues of homosexuality. Then once I have her support, I'll tell my parents."

Despite the closeted state that characterized many Asian American youths, they reported extremely high levels of self-esteem and little clinical symptomatology. Their high levels of mental health may be due to the unconditional support and love that many reported receiving from their mother. The consequential self-esteem did not, however, always translate to a positive gay identity. The following youth finally achieved this dual goal, although at a later age than many of his peers.

It's [his ethnic identity] a part of who I am, because of the way I was raised. I have a positive self-esteem and my gay identity is just a component of that. I don't separate them. I feel much better since coming out to myself. Now that I don't buy into the shame, I have a positive sense of gay identity after I had first developed a positive self-esteem. Some guys carry their self-esteem on their sleeve, but not me. Developing my self-esteem was a long process.

To overcome the obstacles that are unique to Asian American youths may require a level of self-esteem that was often reflected in the narratives of the interviewed youths. Homosexuality was frequently considered a barrier to the fulfillment of their dreams. Eventually, most Asian American youths developed comparable levels of gay self-validation to other ethnic-minority youths.

Reflections on Ethnic Youths Who Are Gay/Bisexual

African American, Latino, and Asian American gay/bisexual youths are in some respects similar to White gay/bisexual youths, and to each other. They also differ from these groupings. Although considerable variation also characterizes youths within each ethnic group, the focus in this chapter has been on interethnic group diversity. African American youths were generally advanced in their sexual identity development, including labeling feelings and self as gay/bisexual, having gay and straight sex, cultivating gay relationships, and disclosing to others. Despite their high level of orgasms, they were not more likely to have more sex partners than most other groups. By contrast were Asian American youths, who were late becoming aware of their same-sex attractions, disclosed to few others, and began gay sex at a late age. They were particularly closeted to their parents, but not to a close sibling. Latinos were, similar to African Americans, early on reaching several developmental milestones: awareness, labeling, recognition, and disclosure to others. They appeared to be out to everyone but their fathers, whom many said they feared, and were very sexually, socially, and politically involved in gay communities.

These ethnic-minority youths developed a positive gay/bisexual identity at approximately the same age as White youths, but reported considerably higher levels of self-esteem and fewer clinical symptoms. Thus, it seems somewhat surprising that a greater proportion of ethnic-minority (one-third) than White (one-quarter) youths reported at the time of the interview that they had not established a positive gay identity. That is, their level of self-worth did not appear to be contingent on their self-acceptance of a gay or bisexual identity.

One explanation of this unexpected finding is that ethnic-minority youths develop high levels of self-esteem in part by having an ethnic family that loves and supports them and that meshes them into an extended family and cultural heritage. Thus, self-esteem in this model emerges at an early age, buffered by an ethnic family that offers its members recluse during frequent attacks by a hostile majority culture.

One thing that youths learn from their families is how to cope with the enduring complexities of being a non-White in North American culture. Little empirical evidence exists, however, that their evolved coping skills and sense of self-worth help them contend with being *sexual* outcasts. Developing a positive sexual identity appears not to be causally linked to, and in reality may be in opposition to, close family and cultural ties. Indeed, none of the youths noted in their interviews this generalization of survival skills, which does not necessarily imply of course that it did not occur. To develop a positive sexual identity, ethnic-minority youths were left to their own devices, similar to the gay White youths, except without the same sources of affirmation and support—role models, media presentations, and gay communities—available to White gay/bisexual youths. What was most clear from the narratives was that ethnic-minority gay/bisexual youths with high self-esteem had not necessarily resolved misgivings they had about their sexual identity.

The following college junior reported a high level of self-esteem but had not yet, by his own admission, reached a satisfactory level of positive feelings about being gay. The first he attributed to his loving, supportive family; the second, to his homophobic, traditional culture.

I am first generation from Southeast Asia. I am still very cultural bound and my family would love to set me up with a woman for marriage. I am proud of my family, a great one. They have always loved and supported me. I know that I can always count on them. I feel good about myself because they've given me everything.

But mother can't fathom homosexuality and many of our friends are the same. So I can't express myself to my culture or to my family. It probably delayed my coming out. I wish I could have done it in high school like other kids.

Complicating their developmental trajectories, ethnic-minority youths faced the task of defining a sexual and an ethnic identity within a White, heterosexual social world. This was most evident, according to the youths in the contentious insistence from peers and the mass media to assimilate, to avoid a stigmatizing identity, and to act White and heterosexual. As a result, many of the Latino, African American, and Asian American youths struggled between who they were and who they felt others wanted them to be. Many felt that they must lead a double life and establish a dual identity. They were often isolated from other gays in their culture, ostracized and stereotyped by both gay and ethnic communities.

One interviewed Chinese American recoiled from the all too often experienced sting of White stereotypes of Asians—as docile, flamboyantly feminine, polite, sly, and untrustworthy.

Well, the Chinese religiously and culturally hate homosexuality and the Chinese and gay identity hate each other. Each community rejects the other. Gays see Asian Americans in a negative way, and so we don't have a voice. They see us as geeks who cannot represent the queer community. We're just "good boys" and we take care of our lovers. I'm trying to change that, so I'm more involved in gay politics than Asian American politics.

The switch in political activism represents, in part, an expectation that as a gay man he will have little opportunity to alter the Chinese community and its attitudes and beliefs.

Several ethnic-minority youths believed that they could not successfully negotiate the development of a positive gay or bisexual identity until they had disclosed to their parents. One Latino youth disclosed to his mother, his brothers and sisters, and everyone in his collegiate environment, but was still waiting "for the right moment" to share his sexuality with his father in order to feel good about his sexuality. Homosexuality was often considered by parents to be a manifestation of adolescent rebellion against traditional culture or a secularization imposed by a decadent, urbanized Anglo-American culture. Although they disagreed, youths did not know how to refute the charge.

Overcoming these barriers was seldom a simple task. If a youth had a deep history of family relationships that strongly emphasized loyalty and honoring both parents and extended family ties, he risked disgracing not only himself by disclosing his sexual orientation but his family, including those long deceased. To neglect these responsibilities was to be selfish, to embrace his own pleasure rather than the good of the community. Perhaps he too had accepted without question parental assumptions regarding fulfilling cultural obligations of marriage and perpetuating the family name. Thus, a wall of silence often formed around a family with a gay or bisexual son. Even if he advanced to the point of self-recognition of his sexual status, the inhibitions against stating this publicly could block further self-development—including disclosing to others, initiating sexual contact, and evolving a positive gay/bisexual identity.

This portrait more characterized Asian American than Latino or African American youths, perhaps because the family and its heritage loomed so large in the lives of the Asian American youths. It dictated their behavior, if not always their attitudes. They had not and could not simply turn the family aside. By contrast, Spanish Catholicism and Black Protestantism appeared to be the primary arbitrators of repressing sexuality among Latino and African American youths. Although religion could be a powerful factor in some lives, Latino and African American gay/bisexual youths appeared to have had an easier time discarding or dismissing this cultural albatross than Asian American gay/bisexual youths had in countering their impediment toward a publicly avowed nonheterosexual identity, their family.

In the following narrative, the problem for a Native American Indian youth was not his family heritage but his family's religion. He had to overcome seventeen years of religious indoctrination and a Bible-toting mother before he could see his way through to self-acceptance and a positive gay identity. He had a distinct advantage in that historically his culture respected and honored those with same-sex attractions or gender-atypical behavior.[6] Thus, to non-Christian Native American Indians, his sexuality was acceptable. This was a situation in which an ethnic culture steeped in traditions overcame the homophobia of a family that had forsaken traditional religion by adopting a foreign one.

> My tribe was very accepting and easygoing and as a result I learned to accept it. I was sick of trying to find my answer in the Bible and I began to see the hypocrisy of much of my mother's religion. This allowed me to let go of the religious thing. So, by the second half of my senior year in high school my self-esteem and self-concept shot up.

Two factors may be changing attitudes within ethnic families toward homosexuality. One is that the growing visibility and diversity of gay life may be chipping away at the rigid stereotypes preserved in some ethnic communities. Cultural shifts toward more tolerant attitudes are often life-affirming for youths striving to accept their homoerotic attractions without rejecting their family and ethnic communities. Perhaps most important for gay/bisexual youths is the increased liberalization of what is deemed acceptable gender behavior and sexual relations. The second is that the longer the family is in the United States, the more it assimilates into American society and ceases to be bound by traditional religion and culture. This impacts subsequent interpretation of behavior that may not have been acceptable in the "homeland." Native American Indian families may be the exception—assimilation into White culture and a decline of traditional tribal religion may portend an *increase* in homonegativity.

Given the dearth of gay organizations and activities for youths of color as well as their inability to explore and assert their sexuality within the historic and cultural context of their ethnic heritage, many of the interviewed youths found it excruciatingly difficult to create a distinctive ethnic/sexual identity. To be uniquely gay and ethnic was the dream of one Japanese youth.

> Well there's never a mixture of gay culture and Japanese culture. It has forced me to choose one, and I can't put the two together. If I'm Japanese, then I have to marry and have two kids and lead a normal life. If I'm gay, then there is no way I can survive in traditional Asian society outwardly. I can only fuck guys on the side.

However, increasing opportunities to "put the two together" have emerged. Cultural expectations are shifting, easing pressure on ethnic minority youths and allowing them to celebrate their singular sexual/ethnic status. Within the last several years, ethnic communities with various support and political organizations for sexual-minority individuals have begun to form, usually in large urban areas. This development may very well benefit several generations of ethnic/sexual-minority youths.

For the most part, the lives of the ethnic/sexual-minority youths I interviewed did not fit the dire descriptions portrayed in the literature. Their relatively high self-esteem and infrequent endorsement of clinical symptomatology indicate a level of mental health superior to White gay/bisexual youths. Whether this difference is a result of a selection bias (ethnic youths with good mental health are overly willing to participate in research conducted by a White researcher) or truly represents the psychological status of gay/bisexual youths of color cannot be determined by the methods used for this study.

Regardless of ethnicity, the youths resolved their sexual identity at approximately the same age, feeling positive about their sexuality, on average, prior to their twentieth year. What is most clear from the narratives is that ethnic-minority youths reached this point in a *healthier and stronger* state of being than did their White gay/bisexual brothers—for reasons worthy of future investigation.

11.

The Diversity of Gay Youth

Throughout this book developmental continuities and discontinuities, both within a population and among populations of gay/bisexual youths, have been the focus. At the conclusion of each chapter, summaries or "reflections" highlight the ways in which gay/bisexual youths are similar to each other in their developmental trajectories and the ways in which subgroups of these same youths differ. The personal narratives illustrate a third point—the total singularity of each individual life. Some never labeled their sexual attractions apart from also self-identifying as gay (i.e., no time gap existed between the two); some have never had gay sex, others have never had straight sex, and still others have never been involved in a same-sex relationship. All these factors should influence our thinking about and interactions with sexual-minority youths.

Many of the interviewed youths faced comparable developmental milestones, which was a source of continuity, but at disparate times, a source of discontinuity. These developmental milestones were often turning points in a youth's life. They provided evidence that one invariant chain of events occurring at set periods of time did not characterize all youths. Once youths were placed into distinctive subassemblies based on the timing of these turning points, it became clear that not all youths passed the next milestones at the same or in the same sequence.

I willingly concede that the basis for subdividing the youths, articulated in each chapter, reflects my developmental bias. Youths were frequently clustered according to the time period when they experienced a particular developmental milestone (e.g., childhood, adolescence, young adulthood). Other criteria for parceling the youths are readily conceivable and should be considered by other investigators. For example, the ease of the transitions or the emotions that were expressed could be bases for division. Similarly, researchers who are biased toward investigating personal or social characteristics of individuals could assemble the youths based on their degree of masculinity or femininity, level of outness, reported psychological health, geographic location during childhood, social-class status, or parental marital status. For each of these a defensible justification is easily fashionable for considering subpopulations of gay/bisexual youths.

My point, however, would be the same. A singular or normative developmental lifestyle for gay/bisexual youths simply does not, and could not, exist. Those who advocate such a position are usually adherents to a *straight versus gay* psychology. This approach might satisfy those who desire to draw attention to either the "Look, we are just like them!" assimilationists or the "We are different from them!" separatists, but it also results in a misrepresentation of gay/bisexual life. No two lives are identical, nor are two lives irrevocably distinct. Both concepts should be assumed concurrently if we are to ever understand how development among sexual-minority individuals moves from first memories of same-sex attractions to feeling positive about a sexual identity.

In this last chapter I mean to belabor this point. First, another demonstration of intrapopulation diversity and sameness among the gay/bisexual youths is broached, not by focusing on each specific milestone but by examining sequences of milestones across individuals within a life course. Second, gay diversity is placed in historic and cultural context. Despite our contemporary North American tendency to characterize "gays" as a single entity, ample evidence exists in the social sciences and in popular culture to contradict this assumption. This chapter and hence the book closes with final reflections regarding the importance of assuming a differential developmental trajectories approach with sexual-minority youths.

Differential Sequences of Developmental Milestones

Two recent investigations conducted by our research team at Cornell University on gay, lesbian, and bisexual youth have convincingly demonstrated the usefulness of questioning previous conceptualizations of identity development. First, Lisa Diamond revealed that relatively few young lesbian and bisexual women follow the male-oriented "master narrative" of identity development that has been articulated in the social-science literature.[1] Counter to this proposed sequence of events, many of the women she interviewed could not recall having childhood behaviors that researchers have assumed to characterize the development of all sexual minorities. Although these predictors of sexual identity have worked quite well as descriptors of gay male development, many of the women Diamond interviewed defined themselves not on the basis of sexual attractions or behavior (as is usually seen in males) but on affectional and emotional attractions toward women. Subsequently, Eric Dubé demonstrated that while many older White gay men follow the *sex-centric* master narrative described by coming-out models of identity development, younger cohorts of White gay men were less likely to follow this assumed script for gay identification.[2] Rather, many of these post-Stonewall young adults identified themselves as gay or bisexual *before* engaging in same-sex encounters. Identity development among his Latino, Asian American, and African American gay/bisexual youths was a different matter altogether, the trends of which were similar to the pathways described by the ethnic youths in Chapter Ten of this book.

The research of Diamond and Dubé casts doubt on the archetypal developmental ordering of milestones that was previously thought to characterize the gay life course:

> becoming aware of same-sex attractions —›
> labeling these attractions as "homosexual" —›
> having same-sex encounters —›
> having other-sex encounters —›
> labeling self as gay, lesbian, or bisexual —›
> disclosing this information to another —›
> developing a same-sex romantic relationship —›
> disclosing to a family member —›
> developing a positive sense of being gay

This assumed master trajectory sequence fits only two of the interviewed gay/bisexual youths. For example, regarding the timing of first sex with another boy or man, the usual pattern was to have gay sex after becoming aware of same-sex attractions and labeling the attractions as "homosexual" and before labeling self as gay/bisexual, disclosing this status to another, and feeling positive about one's sexual identity. However, 30 percent of the youths labeled their attractions as "homosexual" *only after* having gay sex. Furthermore, one-third of these boys were unaware of their general attractions to men until after they had engaged in sex with another boy. Thus, for nearly one-third of the gay/bisexual youths interviewed, gay sex was a very early event and from it followed all other developmental milestones.

This highly *sexualized trajectory* stands in contrast to that experienced by youths who engaged in gay sex *only after* many other developmental milestones had been reached. Nearly 40 percent of the youths did not engage in gay sex until after they had labeled their sexual identity as gay/bisexual. Thirty percent disclosed to another their sexual status prior to having sex with another male, and 15 percent reported feeling good about their sexual identity in advance of having gay sex.

Other minor sequence alterations, reported by fewer than one-quarter of the interviewed youths, included having sex with girls prior to having sex with boys, having heterosexual sex before labeling attractions as "homosexual," feeling positive about their sexual identity before disclosing it to another person, and entering a romantic relationship with a man only after feeling good about a gay/bisexual identity.

These "irregularities," as well as the many others reported throughout the book, attest to the remarkable developmental diversity that characterizes gay life. This heterogeneity should cause one to pause before attempting to depict *the* gay lifestyle or *the* homosexual. One final example from the youths' narratives illustrates the futility of trying to fit all gay/bisexual men into one configuration. A twenty-three-year-old young adult, although aware since age eight of his same-sex attractions, delayed labeling those attractions "homosexual" for eleven years. At age nineteen he had sex with both males and females but was still not prepared to label himself as gay or bisexual. Within a year, he established a romantic relationship with a man he met while grocery shopping and disclosed the nature of this new romantic interest to his best female friend, with whom he had been romantically involved several years prior. He was not yet ready, however, to label his identity as gay or bisexual, "because it seemed to me that it was the *situation* that was gay rather than me as an individual. It was only really when I could stand up for myself that I could then call myself gay." This occurred three years after the relationship ended, just prior to the interview.

Decisions about sexuality and personal identity often reflect the sometimes radically different experiences of individuals growing up gay in our culture and time. Documenting this diversity as a general construct within sexual-minority populations is an enormous proposition and is thus not comprehensively attempted in this book. I seek merely to capture some of the variability that characterizes the lives of sexual-minority individuals.

Further Evidence for Gay Diversity

Although diversity is the "correct" position to assume regarding issues of sexuality in the 1990s, remarkably few behavioral scientists have explored the diversity of gay, lesbian, and bisexual lives. This may be because sexual-minority individuals are often perceived to be carbon copies of one another's physical attributes, experiences, psychological make-up, sex roles, lifestyles, and spiritual qualities. When their complexity is ignored, sexual-minority individuals are simplified, resulting in shallow, thoughtless stereotypes that mask the intricacies of their lives.

Contemporary research and theory still lag far behind concepts advanced some seventy years ago by sexologists Richard von Krafft-Ebing and Havelock Ellis. They proposed multiple types of male and female homosexuality based on psychic disposition, physical constitution, and sex-role behavior.[3] Twenty years ago researchers Arthur Bell and Martin Weinberg addressed the complexity of similarities and differences observed in their sample of sexual minorities by titling their book, *Homosexualities: A Study of Diversity among Men and Women.*[4] Their data helped refute the myth of a homogeneous bisexual, gay, and lesbian population.

Yet, we have not understood the message. For example, one contemporary, scholarly, singular lens perspective is the scientific obsession with discovering the *one* explanation, either genetic or environmental, for homoeroticism. Despite empirical evidence that strongly suggests that different "causes" of sexual orientation may operate for different individuals,[5] few are pursuing multifarious causes of homosexuality, either within an individual or across individuals. If researchers were so concerned, it might be easier for the general population to accept the possibility that there are multiple types of gay people who have become gay for various and particularistic reasons. For example, prenatal hormones may be etiologically significant in the development of gender-atypical gay individuals, while those who conform to culturally prescribed sex-role behavior may be gay or bisexual because of early psychosocial factors.[6]

Even though the most recent theory of homosexuality, Daryl Bem's "Exotic Becomes Erotic," creatively blends biological and environmental agents, it proposes *one pathway* to homosexuality; this has, not unexpectedly, raised the ire of several researchers of women's issues.[7] In most other theories, becoming lesbian and becoming bisexual are ignored or are assumed to be the same as, the opposite of, or halfway like becoming gay. A broader perspective asserts not merely that gays are born or made "that way," but that a unique blend of biological, psychosocial, and cultural factors shape sexual orientation and that these factors differ across individuals and within subgroups of populations.

Regardless of whether the etiology of sexual orientation is singular or multiple, knowing the precise origins of sexual orientation tells us little about the manifest and internalized aspects of same-sex sexuality in different cultural and historic circumstances and for different sexes, ages, social classes, and ethnic groups. Individuals respond differently to their social and physical environments, and this complex interaction was described by researchers Bruce Compas and colleagues in the following way:

> Adolescents evoke differential reactions from the environment as a result of their physical and behavioral characteristics, and environments contribute to individual development through the feedback that they provide to adolescents. The quality of this feedback is dependent on the degree of fit or match between the characteristics of the individual and the expectations, values, and preferences of the social environment. (p. 270)[8]

The vast diversity that is possible among individuals in their timing and sequencing of developmental milestones is undeniable. If this diversity is ignored, as it usually is, misleading, simplistic straight-versus-gay paradigms become viable, but ultimately incorrectly adopted. The acknowledgement, however, that sexual minorities are diverse both in etiology and manifestation may frighten those who wish to characterize gay people by predictable myths and stereotypes.

Especially distorted by these views is an understanding of lesbians and bisexual women. Developmental models that predominantly rely on data collected from gay males to generalize to women falsify differences by erasing them. Lisa Diamond contends in her review of the literature on lesbian and bisexual development, "Women are more likely than men to experience non-exclusive sexual and romantic attractions, to experience changes in attractions and behavior, and to ascribe a role for circumstance and choice in their same-sex orientation" (p. 1). Diamond concludes, using the argument of Laura Brown, "Psychologists must develop models focusing on lesbians and bisexuals *as women* with distinctly female developmental and socialization experiences rather than viewing them as variants of gay men" (p. 3).[9] Otherwise, not only are the experiences of women neglected but the diversity within populations of lesbian and bisexual women—especially those who do not follow the prescribed developmental hurdles in a temporal sequence of recognition, acceptance, and disclosure of same-sex attractions and identity—is relegated to invisibility.

Sociologist Kristin Esterberg, an alumnus of the Cornell research team, documents this diversity in the construction of identity within a population of lesbians and bisexual women. She notes that, "People talk about lesbian identity as if its meaning were transparent and as if it were unvarying across persons, time, and space" (p. 58).[10] In an upstate New York lesbian community, she identified three varieties of identity formation:

> One account emphasizes the importance of being out and its political implications; a second emphasizes social and emotional relationships with other women; and a third emphasizes bisexuality and an openness toward relationships with men. (p. 78)

Notably absent from the women's stories was a focus on sexual encounters—the variable most often used by conservative politicians to justify including lesbians and bisexual women with gay and bisexual men for exclusion from mainstream culture.

Similarly, psychologist and author April Martin observes that the realities of lesbian lives are not easily cataloged. This multiplicity was illustrated in her article for *The Harvard Gay and Lesbian Review*.

> Among self-designated lesbians, there are some who have sex occasionally or even exclusively with men, some who have deep, committed love relationships with men, some whose primary buddies and comrades are men. . . . Some who want little to do with men, who feel most emotionally safe and comfortable with women, who live in the company of women and choose a woman as their most intimate and committed

relationship. . . . Women who feel strongly erotically attracted to women and always have. Their interest in women feels primarily like an interest in getting them into bed. . . . Other self-designated lesbians say they have chosen a woman partner simply because they happened to fall in love with a particular person, and that person's gender was an incidental aspect of their choice. . . . Some women say their primary reason for exclusive involvement with women has to do with the strong feminist feelings they have, and their feeling that relationships with men contain unacceptable power inequities. Yet there are strong and vocal feminists who choose male partners. . . . Some women who are attracted to women do not identify themselves as lesbians because they feel that their other identities, for example memberships in ethnic or racial minorities, take precedence over their sexuality.

Martin notes that this heterogeneity also characterizes the lives of many heterosexual women.[11]

Debate regarding diversity also occurs within sexual-minority communities, often fracturing communities across political lines. For example, despite the public image that nearly all lesbians, gays, and bisexuals are liberal or leftist, nearly one-third of gay people are "pro-life"—some would say "anti-choice"—and nearly the same number did not vote for Bill Clinton in 1992 or 1996.[12] Some community members would probably favor expulsion of such individuals and political organizations (e.g., the Log Cabin Republicans) from the "queer" umbrella.

The most visible display of disparities within gay communities occurs during annual gay pride parades and festivals. Debate often centers on such questions as: Should restrictions be placed on particular community members or subgroups who deviate too far from the message, dress, and behavior intended by pride organizers? Should a show of unity be presented to the straight world? Community members are seldom of one mind regarding the purpose or form of their pride, or even that all share a single attribute of which they are proud. For example, the 1996 Boston Pride Parade became an intense issue in the mainstream media. Local newspapers reported women "rolling about topless in a foreplay frolic atop a mattress" on a float and a nude man atop stilts. Most divisive, according to one writer, were the fault lines these incidents created within the gay community— damage difficult to mend.[13] While conservative elements in the community emphasized the isolated nature of the offending events, the large percentage of marchers who did dress for the occasion, and the unauthorized status of the Lesbian Avengers float, activist elements of the community called the sexual explicitness a legitimate, confrontational, in-your-face response to the increasingly regulated and nondescript nature of the Boston Pride Parade.

In other dominions such diversity has had less of a polarizing and more of a liberating effect. For example, with the recent increase in films by and about lesbians, bisexuals, and gays, not every film needs to show only the strong, positive, "normal" aspects of gay communities. At the San Francisco Lesbian and Gay Film Festival, director Michael Lumpkins noted this change after observing films such as "I Shot Andy Warhol" and "Butterfly Kiss." No longer is it necessary that all lesbians be portrayed as the "nice girl next door."

> Ten, fifteen years ago, with so few films to make up a festival program, it would be so problematic to show those films. This year that's not a problem, because there's so much diverse work, there's something for everyone. One film does not have to represent everything to everyone. For a long time there was that burden. It's nice that we've gotten away from that.[14]

In matters that directly affect gay youths, considerable controversy reigns in several domains. One is in terms of what it means to be gay. Although youths seldom question the direction of their attractions, they more often are perplexed as to what their desires mean. This disorientation was given voice in the November 1996 issue of *Esquire*. In his "The Post-Gay Man" article, Jonathan Van Meter recounts his youthful uncertainty and that of his male friends.

> I did not walk around high school knowing that I was gay and trying not to be. I *just didn't know*. When I was teased or called a faggot or a sissy, it humiliated and wounded me, but it also made me wonder: What do other people see that I don't? (Or, as I now like to say, "Why is it that everybody knew I was gay before I did?") (p. 132)[15]

He had sex with Richard until "he cheated on me with another man" (p. 88); Richard is now married and has two children. Other friends included Christian, who had an eight-month relationship with Van Meter but also slept with women. Christian eventually left him for a woman and currently describes himself as "straight with a shade of gay" (p. 89). Alan dated the same girl throughout junior and senior high school, part of the "perfect couple." Allegedly he has since been caught in the shower with a man, is a born-again Christian, and has a wife and children. Matt lost his girlfriend to another woman and now describes himself as gay. Daron is attracted to lesbians and defines himself as a heterosexual who likes boyish women.

How to reconcile these sexual behaviors, romances, attractions, gender-related behaviors, identifications, and fantasies would challenge even the most sexually sophisticated. Although Van Meter wonders if the term *blends*, for "people whose sexual and gender identities appear to change from day to day, and yet they seem completely oblivious to that fact" (p. 132), is an apt designation for many men and women today, the term may more characterize his friends and lovers than it does the gay/bisexual youths who were interviewed for this book. Blends, ambivalent fags, and post-gays give voice, however, to a decade-long struggle confronting many modern youths trying to piece together the complexities of their fantasy worlds, the secrecies of their attractions, and the concreteness of their sexual behaviors with the realities of social prohibitions and prescriptions.

One of the societal realities that many sexual-minority youths encounter is the presentation of how to be gay. For example, the predominant portrait of gay men and women—one that has direct impact on youths—is that they are by definition gender atypical in their behavioral and personality characteristics. The research of Gabriel Phillips and Ray Over documents a different perspective. Although on a group level various sexual orientations can be distinguished based on memories of childhood preference for dolls or sports, physical appearance as sissy or butch, and desire to grow up to be like mother or father, considerable diversity also characterizes gay populations. For example, nearly one-third of the gay men were "indistinguishable from the heterosexual men in terms of their profile of recalled childhood experiences.... There appear many paths to the development of an adult homosexual orientation" (pp. 556–557). The same conclusion was reached after examining their data on women: "Although there was, overall, an association between sexual orientations and adult and recalled childhood experiences, there was diversity in the ratings given by women in each group, and some overlap in profiles of recalled childhood experiences between groups" (p. 17).[16]

Findings such as these emphasize diversity and serve as a warning against reifying sexual minorities into types. This point is one that actor Dan Butler feels must be conveyed within gay communities: "There are so many different camps about what being gay means. The danger comes when each one is so rigid that it sees itself as the true picture."[17] Although most gay adults eventually discover multiple ways to be gay, the need for articulating the diversity inherent among gay people is glaringly magnified when the experiences of youths are considered. During this time when decisions are frequently made regarding whether to cross the line and irrevocably declare a nonheterosexual identity, a multitude of images is necessary. If options are limited, if a male adolescent comes to believe that to be gay means that he must be sexually active and promiscuous, act effeminate or be a clone of masculinity, live in New York or San Francisco, move in and out of relationships on a weekly basis, adore Broadway musicals and desire to sing in them, stop having sex with girls, and read only the Arts and Leisure and never the Sports sections of the Sunday *New York Times*, then it is easier for him to say, "I don't fit that, so I must not be gay." However youths eventually complete the puzzles of their lives, few put them together in an identical fashion. This is the essence of the diversity documented in our culture and the lives of the interviewed gay and bisexual youths.

Final Reflections

The study of lesbian, gay, and bisexual adolescence has finally come of age, nearly three decades after data were first collected on a sample of gay and bisexual male youths, and one decade after researchers and clinicians Andrew Boxer and Bertram Cohler proposed a research agenda for future investigations of sexual-minority youths.[18] Their exhortation to investigate developmental continuities and discontinuities, especially issues pertaining to critical developmental transition points such as identity formation and the coming-out process, defines the major objectives of the project described in this book.

The developmental diversity alluded to by Boxer and Cohler were readily apparent in the lives of the interviewed youth. It was both exhilarating and arduous to grow up gay or bisexual during the 1980s and 1990s. Some youths appreciated the unique opportunities afforded them by coming of age in a liberal family, an accepting school/community, and a society that had become increasingly tolerant and accepting. Others, however, recalled an abusive family, peers who would not stop harassing them, and societal institutions, such as religion, that were the bane of their existence.

Although focusing on the coping mechanisms that gay/bisexual youths use during their developmental years was not an expressed aspiration of the current investigation, the youths volunteered a variety of strategies that they used. For some, resiliency was notable in their love of self and desire to survive and not succumb to the hatred and bigotry of others; for others, a loving, accepting family or several special friends facilitated resilience. Numerous youths found solace in gay communities, among gay and straight friends, or in a gay culture that became more accessible to them as they grew older. Their vulnerabilities, however, were real, sufficiently tangible that several reported attempting suicide and others had strong suicidal ideation. But these appeared to be relatively rare, the exceptions rather than the norm.

The interviewed youths were usually resilient, but perhaps no more or less than the vast majority of adolescents trying to survive in today's world. They too had to negotiate separation and individuation issues with parents, decide which peers with whom to associate, integrate current conceptions of the world with that presented by parents, and evolve tentative values and beliefs. Although most adolescents must mediate these tasks, the accomplishments of the gay/bisexual youths are noteworthy because they were likely intensified by the youths' sexual orientation or may have necessitated different negotiation strategies. But it is wrong to necessarily assume that because of their gayness they had a more difficult life. Some did, but others felt that their lives had been animated and empassioned by their sexuality. Because of their minority status many felt unique, their own person; they reveled in the secret life they had.

By listening to the youths it becomes readily apparent that few conceived of their lives as following a linear progression from one developmental milestone to the next. Based on statistical averages a series of developmental milestones was discerned, a normative sequence based merely on the mean age that particular landmarks were reached. Within this framework the youths reported deviations and brandished the multidirectionalities of their life course. For example, although most youths had sex with a male prior to labeling themselves as gay or bisexual, before beginning a relationship, and before evolving a positive sexual identity, many exceptions emerged. Virgins would be the most obvious. Some youths decided that they did not need sex to define their sexual identity and that they did not want to have sex with another male until they were in a romantic, committed relationship. A positive gay/bisexual identity could come before sex, after sex, before a relationship, without a relationship, or concurrently with labeling a sexual identity. Some felt that because of their solid sense of self-worth they were able to think positively about their sexual identity; others professed that their high self-esteem was the result of resolving their gay identity in a positive direction. Heterosexual sex could be desired because a youth wanted to test his sexual identity—"Am I really gay?" Other youths had sex with girls after they self-identified as gay or bisexual; it was a novel, fun thing to do or perhaps an expression of their self-defined rebel status.

To assess developmental trajectories most accurately prospective, long-term longitudinal studies on gay youths are needed. The complications inherent in constructing and carrying out such a project are legendary. Far more feasible are short-term longitudinal studies. Several of these are currently being conducted by the Cornell team of sexual-minority investigators. For example, Lisa Diamond is re-interviewing her sample of one hundred women two years after she initially assessed their sexual-identity development. Many of these women initially reported being in transition regarding their sexual self-definition; perhaps over the past two years they will have gained greater clarity. Diamond will assess and predict the fluidity of women's sexuality over time. Eric Dubé is following his sample of gay/bisexual youths to assess their romantic relationships and levels of identity/intimacy over the next two to three years. Dubé will then be able to predict from data previously collected the evolution of romantic and identity statuses.

Missing from the narratives and the interpretations reported in this book are the perspectives of those with whom the gay/bisexual youths interacted. For example, did a female sex partner know or suspect her male partner's sexual status before, during, or after their encounter? Why was she so willing to initiate sex with a gay boy? How did she interpret her male partner's low motivation for sex? If she strongly suspected that he was gay (and sometimes she knew this to be the case), why have sex? How did these sexual encounters affect her self-image and self-esteem? Many of these same questions should be posed to the first male sex part-ners—many of whom were thought to be heterosexual. A complete story can only be achieved if all principals tell their version of the events. This is particularly needed when considering the disclosure of youths to their parents; the two sources may vary quite diametrically in their accounts of the disclosure moment and the aftermath.[19]

The narratives of the interviewed adolescents and young adults cast serious doubt on many of the traditional images of gay youth and their development that have been portrayed in coming-out models. These paradigms were concocted years ago primarily with samples of older White gay men; they appear to fit poorly with the experiences of lesbians, bisexual men and women, questioning individu-als, ethnic/sexual-minority youths, and younger cohorts of gay White men.

Perhaps twenty-four-year-old poet and writer Robin Bernstein was most elo-quent in her objections to previous portrayals of gay youths. She rebels against images of gay youths that have been depicted in social-science research, public policies, and the media.

> I am part of a new generation of lesbians, gay men, and bisexuals. We come out in col-lege, high school, and even junior high. We're savvy and assertive. We know who we are, and even if we're not sure, we know our options. We know we're not sick. We know we're not "the only one." We don't worry about going to hell. We worry about getting laid and joining a community. (p. 23)[20]

Many of the interviewed gay and bisexual youths would agree with her.

My position is that as researchers, clinicians, educators, and parents we have been too raptured with characteristics thought to distinguish "homosexual" from "heterosexual" youths and too lax in pursuing variations in origins, developmen-tal processes, and outcomes within diverse gay, lesbian, and bisexual adolescent populations. Thus, the task of developmental research is not only to investigate general characteristics of sexual-minority individuals but also to explore similar-ities and differences *throughout* their life course.

Indeed, an emphasis on diversity among sexual-minority individuals and com-munities has become a more common and acceptable perspective in popular cul-ture during the last several years. This may have been an inevitable consequence of the increasing numbers of individuals who have allowed themselves to be publicly identified as gay, lesbian, or bisexual. The "love that dare not speak its name" now has many; the silence has been broken with a chorus that, for better or worse, seldom harmonizes.

Scientific and clinical inquiry into the lives of gay youths, however, remains almost universally focused on one aspect of their lives—the problems they face, including their suicides, substance abuse, prostitution, and diseases.[21] The need to broaden our inquiry into the promises as well as the problems of gay youths was a theme with which I closed my 1990 book[22] and reflects the ongoing need to challenge the erroneous belief that one cannot possibly be "young, gay, and proud." Viewing all sexual-minority youths as overwhelmed or defeated with problems in living diminishes the reality that such individuals are a minority of gay youths. Indeed, many youths with same-sex attractions have unique skills that allow them to cope and even thrive in a culture that seldom recognizes them and actively attempts to suppress them. To deny their diversity and resiliency is, in short, to silence gay, bisexual, and lesbian youths.

Notes

1. Personal Stories and Sexuality

1. The particular lives of lesbian and bisexual female youths are not included here but are being collected, interpreted, and reported by Lisa Diamond, a colleague at Cornell University. Her longitudinal study is based on one hundred women between the ages of sixteen and twenty-three years.
2. See books by G. Herdt (Ed.) (1989), *Gay and Lesbian Youth* (New York: Harrington Park Press); G. Herdt and A. Boxer (1993), *Children of Horizons: How Gay and Lesbian Teens Are Leading a New Way Out of the Closet* (Boston: Beacon Press); R. C. Savin-Williams (1990), *Gay and Lesbian Youth: Expressions of Identity* (New York: Hemisphere); and J. T. Sears (1991), *Growing Up Gay in the South: Race, Gender, and Journeys of the Spirit* (New York: Harrington Park Press).
3. See discussion of the fluidity of some women's sexual orientation in L. Brown (1995), "Lesbian Identities: Concepts and Issues," in A. R. D'Augelli and C. J. Patterson (Eds.), *Lesbian, Gay, and Bisexual Identities over the Lifespan*, pp. 3–23 (New York: Oxford University Press); C. Golden (1996), "What's in a Name? Sexual Self-Identification among Women," in R. C. Savin-Williams and K. M. Cohen (Eds.), *The Lives of Lesbians, Gays, and Bisexuals: Children to Adults*, pp. 229–249 (Fort Worth, TX: Harcourt Brace); C. Kitzinger (1987), *The Social Construction of Lesbianism* (London: Sage); C. Kitzinger and S. Wilkinson (1995), "Transitions From Heterosexuality to Lesbianism: The Discursive Production of Lesbian Identities," *Developmental Psychology, 31,* 95–104; and P. Rust (1992), "The Politics of Sexual Identity: Sexual Attraction and Behavior among Lesbian and Bisexual Women," *Social Problems, 39,* 366–386 and (1993), "Coming Out in the Age of Social Constructionism: Sexual Identity Formation among Lesbians and Bisexual Women," *Gender and Society, 7,* 50–77.
4. V. Cass (1984), "Homosexual Identity: A Concept in Need of a Definition," *Journal of Homosexuality, 9,* 105–126. See also, J. Sophie (1985/1986), "A Critical Examination of Stage Theories of Lesbian Identity Development," *Journal of Homosexuality, 12.* 39–51.

5. Theoretical models have included psychoanalytic, cognitive, symbolic-interaction, and social learning perspectives. For examples of coming-out models see two articles by V. Cass (1979), "Homosexual Identity Formation: A Theoretical Model," *Journal of Homosexuality, 4,* 219–235, and (1984), "Homosexual Identity: A Concept in Need of a Definition," *Journal of Homosexuality, 9,* 105–126; E. Coleman (1981/1982), Developmental Stages of the Coming Out Process," *Journal of Homosexuality, 7,* 31–43; K. Plummer (1975), *Sexual Stigma: An Interactionist Account* (Boston: Routledge & Kegan Paul); and two articles by R. R. Troiden (1979), "Becoming Homosexual: A Model of Gay Identity Acquisition," *Psychiatry, 42,* 362–373 and (1989), "The Formation of Homosexual Identities," *Journal of Homosexuality, 17,* 43–73. Note the omission of bisexual development.

6. The narratives are usually a very close approximation of the youths' words. My own limitations of note-taking often prevented exact quoting. I also took the liberty of adding grammatical details, punctuation, and transitional phrases to aid understanding of the narrations.

7. M. Rutter (1992), "Adolescence as a Transition Period: Continuities and Discontinuities in Conduct Disorder," *Journal of Adolescent Health, 13,* 451–460. See also his 1989 article, "Pathways from Childhood to Adult Life," *Journal of Child Psychology and Psychiatry, 30,* 23–51.

8. Alyson Publications has produced such outstanding contributions as A. Heron's (1983) *One Teenager in Ten* and (1994) *Two Teenagers in Twenty* and W. Curtis's (1988) *Revelations: A Collection of Gay Male Coming Out Stories.* See also J. Penelope and S. J. Wolfe (Eds.) (1989), *The Original Coming Out Stories: Expanded Edition* (Freedom, CA: Crossing Press).

9. V. Cass (1979), "Homosexual Identity Formation: A Theoretical Model," *Journal of Homosexuality, 4,* 219–235.

10. J. H. McConnell (1994) discusses additional limitations and uses of these stage models in "Lesbian and Gay Male Identities as Paradigms," in S. L. Archer (Ed.), *Interventions for Adolescent Identity Development,* pp. 103–118 (Thousand Oaks, CA: Sage). He also identifies the homophobic and heterosexist assumptions on which the stage models are often based.

11. See, respectively, chapters by P. Davies (1992), "The Role of Disclosure in Coming Out among Gay Men," in K. Plummer (Ed.), *Modern Homosexualities: Fragments of Lesbian and Gay Experience,* pp. 75–83 (London: Routledge) and B. Ponse (1980), "Lesbians and Their Worlds," in J. Marmor (Ed.), *Homosexual Behavior: A Modern Reappraisal,* pp. 157–175 (New York: Basic Books).

12. See endnote 7.

13. L. Steinberg (1995), "Commentary: On Developmental Pathways and Social Contexts in Adolescence," in L. J. Crockett and A. C. Crouter (Eds.), *Pathways through Adolescence: Individual Development in Relation to Social Contexts,* pp. 245–253 (Mahwah, NJ: Lawrence Erlbaum).

14. Researcher Lisa Crockett notes that conceptions of development are inherent in the terms that are used. "Trajectory" implies an organismic, active role for the adolescent and "that development follows a fairly predictable course." As a concept, "pathway" is more mechanistic, connoting a "course that is already laid out, which the individual simply follows," and giving more power to external than internal forces (p. 75). See

her commentary (1995), "Developmental Paths in Adolescence: Commentary," in L. J. Crockett and A. C. Crouter (Eds.), *Pathways through Adolescence: Individual Development in Relation to Social Contexts*, pp. 75–84 (Mahwah, NJ: Lawrence Erlbaum).

15. Two frequently cited early studies, both of which brought keen awareness concerning the unique issues of gay/bisexual youths, are T. Roesler and R. Deisher (1972), "Youthful Male Homosexuality," *Journal of the American Medical Association, 219,* 1018–1023, and G. Remafedi's two 1987 articles, "Male Homosexuality: The Adolescent's Perspective," and "Adolescent Homosexuality: Psychosocial and Medical Implications," *Pediatrics, 79,* 326–330 and 331–337.

16. See discussion of this issue in A. Boxer and B. Cohler (1989), "The Life Course of Gay and Lesbian Youth: An Immodest Proposal for the Study of Lives," *Journal of Homosexuality, 17,* 317–355.

17. R. L. Sell and C. Petrulio (1996), "Sampling Homosexuals, Bisexuals, Gays, and Lesbians for Public Health Research: A Review of the Literature from 1990 to 1992," *Journal of Homosexuality, 30,* 31–47.

18. R. C. Savin-Williams (1990), *Gay and Lesbian Youth: Expressions of Identity* (New York: Hemisphere).

19. For examples, see R. C. Kessler and E. Wethington (1991), "The Reliability of Life Event Reports in a Community Survey," *Psychological Medicine, 21,* 723–738, and M. Ross (1984), "Relation of Implicit Theories to the Construction of Personal Histories," *Psychological Review, 96,* 341–357.

20. The first study was intended as an in-depth exploration of the unique role that sexual *behavior* during childhood and adolescence plays in forming a gay/bisexual identity during young adulthood. It was originally planned in conjunction with a female colleague's parallel study of lesbian/bisexual youths. We believed that youths would feel most comfortable with a same-sex interviewer. However, due to the pressures of tenure and her changing research interests, my colleague was not able to undertake the female equivalent study.

Of interest were the sexual experiences that youths had prior to, during, and after they became aware of and labeled their sexual identity. The youths heard about the study through classroom lectures and from those who had previously volunteered for the study. I conducted face-to-face interviews using a semistructured script. Tape recorders were considered too intrusive for the material requested, so I took elaborate notes. The youths were sensitive to my method and were careful to pause so that I could catch up when I fell behind. Their many long pauses and hesitations also made it easy to take notes, which were transcribed onto tape and later typed and coded. Confidentiality was assured, and consent for participation—consistent with the Cornell Human Subjects Committee—was secured.

The interview began with questions about sexual outlets and frequency of orgasms during the junior and senior high-school years, especially regarding the ways in which orgasms were achieved: heterosexual contact, homosexual contact, masturbation, wet dream, and bestiality. Circumstances of first orgasm and first infatuation were probed. Youths recounted their personal history of how they experienced their sexual identity during childhood and adolescence.

After completion of the study described above, a second sample was recruited. A larger number of youths were interviewed and a concerted effort was made to broaden the ethnic composition of the sample and the content of the interview in order to more systematically cover the identification process from first memory to final positive recognition of a gay/bisexual identity. Thus, the focus was removed from sexual activities per se, although such questions remained a central tenet of the interview.

Announcements were made in appropriate classes at Cornell University and other local colleges, posters and flyers were posted on campus bulletin boards and relevant public establishments (local bar, bookstore, cafe). Advertisements appeared in local gay newsletters and Internet list-servers. Many of the youths reported that previous interviewees had told them about the research project. Procedures followed those described in the first sample.

In conjunction with Katherine Wright, a pediatrician, a questionnaire was given to a third sample of sexual-minority youths, those attending Affirmations, a gay, lesbian, and bisexual support group in a Detroit suburb. The purpose of the study was to assess various risk factors for HIV infection, suicide, drug usage, and poor mental health. Given the research design of the study—anonymous questionnaires—none of the narratives reported in this book was elicited from these Detroit youths. The questionnaire did provide data, however, on age of first awareness; first gay and heterosexual sex; and disclosure to mother, father, and sibling.

All questionnaires and interview protocols used in these studies are available on request from the author.

21. Although the stories in this book are about growing up gay or bisexual, heterosexuals should be interested in topics pursued in the interviews. Issues of concern to homoerotically inclined individuals may overlap those of straight youths. Indeed, during oral presentations of the life histories at conferences or in classes, I have been struck by the degree to which heterosexual members of the audience quiz me regarding the data presented and whether comparable data exist for heterosexual children and adolescents. They do not.

22. Recent discussions of these issues can be found in articles by Y. B. Chung and M. Katayama (1996), "Assessment of Sexual Orientation in Lesbian/Gay/Bisexual Studies," *Journal of Homosexuality, 30*, 49–62 and R. L. Sell and C. Petrulio (1996), "Sampling Homosexuals, Bisexuals, Gays, and Lesbians for Public Health Research: A Review of the Literature from 1990 to 1992," *Journal of Homosexuality, 30*, 31–47.

23. Delivered at Cornell University, Ithaca, NY, February, 9, 1995.

24. References for the citations in Table 1.3 are as follows: H. Kooden., S. Morin, D. Riddle, M. Rogers, B. Sang, and F. Strassburger (1979), *Removing the Stigma. Final Report. Task Force on the Status of Lesbian and Gay Male Psychologists* (Washington, DC: American Psychological Association); R. R. Troiden (1979), "Becoming Homosexual: A Model of Gay Identity Acquisition," *Psychiatry, 42*, 362–373; G. J. McDonald (1982), "Individual Differences in the Coming Out Process for Gay Men: Implications for Theoretical Models," *Journal of Homosexuality, 8*, 47–60; R. A. Rodriguez (1988), "Significant Events in Gay Identity Development: Gay Men in Utah" (Paper presented at the Ninety-Sixth Annual Convention of the American Psychological Association, Atlanta, GA); A. R. D'Augelli (1991), "Gay Men in College: Identity Processes and Adaptations," *Journal of College Student Development, 32*, 140–146; G. Herdt and A. Boxer (1993), *Children of Horizons: How Gay and Lesbian Teens Are*

Leading a New Way Out of the Closet (Boston: Beacon); A. R. D'Augelli and S. L. Hershberger (1993), "Lesbian, Gay, and Bisexual Youth in Community Settings: Personal Challenges and Mental Health Problems," *American Journal of Community Psychology*, *21*, 421–448; and M. Rosario, H. F. L. Meyer-Bahlburg, J. Hunter, T. M. Exner, M. Gwadz, and A. M. Keller (1996), "Psychosexual Development of Lesbian, Gay, and Bisexual Youths: Sexual Activities, Sexual Orientation, and Sexual Identity" (Paper presented at the Second International Conference on the Biopsychosocial Aspects of HIV Infection, Brighton, United Kingdom).

2. Childhood: Memories of Same-Sex Attractions

1. See early account in A. P. Bell, M. S. Weinberg, and S. K. Hammersmith (1981), *Sexual Preference: Its Development in Men and Women* (Bloomington, IN: Indiana University Press). For data on gay youths see G. Herdt and A. Boxer (1993), *Children of Horizons: How Gay and Lesbian Teens Are Leading a New Way Out of the Closet* (Boston: Beacon) and R. C. Savin-Williams (1990), *Gay and Lesbian Youth: Expressions of Identity* (New York: Hemisphere).

2. J. Sophie presents a synthesis of coming-out models in her 1985/1986 article, "A Critical Examination of Stage Theories of Lesbian Identity Development," *Journal of Homosexuality*, *12*, 39–51.

3. Revised in his 1989 article, R. R. Troiden, "The Formation of Homosexual Identities," *Journal of Homosexuality*, *17*, 43–73. Additional empirical evidence is available in references in endnote 1 and B. S. Newman and P. G. Muzzonigro (1993), "The Effects of Traditional Family Values on the Coming Out Process of Gay Male Adolescents," *Adolescence*, *28*, 213–226, and S. K. Telljohann and J. P. Price (1993), "A Qualitative Examination of Adolescent Homosexuals' Life Experiences: Ramifications for Secondary School Personnel," *Journal of Homosexuality*, *26*, 41–56.

4. For a comprehensive review of this literature see J. M. Bailey and K. J. Zucker (1995), "Childhood Sex-Typed Behavior and Sexual Orientation: A Conceptual Analysis and Quantitative Review," *Developmental Psychology*, *31*, 43–55.

5. For a review of studies using these measures, see endnote 4 and J. M. Bailey (1996), "Gender Identity," in R. C. Savin-Williams and K. M. Cohen (Eds.), *The Lives of Lesbians, Gays, and Bisexuals: Children to Adults*, pp. 71–93 (Fort Worth, TX: Harcourt Brace); R. Green (1987), *The "Sissy Boy Syndrome" and the Development of Homosexuality* (New Haven, CT: Yale University Press); G. Phillips and R. Over (1992), "Adult Sexual Orientation in Relation to Memories of Childhood Gender Conforming and Gender Nonconforming Behaviors," *Archives of Sexual Behavior*, *21*, 543–558; and B. Zuger (1984), "Early Effeminate Behavior in Boys: Outcome and Significance for Homosexuality," *Journal of Nervous and Mental Disease*, *172*, 90–97.

6. From R. A. Isay (1989), *Being Homosexual: Gay Men and Their Development* (New York: Farrar Straus Grove).

7. See sources in endnotes 1 and 4.

8. Experimental evidence is supplied in K. J. Zucker, D. N. Wilson-Smith, J. A. Kurita, and A. Stern (1995), "Children's Appraisals of Sex-Typed Behavior in their Peers," *Sex Roles*, *33*, 703–725.

9. See references in endnotes 4 and 5.

3. Labeling Feelings and Attractions

1. It is not unusual, however, especially among women, for the resolution of self-labeling to be fluid and to undergo reevaluation during the life course. For discussion, see C. Golden (1996), "What's in a Name? Sexual Self-Identification among Women," in R. C. Savin-Williams and K. M. Cohen (Eds.), *The Lives of Lesbians, Gays, and Bisexuals: Children to Adults*, pp. 229–249 (Fort Worth, TX: Harcourt Brace); C. Golden (1987), "Diversity and Variability in Women's Sexual Identities," in Boston Lesbian Psychologies Collective (Eds.), *Lesbian Psychologies: Explorations and Challenges*, pp. 19–34 (Urbana, IL: University of Illinois Press); P. Rust (1993), "'Coming Out' in the Age of Social Constructionism: Sexual Identity Formation among Lesbian and Bisexual Women," *Gender and Society*, 7, 50–77; P. Rust (1992), "The Politics of Sexual Identity: Sexual Attraction and Behavior among Lesbian and Bisexual Women," *Social Problems*, 39, 366–386; and L. M. Diamond's master's thesis (1996), "Attraction and Identity: Evidence for Sexual Fluidity among Young Lesbian, Bisexual, and Heterosexual Women," Cornell University, Ithaca, NY.
2. K. Painter (June 5, 1996), "The Epidemic's Legacy of Change," *USA Today* (pp. 1D & 2D).
3. A comprehensive discussion of these issues is available in K. M. Cohen and R. C. Savin-Williams (1996), "Developmental Perspectives on Coming Out to Self and Others," in R. C. Savin-Williams and K. M. Cohen (Eds.), *The Lives of Lesbians, Gays, and Bisexuals: Children to Adults*, pp. 113–151 (Fort Worth, TX: Harcourt Brace).
4. As told by A. Heron (1983), *One Teenager in Ten*, p. 104 (Boston: Alyson).
5. See his 1993 book, *The Sexual Brain*, p. 119 (Cambridge, MA: MIT Press).
6. See E. Sagarin and R. J. Kelly (1980), "Sexual Deviance and Labelling Perspectives," in W. R. Gove (Ed.), *The Labelling of Deviance: Evaluating a Perspective* (Beverly Hills, CA: Sage).

4. First Gay Sex

1. Published in 1948 by Appleton-Century-Crofts (New York).
2. J. Spada (1979), *The Spada Report: The Newest Survey of Gay Male Sexuality* (New York: New American Library).
3. For a review of coming out and first sexual experiences see R. C. Savin-Williams (1990), *Gay and Lesbian Youth: Expressions of Identity* (New York: Hemisphere).
4. Recently, a popular book on first same-sex experiences among gay men from various time periods has appeared, J. Hard (Ed.) (1995), *My First Time: Gay Men Describe Their First Same-Sex Experience* (Los Angeles: Alyson). These coming-out type stories are presented without commentary.
5. The earliest and best research that found this strong relationship was A. P. Bell, M. S. Weinberg, and S. K. Hammersmith (1981), *Sexual Preference: Its Development in Men and Women* (Bloomington, IN: Indiana University Press).
6. This is, however, a problematic assertion. All statistics on first sex with girls that I could find defined it as first *vaginal intercourse* with a girl. For example, E. O. Laumann, J. H. Gagnon, R. T. Michael, and S. Michaels (1994) in their book, *The Social Organization of Sexuality: Sexual Practices in the United States* (Chicago: The University of Chicago Press), reported that the 50 percent mark for first intercourse was

reached at 16.9 years for White, 16.0 years for Hispanic, and 14.8 years for Black males. It is highly likely, however, that before vaginal intercourse many heterosexual male adolescents experience other forms of genital contact with girls. These statistics would be more comparable to data elicited from the interviewed gay/bisexual youths.

7. Virginity figures for gay youths are available in references for Table 1.3. For heterosexual youths, see E. O. Laumann, J. H. Gagnon, R. T. Michael, and S. Michaels (1994), *The Social Organization of Sexuality: Sexual Practices in the United States* (Chicago: The University of Chicago Press).

5. First Heterosexual Sex

1. The three studies are G. Herdt and A. Boxer (1993), *Children of Horizons: How Gay and Lesbian Teens Are Leading a New Way Out of the Closet* (Boston: Beacon); A. R. D'Augelli and S. L. Hershberger (1993), "Lesbian, Gay, and Bisexual Youth in Community Settings: Personal Challenges and Mental Health Problems," *American Journal of Community Psychology, 21,* 421–448; and M. Rosario, H. F. L. Meyer-Bahlburg, J. Hunter, T. M. Exner, M. Gwadz, and A. M. Keller (1994), *Psychosexual Development of Lesbian, Gay, and Bisexual Youths: Sexual Activities, Sexual Orientation, and Sexual Identity* (paper presented at the Second International Conference on the Biopsychosocial Aspects of HIV Infection (Brighton, United Kingdom).

2. G. Herdt and A. Boxer (1993), *Children of Horizons: How Gay and Lesbian Teens are Leading a New Way Out of the Closet* (Boston: Beacon).

3. E. O. Laumann, J. H. Gagnon, R. T. Michael, and S. Michaels (1994), *The Social Organization of Sexuality: Sexual Practices in the United States* (Chicago: The University of Chicago Press).

4. One study noted that the primary reason (51 percent) for engaging in first vaginal intercourse was for curiosity or because the boy was "ready." Other reasons given included affection for female partner (25 percent), physical pleasure (12 percent), wedding night (7 percent), peer pressure (4 percent), and under the influence of alcohol/drugs (1 percent). Nearly 40 percent of the boys knew their partner very well but were not in love; 31 percent were in love. Twelve percent knew her, but not very well; in 10 percent of the cases she was a spouse. Another 5 percent had just met the girl; 3 percent paid for the opportunity; and 1 percent reported that the girl was a stranger. See E. O. Laumann, J. H. Gagnon, R. T. Michael, and S. Michaels (1994), *The Social Organization of Sexuality: Sexual Practices in the United States* (Chicago: The University of Chicago Press).

6. Labeling Self as Gay or Bisexual

1. P. Davies (1992), "The Role of Disclosure in Coming Out among Gay Men," in K. Plummer (Ed.), *Modern Homosexualities: Fragments of Lesbian and Gay Experience,* pp. 75–83 (London: Routledge).

2. R. C. Savin-Williams (1994), "Verbal and Physical Abuse as Stressors in the Lives of Lesbian, Gay Male, and Bisexual Youths: Associations with School Problems, Running Away, Substance Abuse, Prostitution, and Suicide," *Journal of Consulting and Clinical Psychology, 62,* 261–269.

3. G. Remafedi, M. Resnick, R. Blum, and L. Harris (1992), "Demography of Sexual Orientation in Adolescents," *Pediatrics, 89*, 714–721.

4. See E. O. Laumann, J. H. Gagnon, R. T. Michael, and S. Michaels (1994), *The Social Organization of Sexuality: Sexual Practices in the United States* (Chicago: The University of Chicago Press).

5. For data that support the view that current cohorts of sexual-minority youths are self-defining their sexual identities at increasingly younger ages see G. Herdt and A. Boxer (1993), *Children of Horizons: How Gay and Lesbian Teens Are Leading a New Way Out of the Closet* (Boston: Beacon) and R. C. Savin-Williams (1990), *Gay and Lesbian Youth: Expressions of Identity* (New York: Hemisphere). They give examples of the recent visibility of homosexuality in our culture.

6. Lisa Diamond lists facilitative environments for young lesbian/bisexual women in her submitted manuscript for publication (1996), "Discontinuous Development of Sexual Orientation in Young Lesbian, Bisexual, and Questioning Women" (Cornell University, Ithaca, NY). These include exposure to women-studies classes, a liberal college environment, meeting other gay people, and participation in emotionally intimate same-sex friendship.

7. G. J. McDonald (1982), "Individual Differences in the Coming Out Process for Gay Men: Implications for Theoretical Models," *Journal of Homosexuality, 8*, 47–60.

8. See discussion and empirical evidence in R. C. Savin-Williams (1990), *Gay and Lesbian Youth: Expressions of Identity* (New York: Hemisphere) and (1996), "Self-Labeling and Disclosure among Gay, Lesbian, and Bisexual Youths," in J. Laird and R. J. Green (Eds.), *Lesbians and Gays in Couples and Families*, pp. 153–182 (San Francisco: Jossey-Bass); and an in-press chapter with L. Diamond, "Sexual Orientation as a Developmental Context for Lesbian, Gay, and Bisexual Children and Adolescents," in W. K. Silverman and T. H. Ollendick (Eds.), *Developmental Issues in the Clinical Treatment of Children and Adolescents* (Boston: Allyn & Bacon).

7. Disclosure to Others

1. Many of the exact dates have been struck from the record to maintain anonymity. This should not negate the fact, however, that many youths recalled specific dates and even times of the day.

2. P. Davies (1992), "The Role of Disclosure in Coming Out among Gay Men," in K. Plummer (Ed.), *Modern Homosexualities: Fragments of Lesbian and Gay Experience*, pp. 75–83 (London: Routledge).

3. M. J. Rotheram-Borus, M. Rosario, and C. Koopman (1991), "Minority Youths at High Risk: Gay Males and Runaways," in M. E. Colten and S. Gore (Eds.), *Adolescent Stress: Causes and Consequences*, pp. 181–200 (New York: Aldine DeGruyter).

4. R. C. Savin-Williams (1994), "Verbal and Physical Abuse as Stressors in the Lives of Lesbian, Gay Male, and Bisexual Youths: Associations with School Problems, Running Away, Substance Abuse, Prostitution, and Suicide," *Journal of Consulting and Clinical Psychology, 62*, 261-269.

5. G. Herdt and A. Boxer (1993), *Children of Horizons: How Gay and Lesbian Teens Are Leading a New Way Out of the Closet* (Boston: Beacon) and R. C. Savin-Williams (1990), *Gay and Lesbian Youth: Expressions of Identity* (New York: Hemisphere).

6. V. Cass (1979), "Homosexual Identity Formation: A Theoretical Model," *Journal of*

Homosexuality, 4, 219–235; K. M. Cohen and R. C. Savin-Williams (1996), "Developmental Perspectives on Coming Out to Self and Others," in R. C. Savin-Williams and K. M. Cohen (Eds.), *The Lives of Lesbians, Gays, and Bisexuals: Children to Adults,* pp. 113–151 (Fort Worth, TX: Harcourt Brace); E. Coleman (1981/1982), "Developmental Stages of the Coming Out Process," *Journal of Homosexuality, 7,* 31–43; J. C. Gonsiorek and J. R. Rudolph (1991), "Homosexual Identity: Coming Out and Other Developmental Events," in J. C. Gonsiorek and J. D. Weinrich (Eds.), *Homosexuality: Research Implications for Public Policy,* pp. 161–176 (Newbury Park, CA: Sage); R. C. Savin-Williams (1990), *Gay and Lesbian Youth: Expressions of Identity* (New York: Hemisphere).

7. The reactions of parents to the news of having a gay or bisexual son will be reported in a manuscript I am currently writing for APA Press on gay youths and their families.

8. A correction should be offered here. Not all students at Cornell are gay, even though a large gay presence is readily apparent on campus. In existence are several large gay organizations; a gay, lesbian, and bisexual resource office funded by the university; a lesbian, bisexual, and gay studies program at the graduate level; and an undergraduate minor in gay studies. One cannot major in gay studies but can choose it as a concentration. The "gay dorm" was vetoed by the president and board of trustees and thus does not exist.

9. For a personal account, see M. Duberman's (1991), *Cures: A Gay Man's Odyssey* (New York: Dutton).

10. See C. Golden (1996), "What's in a Name? Sexual Self-Identification among Women," in R. C. Savin-Williams and K. M. Cohen (Eds.), *The Lives of Lesbians, Gays, and Bisexuals: Children to Adults,* pp. 229–249 (Fort Worth, TX: Harcourt Brace).

8. First Gay Romance

1. M. Scarf (1987), *Intimate Partners: Patterns in Love and Marriage* (New York: Random House).

2. These points are elaborated, perhaps most convincingly, by J. Bowlby (1973), *Attachment and Loss: Volume 2. Separation* (New York: Basic Books) and C. Hazan and P. Shaver (1987), "Romantic Love Conceptualized as an Attachment Process," *Journal of Personality and Social Psychology, 52,* 511–524.

3. R. A. Isay (1989), *Being Homosexual: Gay Men and Their Development* (New York: Avon) and C. Browning (1987), "Therapeutic Issues and Intervention Strategies with Young Adult Lesbian Clients: A Developmental Approach," *Journal of Homosexuality, 14,* 45–52.

4. C. Silverstein (1981), *Man to Man: Gay Couples in America* (New York: William Morrow).

5. A. K. Malyon (1981), "The Homosexual Adolescent: Developmental Issues and Social Bias," *Child Welfare, 60,* 321–330.

6. J. T. Sears (1991), *Growing Up Gay in the South: Race, Gender, and Journeys of the Spirit* (New York: Harrington Park Press).

7. W. Curtis (Ed.) (1988), *Revelations: A Collection of Gay Male Coming Out Stories* (Boston: Alyson).

8. P. Gibson (1989), "Gay Male and Lesbian Youth Suicide," in the U.S. Department of

Health and Human Services, *Report of the Secretary's Task Force on Youth Suicide, Volume 3: Prevention and Interventions in Youth Suicide* (Rockville, MD).

9. These studies are reported in A. R. D'Augelli (1991), "Gay Men in College: Identity Processes and Adaptations," *Journal of College Student Development, 32,* 140–146; J. Harry and W. B. DeVall (1978), *The Social Organization of Gay Males* (New York: Praeger); G. Remafedi (1987), "Adolescent Homosexuality: Psychosocial and Medical Implications," *Pediatrics, 79,* 331–337; G. Sanders (1980), "Homosexualities in the Netherlands," *Alternative Lifestyles, 3,* 278–311; and R. C. Savin-Williams (1990), *Gay and Lesbian Youth: Expressions of Identity* (New York: Hemisphere).

10. R. C. Savin-Williams (1990), *Gay and Lesbian Youth: Expressions of Identity* (New York: Hemisphere).

11. Published in 1981 by Alyson Press (Boston).

12. Portions of this chapter previously appeared in R. C. Savin-Williams (1996), "Dating and Romantic Relationships Among Gay, Lesbian, and Bisexual Youths," in R. C. Savin-Williams and K. M. Cohen (Eds.), *The Lives of Lesbians, Gays, and Bisexuals: Children to Adults,* pp. 166–178 (Fort Worth, TX: Harcourt Brace). For a provocative, gay-affirming video of romance among young gays, lesbians, and bisexuals, see "Live to Tell: The First Gay and Lesbian Prom in America," produced and directed by Charley Lang (1995) by Dakota Filmworks.

9. Positive Identity

1. E. Coleman (1981/1982), "Developmental Stages of the Coming Out Process," *Journal of Homosexuality, 7,* 31–43.

2. V. C. Cass (1984), "Homosexual Identity Formation: Testing a Theoretical Model," *The Journal of Sex Research, 20,* 143–167. See also her earlier (1979) article, "Homosexual Identity Formation: A Theoretical Model," *Journal of Homosexuality, 4,* 219–235.

3. R. R. Troiden (1988), "Homosexual Identity Development," *Journal of Adolescent Health Care, 9,* 105–113.

4. J. A. Lee (1977), "Going Public: A Study in the Sociology of Homosexual Liberation," *Journal of Homosexuality, 3,* 49–78.

5. C. de Monteflores and S. J. Schultz (1978), "Coming Out: Similarities and Differences for Lesbians and Gay Men," *Journal of Social Issues, 34,* 59–72.

6. Cass appears, however, to have changed her perspective somewhat in the 1984 article. There, she emphasizes more self-pride. See references in endnote 2.

7. P. Gibson (1989), "Gay Male and Lesbian Youth Suicide," in the U.S. Department of Health and Human Services, *Report of the Secretary's Task Force on Youth Suicide, Volume 3: Prevention and Interventions in Youth Suicide* (Rockville, MD).

8. Whether gay youths actually make the attempt is seldom verified. This would not be an impossible task (e.g., hospital records, police reports, parent reports).

9. Early studies include M. T. Saghir and E. Robins (1973), *Male and Female Homosexuality* (Baltimore: Williams & Wilkins); A. P. Bell and M. S. Weinberg (1978), *Homosexualities: A Study of Diversity among Men and Women* (New York: Simon & Schuster); and K. Jay and A. Young (1979), *The Gay Report: Lesbians and Gay Men Speak Out about Sexual Experiences and Lifestyles* (New York: Summit).

10. G. Remafedi (1987), "Adolescent Homosexuality: Psychosocial and Medical Implica-

tions," *Pediatrics, 79,* 331–337; S. G. Schneider, N. L. Farberow, and G. N. Kruks (1989), "Suicidal Behavior in Adolescent and Young Adult Gay Men," *Suicide and Life-Threatening Behavior, 19,* 381–394; G. Remafedi, J. A. Farrow, and R. W. Deisher (1991), "Risk Factors for Attempted Suicide in Gay and Bisexual Youth," *Pediatrics, 87,* 869–875; M. J. Rotheram-Borus, J. Hunter, and M. Rosario (1994), "Suicidal Behavior and Gay-Related Stress among Gay and Bisexual Male Adolescents," *Journal of Adolescent Research, 9,* 498–508; and S. L. Hershberger and A. R. D'Augelli (1995), "The Impact of Victimization on the Mental Health and Suicidality of Lesbian, Gay, and Bisexual Youth," *Developmental Psychology, 31,* 65–74. Also see reviews in D. D. Durby (1994), "Gay, Lesbian, and Bisexual Youth," *Journal of Gay and Lesbian Social Services, 1,* 1–37; R. C. Savin-Williams (1994), "Verbal and Physical Abuse as Stressors in the Lives of Lesbian, Gay Male, and Bisexual Youths: Associations with School Problems, Running Away, Substance Abuse, Prostitution, and Suicide," *Journal of Consulting and Clinical Psychology, 62,* 261–269; and S. L. Hershberger, N. W. Pilkington, and A. R. D'Augelli (in press), "Predictors of Suicidality among Gay, Lesbian, and Bisexual Youths," *Journal of Adolescent Research.*

11. See, respectively, J. Hunter (1990), "Violence against Lesbian and Gay Male Youths," *Journal of Interpersonal Violence, 5,* 295–300; G. Kruks (1991), "Gay and Lesbian Homeless/Street Youth: Special Issues and Concerns," *Journal of Adolescent Health Care, 12,* 515–518; National Gay and Lesbian Task Force (1982), *Gay Rights in the United States and Canada* (New York: Author); S. G. Schneider, N. L. Farberow, and G. N. Kruks (1989), "Suicidal Behavior in Adolescent and Young Adult Gay Men," *Suicide and Life-Threatening Behavior, 19,* 381–394; J. Hunter and R. Schaecher (1990), "Lesbian and Gay Youth," in M. J. Rotheram-Borus, J. Bradley, and N. Obolensky (Eds.), *Planning to Live: Evaluating and Treating Suicidal Teens in Community Settings,* pp. 297–316 (Tulsa: University of Oklahoma Press).

12. G. Remafedi, J. A. Farrow, and R. W. Deisher (1991), "Risk Factors for Attempted Suicide in Gay and Bisexual Youth," *Pediatrics, 87,* 869–875.

13. See studies by the following scholars: S. G. Schneider, N. L. Farberow, and G. N. Kruks (1989), "Suicidal Behavior in Adolescent and Young Adult Gay Men," *Suicide and Life-Threatening Behavior, 19,* 381–394; M. J. Rotheram-Borus, J. Hunter, and M. Rosario (1994), "Suicidal Behavior and Gay-Related Stress among Gay and Bisexual Male Adolescents," *Journal of Adolescent Research, 9,* 498–508; and S. L. Hershberger, N. W. Pilkington, and A. R. D'Augelli (in press), "Predictors of Suicidality among Gay, Lesbian, and Bisexual Youths," *Journal of Adolescent Research.*

14. See studies by D. Shaffer, P. Fisher, R. H. Hicks, M. Parides, and M. Gould (1995), "Sexual Orientation in Adolescents Who Commit Suicide," *Suicide and Life-Threatening Behavior, 25* (Supplement), 64–71, and C. L. Rich, R. C. Fowler, D. Young, and M. Blenkush (1986), "San Diego Suicide Study: Comparison of Gay to Straight Males," *Suicide and Life-Threatening Behavior, 16,* 448–457.

15. This has been proposed by E. Coleman (1981/1982), "Developmental Stages of the Coming Out Process," *Journal of Homosexuality, 7,* 31–43 and A. K. Malyon (1981), "The Homosexual Adolescent: Developmental Issues and Social Bias," *Child Welfare, 60,* 321–330.

16. This information will be reviewed in a manuscript I am currently writing for the American Psychological Association Press on gay youths and their families.

10. Ethnic Youths

1. For a more complete discussion of these issues, see my 1996 chapter on ethnic
    youths, "Ethnic- and Sexual-Minority Youth," in R. C. Savin-Williams and K. M.
    Cohen (Eds.), *The Lives of Lesbians, Gays, and Bisexuals: Children to Adults*, pp.
    152–165 (Fort Worth, TX: Harcourt Brace).
2. For a discussion of these issues see a paper E. S. Morales presented at the 91st An-
    nual Convention of the American Psychological Association in Anaheim, CA (1983,
    August), "Third World Gays and Lesbians: A Process of Multiples Identities."
3. See endnote 2.
4. B. Tremble, M. Schneider, and C. Appathurai (1989), "Growing Up Gay or Lesbian in
    a Multicultural Context," *Journal of Homosexuality, 17*, 253–267.
5. B. Greene (1994), "Ethnic-Minority Lesbians and Gay Men: Mental Health and
    Treatment Issues," *Journal of Consulting and Clinical Psychology, 62*, 243–251. See
    also discussion in M. F. Manalansan (1996), "Double Minorities: Latino, Black, and
    Asian Men Who Have Sex with Men," in R. C. Savin-Williams and K. M. Cohen
    (Eds.), *The Lives of Lesbians, Gays, and Bisexuals: Children to Adults*, pp. 393-415
    (Fort Worth, TX: Harcourt Brace).
6. See discussion of this issue in W. L. Williams (1996), "Two-Spirit Persons: Gender
    Nonconformity among Native American and Native Hawaiian Youths," in R. C.
    Savin-Williams & K. M. Cohen (Eds.), *The Lives of Lesbians, Gays, and Bisexuals:
    Children to Adults*, pp. 416–435 (Fort Worth: Harcourt Brace).

11. The Diversity of Gay Youths

1. L. M. Diamond (1996), "Attraction and Identity: Evidence for Sexual Fluidity among
    Young Lesbian, Bisexual, and Heterosexual Women" (Master's thesis, Cornell Uni-
    versity, Ithaca, NY).
2. E. M. Dubé (1997), "Sexual Identity and Intimacy Development among Two Co-
    horts of Sexual Minority Men" (Master's thesis, Cornell University, Ithaca, NY).
3. R. von Krafft-Ebing (1922), *Psychopathia Sexualis: A Medico-Forensic Study* (Brook-
    lyn, NY: Physicians and Surgeons) and H. Ellis (1901), *Studies in the Psychology of
    Sex, Volume 2: Sexual Inversion* (Philadelphia: F. A. Davis).
4. See their 1978 book published in Bloomington, IN, by the Indiana University Press.
5. For recent discussion of these issues see J. M. Bailey (1996), "Gender Identity," in R.
    C. Savin-Williams and K. M. Cohen (Eds.), *The Lives of Lesbians, Gays, and Bisexu-
    als: Children to Adults*, pp. 71–93 (Fort Worth, TX: Harcourt Brace) and L. D. Gar-
    nets and D. C. Kimmel (1993), "Lesbian and Gay Male Dimensions in the Psycholog-
    ical Study of Human Diversity," in L. D. Garnets and D. C. Kimmel (Eds.),
    Psychological Perspectives on Lesbian and Gay Male Experiences, pp. 1–51 (New York:
    Columbia University Press).
6. H. F. L. Meyer-Bahlburg (1993), "Psychobiologic Research on Homosexuality," *Sex-
    ual and Gender Identity Disorders, 2*, 489–500, and A. P. Bell, M. S. Weinberg, and S.
    K. Hammersmith (1981), *Sexual Preference: Its Development in Men and Women*
    (Bloomington, IN: Indiana University Press).
7. D. J. Bem (1996), "Exotic Becomes Erotic: A Developmental Theory of Sexual Orien-
    tation," *Psychological Review, 103*, 320–335. A critique of EBE theory has been pro-

posed by L. A. Peplau, L. D. Garnets, L. R. Spalding, T. D. Conley, and R. C. Veniegas (in press), "A Critique of Bem's 'Exotic Becomes Erotic' Theory of Sexual Orientation," *Psychological Review*.

8. B. E. Compas, B. R. Hinden, and C. A. Gerhardt (1995), "Adolescent Development: Pathways and Processes of Risk and Resilience," *Annual Review of Psychology*, 46, 265–293.

9. L. M. Diamond (1996), "Attraction and Identity: Evidence for Sexual Fluidity Among Young Lesbian, Bisexual, and Heterosexual Women" (Master's thesis, Cornell University, Ithaca, NY).

10. See her 1994 article, "Being a Lesbian and Being in Love: Constructing Identity through Relationships," *Journal of Gay and Lesbian Social Services*, 1, 57–82.

11. See pages 10–14 in Volume 1, Number 1 (Winter 1994), "Fruits, Nuts, and Chocolate: The Politics of Sexual Identity."

12. "Many Gays Are Pro-Life," *The Washington Times*, June 13, 1996.

13. Article by Joseph Mont in *The Tab*, a Cambridge, MA, newspaper, June 18–24, 1996.

14. Stephen Whitty, "Sensitizing a Stereotype—Gay, Lesbian Roles Are No Longer Just Comic Relief in Hollywood," *The San Jose Mercury News*, June 17, 1996.

15. Pages 88–89, 132–134.

16. Research on men was published in 1992, "Adult Sexual Orientation in Relation to Memories of Childhood Gender Conforming and Gender Nonconforming Behaviors," *Archives of Sexual Behavior*, 21, 543–558; on women, in 1995, "Differences between Heterosexual, Bisexual, and Lesbian Women in Recalled Childhood Experiences," *Archives of Sexual Behavior*, 24, 1–20.

17. Cited in an article by Stephen Holden, "Two Solo Performers Embrace Multitudes," *The New York Times* (p. H–5), June 18, 1995.

18. Published in 1989, "The Life Course of Gay and Lesbian Youth: An Immodest Proposal for the Study of Lives," in *Journal of Homosexuality*, 17, 315–355. They proposed the following agenda:

- prospective, longitudinal studies of the life course
- utilization of both predictive *and* narrative/interpretative research models
- exploration of developmental continuities and discontinuities over the life course with an emphasis on individual maturation, social contexts, and historic/cultural circumstances associated with stability and change over time
- reassessment of critical developmental concepts such as identity formation and the coming-out process
- investigations of how youths experience their life as they are living it rather than as it is remembered
- a focus on the resiliency of sexual-minority youths who are confronted by adversity and the unique coping mechanisms of youths who are at risk because of their vulnerabilities
- a consideration of the reciprocal and bidirectional effects of developmental events in lieu of assuming a linear, unidirectional perspective of the life course

19. This is a major point I am currently pursuing in my forthcoming book for the American Psychological Association Press on gay youths and their families.

20. Quoted from her book review of two coming-out books for youths in *The Harvard Gay and Lesbian Review*, Spring, 1994, Volume 1, Number 2.

21. A review of this literature is provided in R. C. Savin-Williams (1994), "Verbal and Physical Abuse as Stressors in the Lives of Lesbian, Gay Male, and Bisexual Youths: Associations with School Problems, Running Away, Substance Abuse, Prostitution, and Suicide," *Journal of Consulting and Clinical Psychology, 62,* 261–269.

22. *Gay and Lesbian Youth: Expressions of Identity* (New York: Hemisphere).